Best Wishes

R Shaw

CHILDREN ARE PEOPLE TOO

UNLOCKING THE SECRETS TO A HAPPIER CHILD
&
A HAPPIER YOU

Sharon Fried Buchalter, Ph.D.

*Clinical Psychologist, Board Certified Diplomate-Fellow in
Advanced Child and Adolescent Psychology*

BRUNDAGE PUBLISHING

First Edition Copyright © 2006 by Sharon Fried Buchalter, Ph.D.
Copyright in the United States of America under all International
and Pan-American Copyright Conventions.

BRUNDAGE PUBLISHING
Executive Office Building, Suite 203
33 West State Street
Binghamton, NY 13901
www.BrundagePublishing.com

Jacket design by Angela Capria
Edited by Rachel A. Edwards and Sheryl Denise Rosen

Library of Congress
Control Number: 2005936172
ISBN Number: 1-892451-39-5

Printed in the United States of America

In memory of my parents, Ruth and Louis Fried, the real heroes of the book. They enabled me to believe in myself and to help make a difference in the world. I would not be who I am today without them.

DEDICATION

*This book is dedicated with love and gratitude
to my husband, David,
who is my battery pack, my soul mate and the love of my life,*

*to my children,
Daniel and Rachael, my two greatest pleasures in life,
whose love inspires me to want to give a voice to all children,*

*in loving memory of my parents, Louis and Ruth Fried,
to my Dad, who taught me to believe in myself, reach for the stars
and follow my dreams,
to my Mom, who taught me the virtues of lending an ear and a
helping hand to everyone,*

*and to all of the children in the world, whose voices can finally be
heard.*

ACKNOWLEDGEMENTS

There are so many people in my life who have helped me get where I am today and who helped make this book a reality. I would like to offer my gratitude to the many individuals who directly or indirectly contributed to this book.

In loving memory of my dear parents, Ruth and Louis Fried. Without you, I would not be who I am today. Mom, you taught me to give with all of my heart and to want to help others. Your kindness and warmth drew everyone close to you. From you, I learned how to open my heart and my home to others. Dad, you will always be my life-coach. You are the person who always made me believe in myself and showed me that I can do anything. From you, I learned that "Life is like a horse race—if you don't bet on the long shot every so often, you can never get the big payoff in the game of life. You can never uncover the beauty of a gem that lies untapped in each person. Similarly, if you don't believe in yourself or your children, you can never uncover the true beauty of a gem that lies within each person in your family." You also taught me that "Life is like a feather in the breeze—never brag about yourself or complain. Instead, work on your personal goals and don't let any obstacles stand in the way of reaching for your dreams."

I'd like to thank my brother, Marty, for his love and support. Thank you for believing in my dream, for being an inspiration to me throughout my life and for always putting a smile on my face and making me laugh.

I extend my gratitude to my Aunt Dorothy and Uncle Murray, who are like parents to me. Uncle Murray, thank you for the countless edits of my manuscript and for providing such sage advice throughout this entire process. Your endless efforts are more appreciated than you'll ever know. Aunt Dorothy, thank you for encouraging me to take care of myself so that I could be strong enough to help others. Thank you for being there for me and helping me see the light. Because of you, I know that "everything is a piece of cake," so there is no need for procrastination.

Thank you to my lifelong friends, Lisa Posner and Beth Kamenitz, my "Yaya" sisters, for always believing in me. Lisa, thank you for listening to me for hours to help cultivate the subtitle of my book and for helping me think outside of the box. Your insights into readers' minds have been invaluable. Beth, thank you for your unbelievable leadership in coordinating focus groups and for spending countless hours helping me come up with inspirations for the future.

Thanks to the entire Noiman family, Avi, Orly, Ori and Samantha, for being like family to me throughout this process. I would like to thank Orly, an unbelievable friend, a very talented professional and an outstanding human being. I love you dearly and I would do anything for you. Thank you for introducing me to Gayle and for looking out for key people to assist in this mission.

Thank you to my cherished friend, my right hand, Gayle Denney. Words cannot express my gratitude for your endless belief in me and everything that I stand for. Thank you for your outstanding writing and for polishing my words into beautiful works of art. You take my words and my vision and help make them a reality. I'll never forget working 28 hours straight to meet a deadline. Always remember the iguana. Thank you to Jay and Samantha Denney for sharing Gayle with me.

Thank you to Sharon Cohen for reminding me that I have the tools within myself to impart my words and to make a difference in the world. Thank you for realizing the true meaning behind my book and for providing your endless advice. You are a cherished friend to me.   Thanks to Moshe Peress and Sharon for all of your feedback and support during this process.

Thank you to the fabulous and hardworking team at Brundage who brought it all together. Thank you, Frank Resseguie, my publisher and my friend, for turning the key in my mind and for believing in me. You saw the virtue and the value of this gem. You used your experience to hold my hand every step of the way. Thank you for writing my beautiful foreword and for lending me your invaluable support throughout this whole process. Thank you to Sheryl Rosen for the countless edits and meticulous attention to detail. I believe we have such good karma. Thank you to Angela Capria for taking my vision of a beautiful cover and making it a reality, more beautiful than I could have ever imagined.

Thank you to my cousin, Liz Geller, who I also consider my friend, for all of your feedback and for going out of your way to ask everyone their opinions, in order to come up with the perfect cover.

To my niece, Mandy Lauro, who is like a sister to me. Thank you for being such a special part of my life and for believing in how much I have to give to the world.

To my cousin, Ryan Quint, thank you for showing immense support for the idea that children should participate in their own life plans. You believed children who've used the program should endorse this book in the hopes it will help empower others.

Thank you to Linda L'Esperance for helping me create a cover that will promote the most positive energy for all.

Thank you to my wonderful photo team, Cindy Cohen, Michelle McMinn and Yigal Malach.

My sincerest appreciation goes to Barbara Killmeyer for her endless help in providing a solid foundation for my book and helping along the way as well. You are an incredible writer, editor and a consummate professional. You would never let me procrastinate and you always taught me that persistence pays off. Thank you for being a dear friend to me and my family.

Thanks to Osnat Yeshurun and her family for motivating me to do things for the goodness of the world and for always reminding me that we are all part of the Creator.

Thank you to Linda Rosenbloom for the many miles you went out of your way to help me and my family. You are always there when we need you—you are a true lifesaver.

To my friend, Jane Sharpington, thank you for reading through my manuscripts so many times.

A special thank you to Alysa Siegel and Phyllis Morgenstern for your wonderful input and diligent reading of my entire manuscript.

Thank you to Steve and Robin Weinfeld for all of your help. Robin, thank you for reading the manuscript by candlelight when the electricity was out. Steve, thank you for spending endless hours reviewing book covers.

Thank you to Rabbi Baruch and Rivka Liberow for giving me your invaluable opinions for my cover. Rivka, thank you for believing that the information I am sharing needs to be spread on an international level and that my work here is so important.

Thank you, Rabbi Yehuda Greenberg, for being a catalyst and believing in my mission here.

A special thank you to the dedicated staff at South Palm Orthopedics and to my family members whose help was invaluable in the book cover selection process. I thank my family for the hours they spent reviewing the potential covers. You were a great focus group.

I would like to thank G-d, who inspires me everyday to be a channel to help others. I am eternally grateful to have been given the privilege of being a messenger of help and hope to so many people.

I thank my precious children, Daniel and Rachael, for their unconditional love and support, and for being so patient with me. I love you with all of my heart. You are my true inspiration. To Rachael, my pumpkin, for being such a special little angel and a blessing in my life. To Daniel, my wise son—you always remind me that "children are the cause of the effect." When children improve or do things well, they are the creator of the positive effects. When I tell you how special you are, you always give me credit for helping you be who you are today. You are a loving, spiritual, warm and caring person and I'm so very proud of you.

*I thank my husband, David, for listening to my countless ideas and for being so loving and wonderful, especially while "Madame Yogi" spoke her words of wisdom. Thank you for making me realize my true mission, which led to the title of my book. Thank you for being the mommy **and** the daddy on those many days and nights when I was working on the book. Thank you for letting me unlock the key to your heart and for unlocking the key to mine.*

TABLE OF CONTENTS

FOREWORD

Do you want a happy you, a happy child and a happy home? Do you want to unlock the secrets of a united and successful family?

Dr. Sharon teaches how parenting can be a joy, full of real happiness and individual success. Her book is realistic and complete, and it will be the last book about parenting you will ever need.

Children are People Too enters a new day in parenting. Dr. Sharon's parenting concepts are ground-breaking and strikingly different from all other parenting books, and hers is the only book in print that directly empowers you to empower others. Her book opens undiscovered doors of opportunity and happiness in both parent and child.

Dr. Sharon combines a Ph.D. in Clinical Psychology, a Master's in Business Administration, years of professional experience with adults and children and experiences with her own children into this one-of-a-kind book. She brilliantly applies both business management concepts and principles of applied psychology to develop the ultimate personal and life success program for both parent and child. Her book guides the parent, the child and the family as a whole to happiness and success.

In Dr. Sharon's *Children Are People Too*, you will discover family togetherness, family unity and family respect. Her book goes far beyond all previous parent-child programs by reaching directly to the very heart of good, enduring parent-child interactions.

Dr. Sharon sees children as human beings who, by knowledgeable interaction, become coaches in their own lives just like other "people." Her book encourages each child to actively participate in the development of his interests, talents and goals in a cooperative, interactive and informational growing adventure.

Dr. Sharon fully confronts the realities of a successful academic, psychological, social and spiritual life-journey in a book that should be required reading for all parents, future parents and caregivers. All parents should read this book, and once they do, they will wish they had read it years ago. Dr. Sharon's deepest-held wish is that those who read this book will be led to find the true success and happiness that is inherent in each family member.

Franklin B. Resseguie
Publisher, Ret. Attorney at Law
Lt. Col. USAF, Ret.

WELCOME NOTE FROM DR. SHARON

By opening this book, you have now joined the many people who are part of an exclusive club—one of happy people with happy children. If you want to be a part of this groundbreaking approach to self-help and parenting, and if you want to see positive results that really work, then this book is for you.

You are about to embark upon a successful, eye-opening journey. Remember—Life is a tapestry to be woven, with your family in the center of this beautiful work of art. Your job is to begin weaving and to help your children do so as well. It is my honor to guide you and your children on this journey toward success and happiness.

Best wishes,

Sharon Fried Buchalter, Ph.D.

Sharon Fried Buchalter, Ph.D.

INTRODUCTION

Parenting can be one of the most rewarding jobs of your life, but it can also be the toughest and most overwhelming endeavor you will ever face. Many people find that they are less prepared for this job than for any other job they have ever encountered. If you are seeking a common sense approach to raising happy and successful children in a loving and caring family, then this book is exactly what you need. It will allow you the opportunity to give your children a head start on the road to success.

Children Are People Too is a revolutionary approach to parenting and self-help unlike any other on the market today. I have developed a unique program with proven results that I have used extensively in my private practice, in my workshops and seminars and in my work with corporate management. My approach recognizes that we, as parents, need to understand ourselves before we can begin to help our children.

This is a book that will not become outdated—you will not read it once and put it aside. It can and should be used for many years to come as a comprehensive guide to success for you and your children. My book combines self-help, management training principles and parenting skills as well as principles of life-coaching to help improve the lives of parents and children alike. After reading this book, you will have a better understanding of your inner-self and how your behaviors and actions affect your children. These methods of change will encourage effective communication, leadership skills, self-esteem, constructive methods in conflict resolution, teamwork, a positive attitude and healthy motivation, ultimately promoting family harmony.

You are about to embark on a journey of self-discovery. I want you to know what to expect from the beginning when you follow the program outlined in this book. It will open your eyes to the obstacles that block you from personal growth and open gates to family success in ways that you could have never imagined. The process outlined in this book will challenge you in many ways, and it will help you to better apply the individual skills that you already have at hand.

As you improve your individual skills, you will then become a mentor to your children. You can influence how your children manifest their lives. You can change the "movie" of your child's life, all by first changing your own mindset. That is the true victory this book helps you achieve.

In this book, you will learn the invaluable skills you need to become a life-coach to yourself and your family. Life-coaching is a relatively new term given to someone who takes the best from all fields of work and life, such as psychology, business, philosophy and spirituality, and uses it to help themselves and others benefit in all areas of their lives. A life-coach approach is extremely effective because it has 3 unique features, unlike other approaches:

- **Expertise:** As you become trained as your own personal life-coach, you will become an expert in helping your children make better decisions and set the best goals. You will help them structure their personal life goals for maximum success and happiness.
- **Synergy:** You and your children become a team, focusing on your goals. You work together to achieve these goals, utilizing a two-way communication process.
- **Structure:** With you as their coach, your children will feel more confident to take action, think bigger and meet their goals, thanks to the accountability that you, as the coach, will provide.

As you read through the chapters, you will find yourself becoming more empowered as a life-coach. You will see life-coaching tips throughout that will remind you of this ultimate goal to become a life-coach. In utilizing this approach for you and your family, you will promote success and happiness. You will find that you benefit in all areas of your life: as a person, a parent and a professional.

I have provided a few unique and fun features in this book to help you along the way. One such feature is that, at the end of the book, there are wallet-sized cards that you can tear out and carry with you to remind you of your goals. These cards reflect simple points to remember, which are also found at the end of each chapter. Each chapter will also contain real-life examples, probing questions, problem-solving strategies and tasks that you and your children can use to develop your skills and become confident in your abilities. Each chapter will provide you with objectives, assessments and practical knowledge that you can implement in your life and in the lives of your family members.

To begin your journey, I will share with you the approach I have developed called "Your Pyramid of Success." As you read this book, you will learn how to climb to the top of the Pyramid of Success, ultimately reaching your full success potential.

Part One of this book will concentrate on you, as an individual. It will help you learn more about yourself, recognize your own strengths and develop your own individual plan for happiness and success. The purpose of this section is to allow you to personally analyze your nature and to provide you with tools to bring about any necessary changes to your behavior—changes that will have a positive effect on your whole family. Each chapter includes tasks to help you grow and understand yourself as an individual. Once you embark on an inner quest for self-discovery, you can then feel empowered to become a mentor to your children.

Part Two of this book helps you put your goals into action and teaches you how to integrate them into your life and your children's lives. When children partake in their own life plans, it helps to develop their self-esteem, increases confidence in their own abilities, gives them more control over their life choices and instills in them the skills they need to flourish throughout their lives. I show you how to learn about your children by having them partake in their own goal-setting and decision-making. I include tasks for you and your children that are developed to enhance your children's interests and involvement in the family and in their own success.

Finally, in Part Three of this book, you are well on your way to reaching your full success potential. I show you how to monitor and modify you and your children's communication and social skills. I also show you how to monitor and modify both you and your children's coping skills. You will learn proper disciplining strategies to use with your children. Then, you will learn how to use teamwork to help your family succeed. By attaining the ultimate goal of reaching your full success potential, you will be prepared to be a life-coach and mentor for your family.

This book will help you recognize who you are and how you presently deal with others. If you truly follow the advice and suggestions for improvement that I have outlined in each chapter, you will discover that you feel more fulfilled, both as a person and a parent. You will then be prepared to become a positive role model and life-coach for your children.

Whether you are a new parent or are coming to the job with previous experience, this book will take you on a journey of self-discovery that will lead to a world of inner strength, emotional independence and self-confidence for both you and your children. When you are done reading this book, you will feel educated, enlightened and empowered for the most rewarding job of your life.

Your Pyramid of Success

The chapters in this book take you on a journey through the steps of a unique approach that I developed to self-help, life-coaching and parenting. These steps, which I call the Pyramid of Success, will help you achieve the ultimate goal of reaching your full success potential. As you read this book and begin to feel educated, enlightened and empowered, you can observe yourself climbing to the top of the Pyramid of Success—one step at a time. The following is an illustration of the Pyramid of Success.

Step 1: Planning your success
During this step, I will walk you through devising a plan that will begin with learning who you really are as an individual.

Step 2: Organizing a path to change
In this step, you will discover innovative ways of doing things and begin to develop new behavior patterns.

Step 3: Putting your goals into observable measures

In this step, you will document your goals. By writing them down on paper, you are putting your goals into observable measures, making you more likely to achieve them. When people write things down, it serves as an affirmation or declaration of those goals.

Step 4: Turning your goals into action

By setting realistic goals and writing down ways of achieving them, you will be able to turn these goals into realities. During this step, you begin to work with your children by helping to put their goals into action. I will teach you how to become a life-coach to your children in order to direct them through the rest of the steps in the pyramid, which will guide them in mastering their life plans.

Step 5: Integrating intra-personal self-improvement and inter-personal social interaction skills

There are eight factors incorporated in this step. These factors are all addressed in Parts Two and Three of my book. When you master these skills, you will unlock the key to maximizing both you and your children's success potential.

First, you will learn why intra-personal factors of self development are crucial for happiness and success; these are internal traits within yourself and your children. These factors include self-esteem, attitude, motivation and a sense of empathy toward others. When these intra-personal skills are uncovered and developed within you and your children, your chance of reaching success is greatly enhanced. In Part Two of my book, I have included chapters that will help you develop these skills. You will discover the secrets of how to cultivate these skills within yourself and your children. You will also learn why each child is special and how to recognize the strengths within your children. Once you have mastered these self-development skills, you will feel more enlightened.

Next, you will learn how internal factors within ourselves impact our inter-personal skills. Inter-personal skills involve interactions with others and our surrounding environment. In Part Three, I have included chapters that provide tips for improving communication skills which will, in turn, impact social skills. You will discover the secrets of constructive conflict-resolution and problem-solving. I will guide you through easy ways to instill self-discipline, which will have an impact on you and your children's daily life. You will also learn how to master the skills needed for true teamwork.

By following the easy guidelines given in this book, you will uncover the master key that will allow you to unlock the secrets to you and your children's success potential. You are well on your way to being a life-coach to yourself and your children.

Step 6: Combining emotional and social health to promote success
In this step, we revisit the issue of success. You will see how your emotional, social and spiritual well-being help you on your way to success.

Step 7: Monitoring your behavior and how it affects you and those around you
In this step, I show you how to monitor your newly acquired behavior so that you have awareness of how it affects your life and the lives of those around you.

Step 8: Modifying your goals and behaviors
During this step, you will learn how to modify your goals and behaviors based on the principles you have learned thus far in the pyramid. As you achieve your goals, you will develop and work toward new goals. This will help you achieve the ultimate goal of reaching your full success potential.

Step 9: Full success potential
When you and your children reach this step, you will feel educated, enlightened and empowered to achieve your greatest happiness and success in life.

Part One

Developing Your Pro-Active Goals

Planning, Organizing and Documenting Your Goals

Chapter One

PLANNING YOUR CHANGE

Developing a Plan to Bring Personal Changes into Your Life

CHAPTER OBJECTIVES

- Learn about behavior patterns and how to avoid unproductive behavior.
- Complete a personal assessment of who you are and what concerns you most in life.
- Learn how to make changes one day at a time.
- Study your past and find out how it relates to your life-coaching skills.
- Re-define success and create a new model for success.
- Learn about and develop positive affirmations to use daily.
- Create your individual plan for change.

"No one remains quite what he was when he recognized himself."
— *Thomas Mann*

No venture can be successful without a plan. Your plan for successful parenting must begin with learning who you really are. To be a successful parent, it is vital for you to understand that before you can help your children[1], you must help yourself. You must work hard to become the best mentor, life-coach and role model that you can be for the sake of your children.

It is time now to learn some personal life-coaching skills that you can use later with your family. In order to do this, this chapter will help you both analyze who you are and make a personal plan for success. Keep in mind that there will be times when taking a good look at yourself may not be easy; there will be times when change is difficult to embrace. Familiar ground is always more comfortable, although it may not be the best for you or your family. Your task now is to enter unfamiliar waters, a little at a time, until you feel comfortable enough to move ahead.

Remember, you must become a successful life-coach to yourself before you can hope to coach your children to success. Knowing that you are doing this to improve your life and the lives of your children will make it that much easier.

INDIVIDUAL BEHAVIOR PATTERNS

In general, people find that accomplishment leads them to fulfillment; fulfillment then leads to increased self-esteem; and

---

[1] I use "child" and "children" interchangeably. This book is equally helpful for single-child and multi-child families, as well as single-parent families, grandparents, adoptive parents, future parents or any other caregivers.

increased self-esteem ultimately results in success. The following are some examples of how achievement can bring about positive results:

> **Fulfillment:** "I never thought I'd finish that project on time, but I did."
> **Self-Esteem:** "Now I know I'm as good as anyone else in this department, and I have a great chance for that promotion."
> **Success:** "I feel great. I'm not going to stop here. I'm going to volunteer to head the new marketing campaign. I know I'll do a great job with it."

It seems simple enough, right? Well, believe it or not, many people tend to sabotage their efforts with their own behavior patterns. Unproductive behaviors inhibit individual growth and obstruct efforts to make progress. Your challenge and responsibility is to determine if your behaviors are detrimental to your personal relationships and/or your job performance. The good news is that every liability can be turned into an asset as long as you are willing to work on it—even small modifications can make a difference.

To start, you will now learn about five common forms of unproductive behavior. As you read, note if any of these behaviors are recognizable in your own life. If you have difficulty placing yourself into one or more of these categories, ask someone you trust to give their input regarding your behavioral patterns. The end of each behavior pattern description includes suggestions on ways to improve that behavior.

Here are some things to keep in mind when making improvements in your life:

- It may be challenging for you to incorporate these suggestions into your life but, if you can, you will see the desired results.

- Master your behavioral changes one at a time. Remember that you cannot rush; you must take it step-by-step. **Do not expect overnight results.** Instead, appreciate each small action as it occurs. Over a period of time, you will realize that things are different and you are becoming a happier person. One action at a time will bring about a changed attitude in the people around you and, thus, a more comfortable life for you.

- Do not worry if you fall back a step by reverting to your old habits—if so, you have not destroyed all of your progress and change. Remember, a setback does not mean a relapse. You must try and try again.

Behavior Pattern 1: The Intimidator

There is more than one way to intimidate others. The authority of your position, your size, your intelligence or your on-the-job effectiveness can all be sources of demoralizing behavior. This can be particularly true if you use these as levers in your interactions.

The Intimidator might lean in close to the person she[2] is talking to, thus giving the other person a sense of being overpowered. The Intimidator will be quick to bring up any errors the victim makes but will not give the practical help necessary to correct those errors. She will make the victim the butt of jokes and try to make others laugh at the victim's expense.

A major weapon in the Intimidator's arsenal is the threat. For example, she might say, "If you don't complete this project on time, your job will be on the line," or "The team is depending on you to get the information we need, and it must be correct and on time. You better not let us down, or else…"

If you discover that you fall into this category, you may find that your friendships might not be long lasting and your co-workers might alienate you to escape your overbearing manner. Intimidation does not result in productive work or solid friendships.

If you feel you might play the role of Intimidator, ask yourself the following questions:

- *What do I get from this behavior? What is the payoff for me?*
    Many people think putting others down makes them a bigger person who deserves admiration. They feel it gives the impression that they are more intelligent and capable

---

[2] I use "she" at times, while I use "he" at other times. The use of one versus the other is random and does not indicate any exclusivity or gender bias.

than the victim. Another factor that influences this type of action is fear. The thought process is something like, "What if he can do the job better than I can?" or, "What if everyone likes him better than they like me, and I'm left out in the cold?" To avoid these situations, the Intimidator will do whatever she can to bring down the perceived offender and make sure everyone thinks she is better than the others.

- *Are the results of this behavior worth alienating others? Are you invited to social gatherings because people feel that they "have" to invite you? When was the last time someone called you to come to an impromptu get-together?*

  As the Intimidator, you may experience a temporary sense of self-importance, but when you look at the big picture, you are probably not getting the desired results from your behavior. The people around you may say one thing to your face, but they might be talking behind your back about how much of a bully you are. When you make someone the butt of your jokes, others may laugh, but it is your victim who elicits the empathy of your co-workers.

- *How would my life be better if I changed my behavior?*

  Take a hard look at your life. Do you feel successful or do you feel that you always have something to prove? Are you happy with your present circle of friends or do you feel that you are always on the outskirts of the group? Making changes to this behavior pattern will help you surround yourself with people who want to be around you and whose company you enjoy.

Here are some suggestions for how you can modify your intimidating behavior:

- Give credit to others when it is due. For example, if someone proposes an idea that turns out to be the best solution for a problem, make sure you give that person the credit. Do not slough it off or—worse yet—take the credit for yourself.

- Rather than pointing out mistakes people have made, go out of your way to find something to praise. We all make mistakes; it is inevitable. You are just as vulnerable to this human failing as anyone else. For example, imagine you are reading an essay your child has worked hard on for his English class. You see that it could use a lot of improvement. Begin by telling your child that he has done a good job and that it is obvious he put a lot of effort into it. After pointing out some of the better aspects of the report, you can then give your child suggestions for improvement. This way, you are telling your child that he did good work and helping him by making suggestions for improvement. This improvement will be a positive reflection on you as a parent, and it will also bring you and your child closer.

- Listen to, consider and, if feasible, use an idea proposed by someone else. Be open to new ideas. This will not only increase the morale of the other person, but will also expand your own knowledge base. Most people are more likely to work *with* another than *for* another. The result will be better productivity on the job and good friends for social situations.

Positive Inspiration: You can use the power that makes you intimidating to instruct and to help. You can become a leader that people look up to and want to emulate.

Behavior Pattern 2: The Doubter

The Doubter is a person who is so unsure of his abilities that he will continually do everything in a way that is tried, true and foolproof. The Doubter lives with his own perceived inadequacies, and he projects those feelings of insecurity onto other people in work and/or social situations. The behavior of the Doubter is rigid, and this puts employees who work for him at a distinct disadvantage, since those people do not have the freedom to be inventive. The result of this could be poor morale and a high incidence of departmental turnover.

Socially, the Doubter may be excluded from activities in favor of those people who are not fearful of new situations and are willing to be more adventurous. The following is an example of a Doubter.

After a number of years of hard work and making sure he did nothing that would reflect poorly on his performance ratings, James rose to the position of department head at his company. Fred, one of the employees in James's department, approached James with a new concept. The following is their exchange:

Fred: "Good morning, James. I wonder if you can spare me a few minutes. There is something I'd like to discuss with you."

James: "Sure. Come on in Fred. I have a half hour until my meeting with Mr. Pensure."

Fred: "Actually, your meeting with the big boss this morning is the reason I wanted to talk to you. I've put a lot of time in lately comparing our profits with the profits of our biggest competitor, and I think I've hit on a good idea to increase our sales. Our target audience is the teenager, and teens follow the latest trends. If we can convince one or more of the top recording artists to wear some of our creations when they give a concert or a television interview, it would make teens sit up and take notice. Our sales would soar and profits would rise. I happen to know someone who is an agent for several of the stars, and I could ask him to talk to them about wearing our creations. Will you approach Mr. Pensure with the idea? I really think it's a good one, and I could help make it happen."

James: "I don't know...it could backfire. What if parents object to the performer? They might not allow their teens to wear the clothing."

Fred: "Since when have teens listened to what their parents want them to wear? The objection of the parents might even make the teens want it more. What do you say? Will you talk to Mr. Pensure about it?"

James: "I'm sorry, but we've never attempted anything like this before, and I'm afraid it might bring more problems than profits. Thanks for trying, but I don't think it will work."

Do you think Fred will put time and effort into thinking up additional ideas for the company from now on? No. He will either do what is expected of him and no more, or he will leave to work for a company that will appreciate his ideas.

James was afraid of two things:

1) He feared the idea would not work and the failure would reflect poorly on him.

2) He feared the idea would work and that Fred, not he, would get the credit for it.

If you feel you might play the role of Doubter, ask yourself the following questions:

▪ *Did you once try a new idea that failed?*

If this has happened to you, you are not alone. Remember and learn from the words of Thomas Edison who stated, "No experiment is a failure." You may have been disappointed and emotionally hurt, but you probably learned something from trying.

▪ *Have former employers influenced you by not giving you the option of trying new ideas?*

Think of how the growth of your creative output might have been stunted. Is this what you want to pass on to others? By allowing your employees to see their ideas pass or fail, you are giving them the opportunity for mental and creative growth, in addition to revitalizing your own thought processes and actions. By encouraging an exchange of ideas and being receptive to the plans of others, you are entering into a win-win situation.

▪ *Have friends laughed at you for not being very adept when something out of the ordinary was attempted?*

Not everyone can be a talented artist, mountain climber, accomplished dancer or Olympic swimmer. No one person can do all things. If you challenged these same people to compete with you in something that you do well, chances are they would not measure up to your performance. Instead of feeling inadequate, one defense is to develop a good sense of humor. For example, say you try ice-skating and find yourself sitting on the ice more than skating on it. Perhaps you could ask if you might have a third skate for your rear end.

- *What would be the worst-case scenario for a failed idea?*

    Would you be fired from your job? Not likely. Instead, you would probably be encouraged to rework the plan to make it feasible. Would you be laughed at? No. It is more likely that you would be praised for having the idea in the first place and for putting it into action, even if it did not work out. Would your friends make fun of you for not being adept at an activity or for not participating if the idea fails to interest you? No. They would appreciate your sense of humor and your honesty. They might even ask you to suggest the next group activity so that you can participate and enjoy it.

    Here are some suggestions for how you can modify your doubting behavior:

- After you discover why you might be lacking in confidence, make some small changes and gradually move on to bigger changes as your confidence grows. For example, when employees notice your receptiveness to new ideas, they will be more open and will try harder to be part of an exciting work environment. Friends will be more likely to call on you when they discover your new attitude about participating in group activities.

- All you can do is try your best and accept that some of your ideas will not turn out as you expected. You can then try to improve upon those ideas. Remember, it is impossible to be all things to all people.

Positive Inspiration: Now that you have begun to build up your self-esteem, you can readily relate to those who suffer from similar challenges. Use this new understanding to build bridges and strengthen relationships in your personal and professional life.

Behavior Pattern 3: The Skeptic

The Skeptic is a person who distrusts any ideas that are not his own. This person can shoot down plans and suggestions for no reason other than distrust. Though it is healthy to question ideas and suggestions so that you are better able to accept them in your own mind, some people delight in consistently rejecting proposals made by others. Through sarcastic remarks, the Skeptic manages to undermine the self-confidence of those around her. Constant ridicule, especially from a manager or parent, can be extremely destructive and shut down creativity.

If you feel you might play the role of Skeptic, ask yourself the following questions:

- *Do you give your full attention to others?*

    Consider your responses over the past three months to ideas that were expressed by co-workers. If you have your mind made up in advance that a proposed plan is not suitable, then your attention is diverted, and you will probably miss some very important aspects that might have influenced your decision-making. As fantastic and wonderful as the human mind is, it requires total concentration to fully understand the main points of a discussion. You owe it to the other person to listen and give your full and undivided attention.

- *Can you honestly say that you gave careful consideration to the proposed thought?*

    Listening with a preconceived notion of negativity is not giving a suggestion the contemplation it deserves. Skeptics usually have somewhat of an enlarged ego, in that they only trust their own judgments and ideas. They usually have experience to fall back on, and they have a difficult time believing that anyone else could come up with better ideas, solutions or plans.

- *Did your remarks cause a room that was alive with the exchange of ideas to suddenly become silent?*

Closed-minded skepticism can stop creativity cold. Those who are skeptics have a very difficult time delegating to others. Thus, skeptics usually are not good team players.

- *If another idea is accepted over yours, do you feel it will undermine your authority?*

    Watch carefully how department heads, managers or foremen operate. You will soon discover that the majority of workable plans do not come from the person in charge, but from the people who work under that person. Does this diminish a manager's authority? Not at all. As a matter of fact, the manager receives praise for having employees who are motivated enough to want to do well for the company. A good manager uses the input from his workers and shares the praise with them, giving them the incentive to try even harder. This makes the manager look even better.

- *Do you think that listening to others will make you less of a leader?*

    No one, no matter what his position in life, can do it alone. The President of the United States has advisors, as do heads of other countries around the world. By utilizing the best people in various fields, these leaders are able to lead with wisdom and authority. Companies have their boards of directors to help guide them along the best course of action. If these leaders depend on advice from others, you should do the same. No one thinks less of these leaders for seeking the best plans from their colleagues. Take a lesson from well-known leaders and find the best plan for your purposes.

Here are some suggestions for how you can modify your skeptic behavior:

- As hard as it may be, try to realize how your comments will affect other people before you speak. Negative comments can curb enthusiasm. Stop yourself before you make a negative comment.

- Be a good listener and be receptive to others' ideas and creativity.

> **Positive Inspiration:** Skepticism can be a valuable asset if used judiciously. It can be the catalyst for re-thinking a plan with possible flaws. There is, however, a fine line between constructive criticism and destructive criticism. Constructive criticism reflects your intelligence while destructive criticism reflects your desire to control by ridicule. Use this new understanding of constructive criticism to your advantage.

Behavior Pattern 4: The Perfectionist/The Hypercritical

Perfectionists are, very often, people who are obsessive and inflexible about how things are done. For example, a homemaker might complain about the amount of work she has to do and the small amount of time available to accomplish all of the cleaning, cooking and managing that is part of running a household. Though this same homemaker could eliminate much of the work by delegating it to other family members, she will not do this because she thinks that no one else can do the job as well as she can.

By not sharing some of your responsibility with others, you may be burdening yourself with unnecessary anxiety and stress that could lead to health-related problems. You are also depriving other people of learning experiences and opportunities to take advantage of your knowledge.

People who are hypercritical demand perfection not only in themselves, but also in others. They often attack others' efforts in a way that promotes fear and self-doubt. If you fall into this category—beware. Nothing can turn a friend into a foe faster than a constant barrage of critical remarks. Consider the following examples of unsupportive or hypercritical behaviors:

- Your spouse surprises you by doing the laundry while you are out, but he accidentally puts your favorite blouse in the dryer. If your reaction is, "I wish you wouldn't have put that blouse in the dryer," do you think he will want to help out with the laundry again anytime soon?

- Your six-year-old son proudly brings you a small bouquet of wildflowers that he discovered on the way home from school. If you say to him, "I hope you didn't bring a lot of dirt into the house," you will deeply hurt his feelings. He will think that you do not like his gift, and probably will not make another gesture like that for fear of a similar reaction.

- One of your employees works through the weekend to complete a report for Monday morning. When she shows it to you, you remark only about a small typo buried in the text, never acknowledging the work she put into the project. A simple "thank you" and a smile or a word of praise for the extra work would have made your employee feel special and valued. Instead, she feels that her efforts were flawed and that she could never measure up to your expectations. She might be wondering why she put in all of that extra effort and probably will not do it again.

If you feel you might play the role of Perfectionist or Hypercritical, ask yourself the following questions:

- *As a child, were you always expected to be perfect?*

  All too often, parents expect their children to be perfect, which is just not realistic. Human beings learn from their mistakes. Children who are bullied into perfection cannot make the mistakes they need in order to learn. By the time these children grow into adults, they abhor errors in themselves and in others.

- *What would happen if you failed to show perfection?*

  Would you be fired? No. Would your family suffer? No. Would your friends wonder what happened to you? They might, but it would be in a positive way. People around you would learn to relax and not always be on guard, trying to do everything as well as you. As a result, there would be a lot more smiles when you were around.

- *Do you feel like your world would fall apart if you made a mistake?*

  Look around and you will see that people make mistakes every day, yet the world still exists. By understanding that everyone makes mistakes, you will alleviate much of the pressure you are under and will feel better physically and mentally.

Here are some suggestions for how you can modify your perfectionist or hypercritical behavior:

- Recognize that while attention to detail can be an asset in some situations, lightning will not strike if everything is not perfect. If you can learn to accept an 80% level of perfection, life will be much easier for you and everyone around you.

- Begin, one small change at a time, to accept imperfection. How do you do this? Allow your children to do the dishes while you remain in another part of the house. Do not make negative comments about the job they do, but simply praise their efforts. So what if there was a crumb left on a plate? Is the Board of Health going to come into your home and haul you off to jail?

- Finally...relax, relax, relax. Ease up on your constant vigilance for errors. Learn to see the funny side of a mistake. Humor is a wonderful way to show that you, too, are human. If you relax, others will feel free to relax around you.

Positive Inspiration: Once you can learn to accept that someone else may do a less-than-perfect job, you will be more willing to delegate and remove some of the burden from your shoulders.

Behavior Pattern 5: The Loner

A positive aspect of loners is that they are usually very intelligent people who work well on their own. On the down side, loners are usually not good team players. They may have problems communicating well-thought-out plans to others. Loners often appear to be distant and uninterested. There are times, however, when loners crave company. They need someone with whom they can celebrate victories and commiserate losses.

Loners are very uncomfortable in group situations. In the workplace (particularly in managerial positions) they will call very few meetings. Members of a loner's team may be at a disadvantage, because they may feel their leader does not care about the outcome of a project. This attitude is likely to produce apathy and disinterest among members of the team. The result could be poor performance and low morale. In social situations, loners are unwilling participants in group activities and are often wrongly perceived to be standoffish when, in fact, they are actually just uncomfortable.

If you feel you might play the role of Loner, ask yourself the following questions:

- *Have I always felt this way? If not, when did I start feeling this way?*

  In some people, the preference for being alone began in childhood. Perhaps you were brought up as an only child and often had no one else to play with. You became accustomed to playing alone and, eventually, began to feel uncomfortable when in a group setting. These feelings might have carried over into adulthood and become a way of life.

  Even if you were not an only child, you may still have developed problems with interaction. You may have had siblings who were active and outgoing, while you were studious and quiet. While they were having summer fun squirting each other with garden hoses, you may have preferred sitting in the shade and reading a book. This would have set you apart and left you out of the loop. Although you probably enjoyed your quiet time, it would have been difficult to have it both ways: to be part of the group *and* enjoy your own solitude. At some point, you may have given up on the group and settled for your own company.

- *Do I feel superior to others? Inferior to others?*

  Someone who has feelings of superiority feels like she is above others, which may make others not want to associate with her. People can sense a superior attitude and thus avoid unnecessary interaction with that person. The opposite of superiority is inferiority. Inferiority can also set you apart from others. Feelings of inferiority could make you think, "They don't want me around. I'm not as intelligent (athletic, friendly, fashion conscious, etc.) as they are. I won't give them the chance to shun me. I'll just stay by myself."

Here are some suggestions for how you can modify your loner behavior:

Socially, there are several ways to modify your loner behavior:

- Learn to spend more time with others. You may not be the life of the party, but you can increase your interaction with others.

- Work to cultivate one or two close friends. Through these friends, you will be drawn into a circle of like-minded people with whom you can feel comfortable.

- Be selective in the social invitations you accept, but make a serious effort to spend time in the company of others on a regular basis.

Professionally, there are several ways to modify your loner behavior:

- Make every effort to call and participate in regular meetings in which all members of your team can voice their opinions.

- Show interest in and comment on the thoughts expressed by others in order to show your concern and regard for their ideas. Give praise for others' good thoughts and insights.

- Develop an open-door policy and encourage co-workers to come to you. If an all-day open-door is too much, determine times when you will be available to listen and talk. As those who work with you become aware of your new openness, they will be more likely to approach you.

- Be sure to participate in office celebrations or get-togethers where you can get to know your co-workers better and they can get to know you.

Positive Inspiration: By modifying your loner behavior and making a few adjustments, you can begin to feel more comfortable in social situations, and other people can begin to feel more comfortable around you.

YOUR PERSONAL ASSESSMENT

The five personality types discussed above are a glimpse into some areas of your life that might need to be restructured for better interaction with others.

Below, you will find ten statements to complete. When you are done, it will provide you with a personal profile that can be used to initiate specific changes for improvement. Every person is unique in his feelings and observations, so the best results are obtained when the assessment is completed separately by all of the adults in your family. Remember, there are no right or wrong answers. Just be honest with yourself.

Complete the following statements before reading further:

1. I am happiest when _____

_____

2. I get angry when _____

_____

3. I wish for _____

_____

4. What helps me through hard times is _____

_____

5. I feel good about myself when _____

---

6. I hate it when _____

_____

7. My worst fear is _____

_____

8. My spouse/partner treats me _____

_____

9. I love to _____

_____

10. As a child, I was treated _____

Statement 1: I am happiest when…

Happiness means different things to different people. What makes you glow? Is it praise for a job well done, or is your answer more along the lines of a new outfit or a night out on the town?

By determining the things that make you happy, you can find a profession that really suits you. Do you feel best when you are outdoors doing something physical, like sports or gardening? If so, then you probably are not at your best when you are confined to an office. You would do better at a job where you could be outside as much as possible. Do you prefer to work alone, or would you be miserable without human contact throughout the day? If you cannot seem to concentrate unless you are alone, then you should work behind the scenes, perhaps as an accountant or computer programmer. On the other hand, if you crave the company of people to make your day more enjoyable, then consider a career in sales, teaching, counseling or consulting. Anything that brings you and the public together would work well for you.

By deciding exactly what it is that makes you happiest, you can determine what direction you want to take in your life, both personally and professionally. It may mean taking your life in a whole different direction. This can be very frightening, but the end result will be a more satisfied and happier you. **Discover what makes you happy, and make it happen.**

Statement 2: I get angry when...

Do you get annoyed at petty distractions, or does it take a major conflict to get you angry? If small, bothersome annoyances cause your anger to flare, you need to look for an underlying cause. How is your health? When you do not feel well physically, it is hard to have much patience with anything. Are you dissatisfied with some aspect of your life, such as your job or your marriage? If you are, then the situation needs to be corrected; otherwise, it can undermine your good nature and may cause you to lash out at trivialities.

If you are constantly angry and your attitude is affecting your job performance or your social life, you should take a course in anger management. Please do this as soon as possible. The earlier you get your impulsive feelings under control, the faster you will regain control of your life.

Statement 3: I wish for...

If a fairy godmother appeared and promised to grant you just one wish, what would your wish be? Money? Health? Happiness?

Did you wish for money? The old saying is that "money can't buy happiness." This might be true, but the lack of money to provide for your family can lead to frustration, anger and depression. If you feel that you need to have more money to properly care for yourself and your family, do not depend on that fairy godmother, and do not gamble away what you do have in hopes of winning more. Instead, sit down and make a plan. Think about ways you can cut back on your current spending. Must you have the most expensive telephone service available? Can you vacation locally this year? Is frequent dining out eating into your budget? In the winter, is it really necessary to keep the thermostat turned up high even when you are not home during the day? When you shop, do you always reach for the high-priced brand name when a generic product might do just as well? If money is an issue for you, examine where you spend the most money, and then try cutting down as much as possible. If you still find that you need more money, you may want to look into getting a part-time job.

Did you wish for good health? If this is the case, then you can do a lot to make your wish come true. The first thing you need to do is visit your doctor for a complete checkup. If the doctor says you are in reasonably good health and places no restrictions on exercise or physical activity, then you can put a health and fitness program into action. Start with the way you eat. Find a plan that works for you, and do not jump into anything too severe. Develop a moderate change in your eating habits that will result in a healthier diet and, if needed, some weight loss. If you have not been in the habit of exercising on a regular basis, then begin slowly. A walk each day will get you started. If you have a treadmill, use it and increase your time daily. Do any other exercises that appeal to you. In just a short period of time, you will begin to notice a difference. You will look and feel better, and you will have done it all on your own.

Statement 4: What helps me through hard times is…

What helps you get through the rough spots? If you do not have a favorite method to employ when the going gets rough, you can become frustrated and irritable, causing your interaction with others to suffer. If you currently have nothing in place to help you through the difficult times, try different things until you hit upon one or two that suit you. Below are some suggestions to help get you through the rough times.

Tell yourself, "In one hour (or two or three) this will be over. I can stand anything for one hour." This gives you a time frame. You will know when the difficult time will be over, and then you can relax. It will be comforting to know that whatever the problem is, it will not go on forever.

Use positive affirmations often. When you encounter a difficult task, repeat to yourself, "I am strong. I can handle this." If you repeat this often enough, you will begin to believe it—and believing is half of the battle.

Try to retain your sense of humor. This is not always easy to do but, if you can manage it, the problem will seem less daunting and will lead to a better mood.

Statement 5: I feel good about myself when...

When do you feel good about yourself? Is it when you know you are looking your best or when you have successfully completed a difficult project? Use whatever makes you feel good about yourself when you need a pick-me-up. When you are feeling down in the dumps, reach into your subconscious and think about the time that you did something that boosted your morale. Think about that moment and how you felt. Even though things may not be as good as you would like them to be right at this moment, you have had some good things happen in the past. Thinking about these things can make you a happier person. Remember, happy thoughts create happy feelings.

Statement 6: I hate it when...

What is it that you hate? What are your pet peeves? Is it when you are working on an important presentation for work and someone interrupts you, causing you to lose your train of thought? Perhaps you are most annoyed when you are in a meeting and one person dominates the conversation and does not give anyone else a chance to talk. You might hate it when you are at home and begin catching up on several chores you have been putting off, when the doorbell rings and your neighbor unexpectedly shows up to have coffee and share gossip.

How do you handle these situations without making enemies? First, be honest and up front. If you are being interrupted while trying to prepare for an important presentation, let your co-workers know that you need to be left alone to work. You could consider a bit of humor such as hanging a sign in your area that reads, "Genius at work. Do not disturb."

What do you do about the meeting hog? Be thoroughly prepared so you will not stumble over your words. Know what it is that you want to say. If you feel you may need to refute some points the other person is making, take notes. The conversation hog will have to stop to take a breath at some point. When there is a small break in the discussion, raise your hand, making sure that the person in charge of the meeting sees you. When you get the floor, simply say, "I have something to contribute to this discussion," then use your notes to make a clear and knowledgeable presentation.

When your neighbor comes to your door and you are busy, be honest. Say, "I would love to have coffee with you, but could we please schedule it for another day? I really need to get this work done now. If I know in advance when you want to do this, I'll make time for you."

You have always heard that honesty is the best policy, and it is true. If you hate it when people continually tease you about something, be honest. Tell them, "It really bothers me when you do that, and if you continue I will have to spend less time around you."

Being honest and up front about your pet peeves and feelings will make people aware of them, and you will find that most people will be sensitive to them. You will then become more productive and fun to be around.

Statement 7: My worst fear is…

Do you fear failure, or possibly even success? Does the thought of being alone fill you with dread? Many people are afraid that others will recognize them as frauds; and that others will discover that they do not really know what they are doing.

First of all, erase the word "failure" from your vocabulary— there is no such thing. Perhaps the results of the long hours you put into a work project were not as good as you had hoped they would be. The long hours spent on the work project gave you valuable information to be used in the future. Maybe you have tried your best but still cannot master the art of skiing. At least you learned something each time you made an attempt. You might not have become a proficient skier, but you did learn a lot about the sport that will be useful in other aspects of your life. Did you know that Perry Mason had to take the bar exam five times before he passed? Despite these challenges, he became one of the most well-known and successful attorneys to date. Keep in mind that everyone, no matter who he is, has times when things do not go exactly as planned. The important thing is to learn from your experiences.

There are people who fear success. What will happen if I move up in the company? Will I lose the friends I have? Will I be able to manage the additional work? What if I have to speak in public? First, you must realize that you have worked hard to get ahead, and you deserve success. All of your hard work is finally paying off. Your friends, if they are true friends, will be happy for your success. Keep the friendships on the same level as they have always been and there should be no problem. As far as managing additional work, if your supervisors did not feel that you could take on the additional work, they would not have offered it to you. The secret is time management. Learn how to manage your time, and you will conquer even more than you thought you could handle.

Speaking in public is the number one fear of most people, but it can be overcome. The best way to do this is to join an organization devoted to public speaking, such as Toastmasters. This organization will teach you tricks to help you relax when called upon to speak. This will allow you to get practice in the company of your peers, so you will be prepared to address larger audiences with ease.

Thinking that you may be recognized as a fraud is a sign of poor self-esteem. You obviously know what you are doing or you would not be in that position. Think of all of your accomplishments. Tell yourself, as often as necessary, "I am good at what I do." Positive affirmations are strong allies in our fight for self-esteem. **Stroke your ego a little.** You deserve it, and it will go a long way in helping you overcome feelings of inadequacy.

Statement 8: My spouse/partner treats me…

How does your significant other treat you? Like a child or like an adult? As an inferior person or as an equal? Is he an expert at manipulating you, or does he appreciate you and treat you fairly?

If your spouse treats you like a child, perhaps it is because—to an extent—you enable that type of behavior. Consider your interactions with him. You may want to work toward a behavioral change. When you have a disagreement, how do you get your way? Do you pout and throw a tantrum? Do you charm your partner into agreeing with you? Who does that behavior remind you of? Does it remind you of a child? Remember the old adage, "If you're going to act like a child, then you'll be treated like one." When a disagreement arises, make your points in a clear, firm manner and discuss your differences like adults—keeping childish actions out of it. It will not take long for your partner to realize that you are acting in an adult manner and begin treating you accordingly. You may not always get your way by acting like an adult, but you will have earned your partner's respect. If you want to be treated as an adult, then you must act like one.

Do you feel that your spouse treats you as an inferior? In what way? Does she have more education than you? Feel free to get more education if that is what it would take to make you feel equal. Remember, however, that there are many people who have schooling but do not have the experience or common sense necessary for everyday living. Recognize your own talents and refuse to allow yourself to be put down. First, try to explain to your partner how hurtful her remarks are to you. If that does not help, then simply walk away when a remark is made. When she gets no reaction, she will stop—it is the reaction that makes her feel superior. A course in assertive, non-aggressive behavior would help you understand that you have certain rights. It may also aid you in achieving the respect and consideration you deserve.

Are you easily manipulated? This is a combination of low self-esteem and non-assertive behavior. Knowing your rights and having the self-confidence to demand those rights in an assertive manner will help you become the person you want to be.

Statement 9: I love to...

Earlier you explored what you hate; now it is time to talk about the things you love. You must see to it that you spend at least a little time each day doing something that you love.

Do you love to walk? Put aside a time everyday when you can get your exercise and take a walk. Make it fun; vary the route and become familiar with your neighborhood. Your mind and body will benefit from the exercise you receive.

If a relaxing bubble bath is your favorite thing, then make it a nightly ritual. Light a scented candle, play some soft music, keep a stack of magazines nearby, put a "do not disturb" sign on the door and make this your own special time.

Perhaps you like to read but never seem to have enough time for it. In this case, declare a certain time every day that is your time only, and do not let that time be disturbed. Go into your bedroom, get comfortable, and spend the next two hours with a good book. You might fall asleep, but that is okay. You will emerge from your hibernation den more relaxed and better prepared to handle life's situations.

Whatever it is that gives you pleasure and helps you relax, it is important enough for you to set a time each day to do it. **Indulge yourself.** You will be a better person for it, and those around you will appreciate the relaxed and easy-going person you become.

Statement 10: As a child, I was treated…

What was your childhood like? Were you pampered? Were you given strict rules to obey? Were you abused? Our childhood may contribute to the type of person we become as an adult.

If you were pampered as a child, then it is very likely that you might expect a continuation of the same pampering as an adult.

Were you expected to adhere strictly to the rules set forth by your parents? If so, you may go in one of two directions; either you will expect the same behavior from others, or you will rebel and throw all of the rules out of the window.

Statistics show that many abusers were abused as children. If you are an unfortunate victim of abuse, this does not have to happen to you. Take steps early, such as professional counseling, to reverse the situation.

Childhood should be a learning experience. We can learn good things and bad things. It is your job as an adult to sift through your own experiences. Take what was good and make it better. Take what was not good and use it as a tool for improvement.

Take Change One Day at a Time

Now that you have completed the exercise above, you should have a good idea of the changes you would like to make in your life. Not all of these statements will apply to you and your own experiences and feelings. Go over the statements again and choose a statement that you feel would make the most difference if you could change your reply to it. It is vital that you do not try to alter your life too much at once; that would just leave you vulnerable to frustration and defeat. Instead, work to develop one modification until you have achieved that goal. Once achieved, choose the next most important change and continue to work through each change.

The mind and body work together as the ultimate team. The body is dependent on the mind to give it commands, and the mind is dependent on the body to carry out those commands. To give your mind the power to lead your body in certain behaviors, you must provide it with a focus. For example, suppose you chose to work on Statement 8 in the above list: "My spouse treats me…" and you completed that sentence with the words, "like a child." How would you initiate a change? The following are some ways that you can make changes.

The first step is to recognize that this is a problem for you. Next, focus on the change you want to make and examine it from every angle. Ask yourself probing questions such as: Is this how I see myself? Do I think of myself as a child? Is my behavior indicative of an adult or of a child?

We are what we believe ourselves to be. Paul Valery, French poet and critic, said, "To know oneself is to foresee oneself; to foresee oneself amounts to playing a part." If you want others to perceive you as an adult, then you must see yourself as such. You cannot act in a mature manner only until something does not go your way, and then revert to childish behavior in order to get what you want. Actions such as these send out mixed messages to those around you. If you truly wish to be treated as an adult, then you must sincerely believe you are an adult and act accordingly in all situations. **If you believe it—you will live it.**

Look the part. Act the part. Believe in yourself. For example, if you have set a goal to become a vice-president of your company, then in your mind, you are the vice-president. You must dress, speak and act as a vice-president. The day will come when you reach your goal—and it will happen because you believed in it.

An illustration of the power of beliefs can be seen in studies conducted by medical groups. In these studies, some participants are administered medication and others are given a placebo. Many of those who receive the placebo exhibit the symptoms of relief that are normally associated with the medication. Their health improves only because they believe they are getting the medicine that causes the improvement.

In seeking change, we need to keep our expectations reasonable. If you have been a loner all of your life, you will not become a social butterfly overnight. You will, however, gradually become more comfortable in the company of others. You will become more tolerant of opinions and ideas that differ from your own, and you will find a life filled with unexpected pleasures. This will all be due to your efforts and your willingness to make self-improvements.

YOUR PROFILE OF LIFE CONCERNS

We all have a priority of concerns that are problematic for us; these will differ on an individual basis. The exercises you completed earlier gave you some insight into what makes you behave the way you do. Now, it is time to prioritize a list of concerns that color your character. Remember, there is no right or wrong way to do this. Just be honest with yourself. This is another way to delve into your inner-self and discover what is topmost in your mind, reflecting on your interactions with friends and co-workers.

Please rate the following list of self-concerns on a scale of 1 to 10; 1 being of very low concern to you and 10 being of very high concern to you:										
	very low concern									*very high concern*
Self-concept, or feelings regarding yourself	1	2	3	4	5	6	7	8	9	10
Relationships	1	2	3	4	5	6	7	8	9	10
Health	1	2	3	4	5	6	7	8	9	10
Money	1	2	3	4	5	6	7	8	9	10
Work	1	2	3	4	5	6	7	8	9	10
Safety	1	2	3	4	5	6	7	8	9	10
Other _____	1	2	3	4	5	6	7	8	9	10

Which items above concern you the most? Which items are of utmost importance? Which ones did you rate as less of a priority for you? To get a better understanding of these self-concerns and how you look at things, I will now give you a few examples of real-life people and their experiences with this same exercise. As you are reading these examples, see if you can relate to any of the experiences. See if your ratings match some of theirs.

You can use the following examples as a guide to examine your own priority list. Through this review, you can discover the hidden meaning for each high-concern element. Once you understand yourself, you will be a happier and more successful person. Once you are happier with yourself, you can then be a better role model for your child and help your child develop traits that are essential for his own success and happiness.

☆ *A Concern Profile for Joan*

Joan was a client who did this very same exercise a few years back. Joan rated self-concept and relationships of highest concern to her, followed by money and work. Over a period of several sessions, Joan was able to develop and prioritize a list of concerns that we worked through.

We began by speaking about her childhood and the day-to-day experiences she shared with her parents. She stated repeatedly (but in different ways), "I could never please them. I was never good enough. No matter how hard I tried, I couldn't live up to their expectations." By the time she was a teenager, Joan's parents' high expectations, coupled with her inability to satisfy them, eroded her fragile self-esteem. The lack of parental encouragement convinced Joan that she could never measure up.

As Joan got older and entered into relationships, she assumed the same inferior role as she had with her parents. She never stood up for herself, because she felt she was not worthy. This eventually took a toll on every relationship she had. She was unable to maintain a meaningful association with another person, which further fueled her feelings of inadequacy.

Joan had a responsible position in her company and earned a good salary, but she constantly worried that the company would find someone who could do a better job. She simply could not convince herself that she was good enough. She felt she was a fraud and that she would eventually be found out, which would lead to unemployment.

It took time and commitment to undo the damage of Joan's childhood. Words of encouragement from her parents, sprinkled liberally with praise, could have prevented years of painful self-doubt. Learning this was a valuable lesson for Joan. From these lessons, she learned to be better prepared for the job of parenthood than her parents were and end the damaging cycle.

Parents who treat their children as Joan's parents did usually do not realize that they are doing something wrong. They sugarcoat their negativity with words like, "We only want you to do well so you'll be better off than we are," "We're only trying to help you" or "We only want the best for you." The problem is that, although they do want what is best for their children, they are going about it the wrong way. In the end, these parents are causing problems for their children that will last into adulthood. If these problems are not treated, it could affect their children (and grandchildren) for the rest of their lives.

☆ *A Concern Profile for Mark*

Mark's highest priority was his health. When we talked about this during our sessions together, I realized that he was allowing his fear of possible health concerns affect his life in a negative way. He stopped going out and having fun with his friends, and eventually lost many of them. He would not go skiing for fear he would break his leg. He avoided swimming pools because of the germs. Picnics were out of the question, because he could never tell if the mayonnaise was left out too long or if the restroom facilities were clean enough. The list went on and on. Mark realized this was a problem, but he could not seem to overcome his health-related fears.

When we delved into Mark's childhood, we discovered that his parents, particularly his mother, were obsessive about his welfare. He was not permitted to be a rough and tumble boy; his mother preferred that he play indoor games and watch television. Mark was an only child, and his parents doted on him. The thought of him being hurt colored every decision they made regarding his activities. He was told, in no uncertain terms, to forget about playing sports in high school—he would have to be content with cheering from the sidelines.

This became such a way of life for Mark that he allowed it to continue into his adult years. He knew no other path to follow, and the fear his parents held transferred to his own way of thinking. He wanted to break the cycle but was afraid— he did not know how to do it.

The first thing I had Mark do was make an appointment with his doctor for a complete physical examination. Once he received a clean bill of health, we slowly started to incorporate activities into his life that he had previously avoided. We began with a trip to a public swimming pool. On his first try, Mark only ventured a short way into the pool area and did not stay very long. His second try was a little better and Mark got a little closer to the pool. By his third try, he actually went into the water for a short time. By the end of the summer, his friends were pleasantly surprised when Mark suggested that they all spend a day at the pool.

One by one, we confronted the rest of Mark's fears in the same way. Although it was a slow process, Mark eventually conquered many of his fears and enjoyed activities with his friends.

☆ *A Concern Profile for Joel*

When I read some background that Joel had given me about himself, I was not surprised that he rated money as his highest priority concern. He grew up in a family where there was very little money. It was drummed into his head that every cent was to be saved and nothing was to be spent frivolously or wasted on unessential purchases. Vacations were either non-existent or were so frugal that they were not fun.

Joel remained true to his upbringing. He was frugal with his own family to the point of embarrassment. His wife finally gave him an ultimatum: get help or get out. This is what brought him to my office. He said to me, "I don't want to lose my family. I know I worry too much about money, but I can't seem to help it." By studying the actions of his parents, we were able to pinpoint the crux of his difficulties when it came to spending money. His parents had set an example, and Joel had followed it.

Although he had a nice savings account, Joel had deprived his family of things like going out to eat or going on vacation. Joel's wife, Anne, agreed to work with us in our sessions. The three of us devised a plan that began with a family dinner at a fast food restaurant. It went well, and Joel was pleased to see how much his family enjoyed going out to eat. We took it step by step and moved slowly. Two weeks later, the family went to dinner again at the same restaurant, but this time, they went to a movie afterward.

During our subsequent sessions together, Joel and I discussed many issues that concerned him. Although the outings with his family were going well, he still had worries. We talked of worst case scenarios. We also talked about making a budget that allowed for entertainment expenses. Most importantly, we talked about sharing his fears and concerns with Anne. Previously, he kept it all inside and just said "no" to expenses he thought were unnecessary. Now, by telling Anne what he was thinking and why he felt they could not afford something, she was more sympathetic to his feelings and helped him work things out.

Although Joel still has moments of frugality, the family is much happier and more secure. An added bonus is that, by discussing options, the family has found ways to enjoy time together without spending a lot of money. They have discovered things to do such as camping, family bowling nights and picnics. It made me so happy when Joel came into my office a few months after the start of our sessions and said, "Making my family happy has made me happy."

Your Past May Impact Your Child's Future

You just read a few examples of how parents can influence their children in a negative way, without even realizing they are doing so. Use those examples as guidelines to examine your own priority list of concerns. Try to discover the hidden meaning for each high-concern topic. Once you understand yourself, you will be better prepared to understand your children. Now that you know yourself a little better and have identified some areas that you feel need to be changed, you are in a better position to coach your children to success.

Some parents, particularly those who had little in the way of material goods while growing up, are determined to see that their children have everything they missed out on. The result can be spoiled children who grow into dysfunctional, unsuccessful adults. On the other hand, we all have some very positive memories of parental actions that left us with a feeling of well-being and positive self-esteem. The key is to focus on these positive behaviors and build upon them when coaching your children to success.

Think, for a moment, about your favorite relative. Why is this person your favorite relative? Is it because he gives you gifts, or because he makes you feel important? Most often, our favorite people are those who make us feel special.

My own personal cheerleader was my grandmother. She could not buy me a lot of gifts because she did not have much money. When I was with her, however, I could feel the love she had for me. I knew that, in her eyes, I was an exceptional person.

Good parenting is not dependent on how much money you have, but on how much love and quality time you share with your family. Below is an example of how one parent's past was affecting her child's life.

☆ *Esther and her Mother*

Esther was fifteen years old when her mother brought her to see me on the advice of the school counselor. The counselor saw that Esther had many friends and good leadership qualities, but she held these qualities back and exhibited signs of low self-esteem. She had many good ideas but was afraid to speak up. She usually just went along with the opinion of the crowd. If she did do something that deserved praise, she assumed it was due to luck, rather than her own abilities. The counselor felt that Esther needed to develop a sense of confidence in order to excel in her high school studies and continue excelling into her college years.

I had several sessions with Esther and a few sessions with Esther and her mother. I was able to determine that Esther's mother suffered from her own deep feelings of inadequacy and had passed these feelings on to her daughter. Esther's mother was the child of immigrant parents and grew up thinking she had to work harder to be accepted because of her background. Using her own childhood feelings of inadequacy as a reference point, she constantly admonished Esther for saying anything that might cause people to think she was different from them. Esther grew up hearing, "What will people think of you?" and "Everyone will laugh at you." By the time Esther entered high school, she had buried her outgoing personality and leadership qualities in an effort to blend into the background and avoid being criticized or laughed at.

After many sessions together, a lot of hard work and soul-searching, Esther began to believe in herself. I knew we had come a long way when she came into my office one day and was excited because she had been elected president of her junior class.

Esther's was a typical case of a parent projecting her own fears and self-doubts onto her child. If her mother had come to terms with the negative forces in her own life, she could have been a better parent to Esther through the use of encouragement and praise. This is why it is so important for you to be serious about personal life-coaching and make any necessary changes in your life—it will enable you to recognize the potential for success in your children.

YOUR PROFILE OF SUCCESS

If fifteen people were asked how they define success, there would most likely be fifteen different answers. Christopher Morely, an American Rhodes Scholar, editor and author once said, "There is only one success—to be able to spend your life in your own way."

All too often success is equated with the amount of money a person has. Some people may be more concerned with quality of life. Others insist that success lies in how much you enjoy life. Believe it or not, there is a proven formula for success, and I will share it with you now:

> **Emotional health + Social health + Spiritual health = SUCCESS**

It is not enough to be emotionally stable if you lack social skills and spiritual awareness. All three elements must be present for you to become a healthy, successful and happy person. The secret is to achieve a balance between the three. To have emotional health means that you love and believe in yourself. You must be happy with the person you are. You must be willing to change the necessary characteristics in yourself to achieve these personal tenets.

Unfortunately, many people do not really know themselves. In order to give you some clues about your inner-self, respond with true or false to the following statements. Remember to be honest with yourself when responding.

Please circle true or false for the following statements:		
1. I love to explore new places and new things.	true	false
2. I am happiest with familiar surroundings and old friends.	true	false
3. I feel a need to be accepted by others.	true	false
4. I have a hard time keeping my temper under control.	true	false
5. I am known as an easy-going person.	true	false
6. I feel underappreciated in my job.	true	false
7. I am comfortable doing things alone.	true	false
8. I always seem to be in debt.	true	false
9. I do not enjoy exercise.	true	false
10. I do all I can to maintain optimum health.	true	false
11. I believe it is "every man for himself" in life.	true	false
12. If I can offer a helping hand, I will do it.	true	false
13. I will only help someone else if it is in my best interests.	true	false

Review the previous statements and think about the ones for which you would like to have different answers. Keep in mind that everyone has different opinions of what makes them uncomfortable. For instance, the statement "I always seem to be in debt" may be bothersome to some, but may not matter to you. If you feel that you are underappreciated in your job, then you must rectify that situation in order to be a happier and more emotionally secure person. You can do this by seeking out promotions within your present company or by finding a position in another company that will make you feel more fulfilled.

When we help others and give of ourselves unselfishly, we feel an inner-sense of well-being and a lift in our spirits. That is why it is so important to think of and share your time with others who need you. For example, perhaps you could volunteer at a soup kitchen nearby or donate your time as a hospital volunteer. When you help others, it not only enhances your spiritual well-being, but also teaches your children similar values. You can even volunteer to do a charitable activity with your children. This gives you an opportunity to spend time with your children, while also helping others.

YOUR PROFILE OF SELF-WORTH

A belief in yourself and in what you can accomplish is crucial to how you assign and evaluate self-worth. Think about the following ten statements and how they relate to you. Be honest with yourself when responding.

Please circle true or false for the following statements:

1. In meetings, I am afraid to voice my opinions.	true	false
2. I recently received a promotion, but I do not really deserve it.	true	false
3. I am comfortable making decisions for a group.	true	false
4. When out with friends, they all look more stylish than I do.	true	false
5. I am as well educated as my peers at work.	true	false
6. I can be trusted with important assignments.	true	false
7. It bothers me when people do not agree with me.	true	false
8. I have a hard time relating to people who are self-assured.	true	false
9. I know that if I set my mind to something, I can do it.	true	false
10. I find it difficult to accept praise.	true	false

In responding to the key elements above, you have the opportunity to see how you relate to others. Strengthening self-belief is, perhaps, the most important step. Therefore, it is crucial that you find ways to strengthen your self-belief.

A very powerful tool that encourages you to believe in yourself is the use of affirmations. An affirmation is a positive statement used to contradict negative feelings, observations or events. For example, if you responded "true" to the statement, "In meetings, I am afraid to voice my opinions," then you should come up with a positive statement that you could repeat to yourself to counteract that negative feeling. An example would be, "My thoughts are important and need to be heard." If you responded "true" to the statement, "I find it difficult to accept praise," you can repeat to yourself, "I am a worthy person and deserve to be praised." Keep in mind that affirmations do not work by themselves and will not change you overnight, but by repeating them often, you will begin to believe in yourself and your abilities.

Return to your responses and note any that pertain to you in a negative way, and then make a list of affirmations to counteract each negative statement. This is your personal tool; it is intended to resolve the issues you have now identified. Carry the list of affirmations with you and repeat them every day.

Be Happy with Who You Are

There is a good reason why jealousy is called the "green-eyed monster." To envy your neighbor's shapely body, your friend's good job or your cousin's new home can eat away at you. It can erode your sense of self-worth and make you chronically unhappy. Are other people's lives really better than yours? Remember, the grass is not always greener on the other side.

Your neighbor may have a shapely body, but does she have your great personality? Does she have as many friends as you? Can she organize a civic event and have others depend on her like they do on you?

Your friend may have what you consider to be a dream job, but how much time is he required to spend away from his family? How many weekends is he at work while you are on the golf course? How have the pressures of his high-profile job affected his health?

Your cousin's new home may be big and beautiful, but how high are her mortgage payments? Will she have to take on a second job to keep up with the payments? How will this affect the time she can spend with her children? Will the family be able to afford a vacation every year like your family can?

Look around your home and notice all of the nice touches that make it yours—appreciate them. If you live in an apartment and plan to purchase a house someday, remind yourself of your goal and begin to prepare for that goal.

It is more important to want what you have than to have what you want. Remember to focus on the positive elements of your life. By looking at the positives, you can eliminate the envy and resentment that may cause emotional pain and anxiety.

YOUR PLAN FOR CHANGE

Be willing to change. When a pool of water does not move, it becomes stagnant. The same can be said for a life that remains the same year after year, month after month, day after day. Change is the one variable that keeps your life from becoming stale and boring. If, for instance, you are truly unhappy in your job, then begin searching for one that offers you a better fit. Do not be in a hurry—plan it on your own terms. Set your goal and work to achieve it one step at a time. Change is not always comfortable or easy, but taken one step at a time and with a definite purpose in mind, it can be the key to a more positive, enriching and happy life.

No two people are alike, and one overall plan will not do. Each plan must be tailored to individual wants and needs. To develop your personalized plan for change, you must take a good look at all of the information you have gathered about yourself in this chapter. Study it carefully, pulling out the changes you want to make in your life.

On the following chart, write down the changes you want to make in your life and define the methods you will use to bring about those changes. Also, write down some positive affirmations that you will use daily. When making your list, develop an order of priority. Never attempt to tackle more than one change at a time. Through the success of these positive changes, you will be able to see how your life has improved. You will then be able to see the impact of your positive behavior on your family, your friends and your business relationships. As you practice your new lifestyle and begin to reach the goals you have set, you will be amazed at how different your life will become.

My Individual Plan for Change

Change I Would Like to Make:

Example: Act more like an adult, so my husband will treat me like an adult.

_____

_____

_____

_____

_____

_____

_____

How I Will Make This Change:

Think before I act; do not respond childishly if I do not get my way.

_____

_____

_____

_____

_____

_____

Positive Affirmations (to be repeated daily):

"I am a mature adult. I deserve to be treated like an adult."

_____

_____

_____

_____

_____

_____

_____

_____

SUMMARY OF CHAPTER ONE

In this chapter, you learned how to avoid unproductive behavior patterns. Through an assessment of your individual profile, you were able to see which areas of your life need the most attention. You learned how to make changes one day at a time. By bringing your past into the picture, you received a glimpse of how it could affect your child-rearing abilities. You learned how to turn negatives into positives by using affirmations. You learned that success means different things to different people.

You can now give yourself the opportunity to discover what success means in your life and learn the steps you can use to reverse the negative feelings that may have impacted you. By developing your individualized plan for change, you are well on your way to becoming a happier and more successful person. You have now begun your journey toward becoming a life-coach to yourself, which will ultimately allow you to help your children.

Below, you will find some simple coaching points to remember. For each chapter, a corresponding wallet card is provided for you in the appendix. Read the points from the end of each chapter, then cut each card out from the back of the book and keep it with you to remind you of your goals.

☆ Focus on my assets.

☆ Offer only constructive criticism.

☆ Work on one change at a time.

☆ Repeat my positive affirmations daily.

☆ Emotional + Social + Spiritual Health = SUCCESS

Chapter Two

THE IMPORTANCE OF INNOVATION AND ADVENTURE

Why "But We've Always Done it That Way" Can No Longer Be an Excuse

CHAPTER OBJECTIVES

- Discover the importance of innovation.
- Assess your adventure profile.
- Learn ways to bring out your innovative side.
- Learn the importance of change, risk-taking and decision-making.
- Organize your desired life changes.
- Learn how to keep your positive qualities but change the negative ones.
- Learn how to embrace change.
- Create your Individual Plan for Innovation and Adventure.

"It is in the nature of a man as he grows older...to protest against change, particularly change for the better."
— *John Steinbeck*

In the previous chapter, you learned a lot about yourself and began some plans for change in your life. You must remember that change, even minimal change, is an essential step on the road to success. In order to help your children grow and succeed, you must first work on improving yourself.

This chapter will help you discover the benefits of innovation. You will assess your adventure profile to see how open you are to new ideas and actions, and you will learn new ways to bring out your innovative side. You will also learn the importance of taking risks, making decisions and embracing change. I will show you how to realize and retain your positive qualities, while discarding negative thought patterns and behaviors. You will learn to embrace positive changes in order to look forward to a brighter future. You will create your own individual plan for adding innovation and adventure to your life. Remember, before you can become a life-coach to your children, you must be willing to make the necessary changes in your own life.

THE IMPORTANCE OF INNOVATION

An important aspect of discovering who you are is learning to think and act innovatively. Through the ages, every invention and discovery has been the result of people who had the foresight to imagine possibilities. These people also had the courage to go against huge odds in order to see their vision become reality. Without the innovative thoughts and actions of men and women throughout the past, we would still be stuck in a cave. Someone had to notice the spark when two stones hit each other a certain way.

These observations had to be processed and projected until man was finally able to ignite materials for fire, thus changing the lives of humans forever.

You may be wondering how this applies to you in your daily routine, such as your job, your home life and your interactions with friends and family. Each person possesses two minds: a logical mind and an innovative mind. When faced with a question or a problem, your logical mind will give you an analytical, sensible and reasonable response. Your innovative mind, however, will jump ahead and say something like, "What if…?" Your innovative mind is a master of creativity and imagination, and it offers a myriad of possibilities and options from which to choose. It is from our innovative mind that we can develop new solutions to old problems.

For instance, say you are asked to chair your town's summer festival, which runs for three days. Your logical mind will say, "Are you crazy? You don't have enough time to fit it in with all of your current activities. How could you even consider taking on such a monumental job? Turn the offer down." On the other hand, your innovative mind will say, "Think of the wonderful opportunity you have been given. You can learn all sorts of things you'll be able to use later in your regular job. You can't let this opportunity pass. Go for it!"

People tend to ignore their innovative mind because of personal concerns and fears of the unknown. They choose instead to remain with the tried-and-true solutions, even if they are less than satisfactory. Many people have an ingrained aversion to change. What many people do not realize is that, while not everyone can be Thomas Edison or Alexander Graham Bell, each of us *can* address our situations with an open mind.

If you give yourself the chance, you will realize you are capable of seeing beyond the obvious and creating a different model to explore. When you do this, you will open the door to adventure and enthusiastically embrace opportunity. By embracing change and innovation, you can become a leader and life-coach; someone others depend on to take them beyond normal boundaries and into exciting new areas.

You might currently be using your innovative mind without even realizing it. How often have you said things like, "Something just told me that I should go for it," or, "It just felt right to do it a different way." **Listen to your innovative mind and follow where it leads you.** Your logical mind might try to tell you that you are being foolish, but it is not programmed for adventure. Remember, a life without adventure is a life full of yearning for a missing element.

Can you think of an instance in which you used your innovative mind and were rewarded with good results? On the other hand, are there any occasions you can think of when you let your logical mind keep you from taking an innovative approach to a problem? Consider your new insight into innovation, and think about how the results may have been different if you had listened to your innovative mind.

It takes a combination of courage and patience to hone your innovative skills, but the payoff is well worth the time and effort. The experience of learning to pay attention to your innovative side will equip you with the right tools to be a life-coach first for yourself and then for your family.

Effective use of your innovation will help you gain a reputation as a visionary; one who is not afraid to take chances or tackle larger problems. If you are just beginning your climb up the corporate ladder, you will probably find that promotions come faster as your talents are recognized and you are set apart as one of the new "innovative performers." If you are at or near the top already, your employees will respond to your actions by demonstrating loyalty to you. They will be quick to follow a leader who is always one step ahead of the pack. People tend to gravitate toward those who demonstrate self-confidence and adventure.

Think about the people you know. Who do you think has the more interesting and robust life? Is it your calm, steady, reliable and logical friend, *or* is it your intuitive, sensible, willing-to-try-something-new friend? Moving toward the point of discovery by executing your intuitive skills can offer you a new path to change. This new path can open a wide variety of doors on your road to success.

AN ASSESSMENT OF YOUR ADVENTURE PROFILE

Those who enter a situation with an open mind and try to bring innovation into play are generally more open to making necessary changes in their lives. Below, you will find an adventure assessment with fifteen true or false statements to answer. When you are done responding, you will analyze your personal adventure profile in order to initiate specific changes for personal improvement. Each of us is unique in our feelings and observations, so the best results are obtained when the assessment is completed separately by all of the adults in the family. Remember, there are no right or wrong answers—just be honest with yourself.

Please circle true or false for the following statements:

1. I like to try new and different activities.	true	false
2. I feel comfortable meeting new people.	true	false
3. My dream is to own a hot new sports car.	true	false
4. My clothing tends to be all one color, so I can mix and match.	true	false
5. My idea of a great vacation would be an African safari.	true	false
6. I tend to frequent restaurants where I know I will like the food.	true	false
7. At a networking event, I usually stay close to people I know.	true	false
8. I am excited by new challenges at work.	true	false
9. I would be willing to visit a strange city without hotel reservations.	true	false

---

10. My favorite ride at amusement parks is the roller coaster.	true	false
11. Concerning sports, I would rather be a spectator than a participant.	true	false
12. During storms, I close all windows and unplug all appliances.	true	false
13. I think people who skydive are crazy.	true	false
14. I dislike traveling alone.	true	false
15. I would like to own a motorcycle or pilot my own plane.	true	false

If you responded mostly with "true" to statements 1, 2, 3, 5, 8, 9, 10 and 15, you are a very adventurous person and look forward to the excitement of not knowing what is around the next bend. If you responded mostly with "true" to questions 4, 6, 7, 11, 12, 13 and 14, you are a solid, reliable and reasonable person, but you may not be quick to try new things. If you have a mix of responses from those two groups, you maintain a healthy balance of adventure and sensibility. You are willing to occasionally try new things in order to keep your life exciting and your skills and relationships fresh.

Bringing Out Your Innovative Side

I have found that when your mind is open to new ideas and potential for change, there is nothing to hold you back from experiencing positive progress in your personal or professional life. Developing your innovative side is the result of a dedicated effort. In turn, your focus on the innovative process will lead you to expanded horizons and an ability to embrace change. Some ways to bring out and develop your innovative side include the use of relaxation techniques and affirmations. These methods are described below.

Gaining Balance Through Relaxation

When your mind is in turmoil and you are struggling with problems, it is difficult to be innovative. Little can be accomplished until you calm your inner-self, clear your mind and let positive thoughts overtake your negative thoughts. Find a quiet place, away from distractions, where you can sit in a relaxed manner for at least three minutes. Once in this quiet place, you will experience a simple form of relaxation that will provide you with the ability to understand your personal situation and the things that impact you the most.

To begin, you need to find a personal comfort zone, which starts with your ability to breathe. When we think anxiously and have aggravating thoughts, our breathing becomes rapid and shallow. If you find yourself anxious and your breathing irregular, sit down and close your eyes. Take a deep breath in slowly through your nose. When you breathe in, feel your stomach expanding. As you exhale through your mouth, contract your stomach muscles for a count of five. Feel your chest expand as your lungs fill with air. Exhale through your mouth, to the count of five, releasing all of your negative thoughts and energy. Repeat this process over and over again until you feel yourself becoming calmer. Notice how it allows you to understand the problems that have disrupted you and your environment.

As you continue to breathe, allow yourself to be receptive to any thoughts that come to you or float through your mind. Focus on positive thoughts. Think about all of the successes you are going to achieve. Continue this process for a few more minutes and then slowly return to your surroundings. Do not jump up and get back into the swirl of things just yet. Take another three to five minutes to examine what thoughts, emotions and reactions you experienced while in your calm state. This reflection has real value and will help you grow and define your perspective of the issues at hand.

Even this simple relaxation may be difficult the first few times you try it. Try to stay focused; do not let other things pull you away. Give this relaxation time the priority it deserves. In time, you will look forward to this solitude and reflection. As you improve your relaxation techniques, you will begin to recognize ideas, answers and solutions that previously could not get through the muddle.

Using Affirmations to Support Your Innovation

As you recall from Chapter One, you can promote positive behavioral changes through the use of affirmations, or clear statements of intent voiced for personal commitment. Affirmations, when repeated often, act as positive reinforcement for thoughts and behaviors that you are working to acquire or improve. To be effective, affirmations must be stated in the present tense and repeated several times throughout the day. This will change any negative, doubt-filled thoughts to positive, pro-active thoughts.

In the previous chapter, you wrote down affirmations of your own, based on personal needs and goals. Here are a few affirmations you can use that are related to innovation:

- My openness to change is leading me on a path to inner happiness.
- My innovative side gets stronger daily.
- My innovation helps guide me in a creative direction.
- My innovation is a powerful tool that leads me along the path to success.

Work on developing your own affirmations that will help bring out your innovative side. Write those affirmations down and place the list where you will see it often, such as on the bathroom mirror or next to the phone. Put this list of affirmations next to the affirmations you wrote down in Chapter One. Repeat your affirmations often throughout the day. Remember, the more often you say them, the more effective they will be.

The Importance of Risk-taking

In order to embrace innovation, you must be willing to take risks. Most people avoid taking risks because they are scared of failure or rejection. They prefer to remain as they are, rather than risk failure. Even the prospect of being successful is not enough for them to take a chance.

In order for you to grow, you must change your attitude regarding risk-taking. Start by putting things into perspective. Just for a moment, and for this *one time only*, think in the most negative way that you can. Now, ask yourself the following questions: If I take a risk and do something that I have always wanted to do, what is the worst thing that can happen to me as a result? Will I lose face? Will I be rejected? Will I be the object of laughter? Will I be considered a failure if it does not work out? The answer to these questions is most likely "No." If any of the above did actually happen, would it be the end of the world? No. You will learn from the experience. Now throw out those negative thoughts and get positive. Remember, in order to make positive changes in your life, you must be willing to take some risks.

Do remember that there are those people who are too risk-taking and will stop at nothing to try something new, regardless of the consequences. However, innovation, coupled with logic, moderation and balance will open new paths of opportunity.

The following is an example of the positive influence risk-taking can have on your life.

☆ *Bridget's Presentation*

In college, I was in a class in which we had to prepare a paper about the United States presidential race happening that year. Each week, someone had to give an oral presentation of his paper. I remember someone I sat next to in the lecture hall, Bridget. She was terrified of giving an oral presentation. Although this was one of her favorite subjects and she was happy to turn in her paper, the notion of putting her ideas and thoughts out there for everyone in the class to hear was more than she could handle. She worried constantly with questions such as, "What if I make a fool of myself?" or "What if my work isn't as good as everyone else's?" Bridget contemplated dropping the class, but she needed the credits to graduate. She wound up staying in the course, but signed up for the last possible slot to give her presentation. She agonized the entire semester about the possibility of failure.

Finally, the day arrived for her presentation. She made her way slowly to the front of the room, her hands and voice both shaking. She knew the subject and had prepared well, but all of her negative thoughts were keeping her in a terrified state of mind. As she warmed up and started presenting, Bridget became more confident until the shaking stopped and she was lost in the topic. At the conclusion of her paper, she received a great amount of applause. On the way back to her seat, she heard comments such as, "Good work," "You really know what you're talking about" and "I wish my presentation was as good as yours."

Bridget was forced to take a risk and found that she spent the whole semester needlessly frightened. She was determined to be more confident of her abilities in the future.

The Importance of Decision-making

In order to develop your innovative side, you must be able to make decisions. Risk-taking involves decision-making. Some people are not decisive; they constantly worry about making the wrong decision and, therefore, make no decision at all. I always remind myself of the 99/1 Rule, whereby most people worry 99% of the time, about things that happen only 1% of the time. To make positive changes in your life, you need to be able to do the following:

1) Have confidence in your decision-making abilities.
2) Do not needlessly delay making a decision.
3) Realize that not every decision you make will be the right one.
4) Do not make your decision just to please others.

Each of these principles is described below, followed by an example.

1) Have confidence in your decision-making abilities.

No one can make the right decision 100% of the time. The fear of being thought of as stupid and unworthy is a problem of low self-esteem. You must tell yourself that whatever decision you make is what *you* consider to be the right one. You must tell yourself that your ideas and thoughts are good. If it turns out that you made a bad decision, at least you will know you did your best.

☆ *Jeremy*

Jeremy worked as the head of human resources for a mid-size electrical firm in Omaha, Nebraska. The firm was seeking a new junior executive in the sales department. Several candidates were interviewed until it was narrowed down to two: Ed and Richard. Since Jeremy had interviewed both men, senior management asked his opinion on which person would be better for the job. His recommendation would carry a lot of weight when the final decision was made. Both men were highly qualified for the job; Ed was outgoing and made friends easily, while Richard was serious and would put a lot of time and effort into the job. Jeremy did not want to make this decision. He thought that if he chose the wrong man, the blame would fall on him and he might be considered incompetent. There was no way to get out of the decision, so he finally recommended Ed for the job based on his easygoing manner and attitude, which were necessary for a job in sales. His decision was a good one, and Ed increased company sales by 8% his first year.

Jeremy had the expertise and was qualified to make the decision all along but was afraid of making the wrong choice. He had to be forced into making a decision. What would have happened to Jeremy if Richard had been the stronger candidate? Nothing. Jeremy made the best decision he could, based on his experience and on personal interviews with both men. That is all he could have done, and he did his best.

This example shows why it is necessary to have confidence in your decision-making abilities. People would not be asking you to make an important decision if they did not think you were capable of it. Have confidence in your abilities and do not be afraid to make decisions.

2) Do not needlessly delay making a decision.

If you put off making a decision, the delay can be more uncomfortable than the making of the actual decision. Have you ever dreaded doing something and then finally went ahead with it? How did you feel then? You probably felt relieved that you made your decision and did not have to worry about it anymore.

☆ *Marcy*

Marcy was twenty-two years old and still lived with her parents. She desperately wanted to move out but kept finding excuses not to do so. She kept telling herself that her parents would feel hurt. She worried about not being able to make it on her own and not being able to afford her monthly expenses. If she did not make it, she would have to crawl back to her parents; then she would never get out on her own, because they would keep reminding her that she tried it once and failed.

Marcy agonized over her predicament for several months and, as a result, was becoming irritable and frustrated. Finally, Marcy made up her mind. She told her parents that she felt it was time to be on her own and that she would be looking for a place she could afford. Once she found a place, she would be moving out. To her surprise, they were very receptive to the idea. She searched the newspaper for a nice apartment in her price range. It took four months, but she finally rented an apartment in one of her favorite areas of town and moved in.

Once Marcy told her parents about her decision, her entire personality changed for the better. She was doing something about a situation she had been putting off for quite some time. She took her time and waited until she found just what she was looking for—and she was able to do this because she finally made a decision. Marcy could have saved herself many months of anxiety and frustration if she had not put off her decision based on needless worry and anxiety. Once Marcy put her fears aside and forged ahead with her plan, it worked out for the best.

3) Realize that not every decision you make will be the right one. You can never be 100% sure of anything. You cannot know if a decision is the right one until you make it and see the results. If there is no way of knowing whether your decision is right or wrong until after the results, then you are wasting your time worrying instead of taking action. You could miss out on valuable opportunities while you are waiting to make a decision.

☆ *Mandi*

Mandi was offered a better job with a larger company. She had been with her present company since she graduated from college, and she was loyal to it. She also had many friends where she worked and did not want to lose them. On the other hand, the other job offered more money and more chances for advancement.

Mandi was indecisive and kept weighing the pros and cons of each place. It took her a long while to decide, but she finally called the new company and told them she would accept their offer. Unfortunately, the position needed to be filled as soon as possible, and they could not wait for Mandi to make up her mind; they had hired someone else. Mandi learned an important lesson from this experience: the next time an opportunity came her way, she would not hesitate to take it.

If you put off making a decision, the process of delaying it can be a painful one. You can miss out on great opportunities while you are waiting to make a decision. While you may not want to rush into any decisions, you should not needlessly delay an important decision—the opportunity could pass you by. Every decision you make may not be the right one, but at least you will have taken action.

4) Do not make your decision just to please others.

We all seek approval, but you should not base decisions on the opinion of others. Gather all of the information you can about the situation. Consider all angles and ramifications of that decision, and then make your decision based on the facts. If the outcome is not what you expected, then you will learn to accept it, knowing that you did your best and made the decision on your own.

☆ *Glenn*

Glenn was sure that the way to advance in his career was to go along with the ideas and decisions of his superiors. When he had to make an important decision, he tried to find out how others, especially those higher up the ladder, felt about the situation. This is what he used as a basis for his judgment. Even when he formed his own opinions, he kept his opinions to himself because he feared his superiors might not like them. He was too careful never to offend anyone of importance.

Glenn would have been much better off had he done research and reached a conclusion based on his own knowledge, rather than just trying to please others. If you always base your decisions on what you think others want, you are not learning anything new. You are not experiencing things on your own and might be missing out on great opportunities.

LEARNING MORE ABOUT THE IMPORTANCE OF CHANGE

As you learned in the previous chapter, change is a necessary element for life success. As an example, think of what happens to a body of water that does not move. Before long, it becomes stagnant. You are like a body of water; you must keep moving, keep active and change with your environment in order to stay fresh and alive.

The following is a real-life example of change from one of my counseling sessions.

☆ *The Kastor Family*

When the Kastor family entered my office for their first counseling session, all three family members were nervous. I checked my notes before they arrived and found that this was not a typical family. Kevin, fourteen years old, was being raised by his grandparents, John and Ellen, sixty-seven and sixty-six, respectively. Kevin's parents had divorced when he was five years old. His father remarried and began a family with his second wife, choosing to leave the raising of his son to Kevin's mother. Kevin's mother, however, wanted a life of her own without the burden of a child, so she had her parents adopt Kevin. She moved to another part of the country and was seldom heard from again.

Kevin was very much in need of some life-coaching to keep him from straying into unwanted behavior. His grandparents, however, were unable to provide the coaching he needed. They had no experience with coaching either in their own lives or with their daughter.

John and Ellen loved Kevin with all of their hearts, but problems had been popping up and they were at a loss as to what to do about them. In short, Kevin had been ignoring the rules they had set for him. His once good grades had steadily fallen, and he had been involved in several incidents at school in which he was bullying other students. The school counselor required the Kastors to seek family counseling, which is what brought them to my office. The day outside was a typical sunny Florida afternoon, but the atmosphere inside the office was dark and gloomy. John sat in his chair with his arms folded across his chest, while Ellen despondently twisted a handkerchief in her nervous hands. Kevin slouched in his chair with a practiced, bored expression on his face. He studiously cleaned the dirt from under his fingernails with a small penknife. My questions, designed to put Kevin at ease, were answered with one-word responses that offered no information.

I moved on to John and asked him to tell me what he thought the issue was. John's voice boomed, filling the room. "He's runnin' wild. He don't wanna follow our rules. He sneaks out at night, he's goin' with a bad crowd and he talks smart to his grandma."

Next, I turned my attention to Ellen. I asked her to tell me what she thought was the problem. Her voice trembled and she said softly, "It's like John said, he won't follow our rules anymore. Sometimes he goes to bed and then sneaks out to meet his friends. Everything was fine 'til about a year ago, then he changed, and that's when all this trouble started."

During this exchange, Kevin continued to clean his nails while slouching in the chair. I turned to him and asked, "What do you have to say, Kevin?" His answer was short and to the point, "Nothin'." I explained that we were all there to get to the bottom of the problem and to find some answers that would bring them back together as a family. Suddenly, Kevin opened up and started shouting.

"It's their dumb rules. I changed, but the rules didn't. I have to be in the house by nine. I can only watch certain television shows. I always have to let them know exactly where I'm goin' and who I'm gonna be with. And look at these clothes they make me wear; the kids at school think I'm some kind of geek!"

"We have these rules because we love you," Ellen stammered.

"There's nothin' wrong with these rules. They were good enough for your mother," John bellowed.

"Yeah, and where is she now?" Kevin shot back. "She left to get away from all your dumb rules." This obviously hurt everyone. John turned his face away, while a tear rolled down Ellen's cheek. Kevin looked miserable.

From this exchange, I found a link to work with—"They were good enough for your mother." This comment gave me a place to start. Ellen and John's rules were strict and, though they had been put in place with love, they were outdated and inflexible. It was clear to me that John and Ellen had to learn that times were different and that they would need to consider change. Kevin also had some learning to do. He had to understand that these rules were for his own good and that he had to learn to work with them. While many of the rules could be modified, some rules, such as having to let his grandparents know where he was and who he was with, would not go away.

We set up a schedule of appointments, some with all three family members, some with Kevin alone and some with Ellen and John alone. After several sessions, I was able to convince John and Ellen that times were different and that, although Kevin still needed them and their guidance, he should be allowed a few more freedoms. As a result, several adjustments were made. They modified his time to come home, increasing it by one hour during the week and two hours on weekends. This eliminated his nocturnal escapes to be with his friends. He was permitted to choose his own clothes, with the stipulation that he would not go too far out. Ellen agreed to this, provided that if she absolutely disapproved of something, he would not wear it. Most importantly, John and Ellen agreed that they would be non-judgmental when he brought friends home, trusting in Kevin's good sense to choose the right friends.

For his part, Kevin agreed to abide by the new rules and also agreed, reluctantly, to let them know who he was with and where he was going. Trust had to be rebuilt between Kevin and his grandparents, and that would take time. Their willingness to change and to consider each other's needs was a powerful step. This family learned how to negotiate without manipulation.

I am pleased to say that, after one year, the family was happy once again and Kevin's grades started to climb back up. I am not saying that their lives are problem free; no family is immune to problems. By working together, however, and being open to change, we were able to resolve many issues and problems and make everyone happier.

The big hurdle for John and Ellen boiled down to just one word: **change**. Though they eventually made the necessary changes, it was a long process for them. The love of their family, however, overcame their stubbornness; it was important for them to be finished with the bickering and anger that had invaded their home. They wanted to enjoy the time remaining with the beloved grandson they had raised.

We worked on one issue at a time. The first issue was to get John and Ellen involved in a parenting group. Ellen was hesitant, because she felt she was much older than the other parents. Once there, however, she discovered that age did not matter and that her family's problems were not unique. In fact, many other families were experiencing the very same issues. Eventually, both John and Ellen were able to relax and became active members of the group. Kevin lived up to his part of the deal as well. He came in on time every evening. After a while, John and Ellen knew they could trust him and allowed him other liberties as well.

From this experience, the Kastors have found that balance offers many opportunities. John was an avid chess player, and he showed Kevin and a few of his friends how to play the game. This evolved into a chess group that met in Kevin's home. This chess group allowed John and Ellen to get to know Kevin's friends, and they found that they were good kids.

During my sessions with the Kastors, we incorporated steps from the Pyramid of Success. We identified changes that were necessary, developed and organized a plan, wrote down goals and put those goals into action. They learned to communicate with each other. I taught them the importance of embracing change. We worked on their emotional, social and spiritual health. We monitored how each of their behaviors affected themselves and those around them, and then discussed how to modify their behavior and set new goals. Ultimately, this allowed members of the Kastor family to achieve their full success potential, both as individuals and as a family.

What the Kastors found is that, through change, the elements that did not work previously could be reformed to fit today's standards. When they opened themselves up to change, their lives improved dramatically.

Organizing Your Desired Personal Life Changes

In the previous chapter, you completed your "Individual Plan for Change" and wrote down some changes you want to make in your life and ideas of how you are going to make those changes. Now that you understand the importance of risk-taking and decision-making, it is time to go over some of those life changes. You will now review and organize how you are going to make those changes happen. Remember, this may be a slow process, so results will not be achieved overnight.

First, look at the list of changes you wrote down. Now, refer to what you wrote down as the method for achieving these changes.

Try to think of some other ways you can accomplish these changes. Next, prioritize your list of changes, putting the changes you feel are most important at the top of the list. These are the ones you will concentrate on first. Ask yourself why you want to change that particular behavior pattern, then think about your behavior and why you act as you do. What can you do differently? What should you keep as-is? Identify the steps you need to take in accomplishing each change, and then make that change happen. Practice, practice, practice until the new behavior pattern becomes a part of who you are. Eventually, you will discover that change is not so difficult.

The following is an example of identifying and accomplishing a change:

1) Identify the desired change: *Become a more assertive person.*
2) Write down ways to bring about this change:

- *Pay attention to people whose assertive style I would like to emulate.*
- *Read a book on assertiveness.*
- *Take a course in assertive behavior.*
- *Practice with small points, like sending back a restaurant meal I am not satisfied with or saying no to a request I would rather not fulfill.*

The above example can be used as an outline for changes you want to make in your own life. It is well worth the time and effort to do these exercises. You will find that your life can be improved, and you can feel stronger as a person.

Note: Do not confuse assertive behavior with aggressive behavior. This will be discussed in greater detail later.

Keep the Positive and Change the Negative

Have you ever heard the old saying, "Don't throw out the baby with the bath water," or "Don't cut off your nose to spite your face?" These adages, though old, still hold as true today as when they were first uttered.

What those wise people were saying is that you should keep what is good from every situation and discard only what no longer works. While we are discussing changes within yourself, you must decide which qualities to keep in your present behavior and which qualities to change.

NON-ASSERTIVE, AGGRESSIVE AND ASSERTIVE BEHAVIORS

Look at the previous example of wanting to become a more assertive person, and view this example in light of these adages. Perhaps you are a non-assertive, but really nice person. In making your change and becoming assertive, you want to make sure you do not rid yourself of your "nice guy" reputation. **In order to be happy, you must like yourself.** If you lose the nice image, you might lose your ability to think well of yourself. An easy way to lose that nice-guy quality is if you step over the line from assertiveness to aggressiveness. While you *do* want to change your behavior from meek to assertive, you also want to retain your nice-guy personality by not being overly aggressive. What you are doing is keeping the positive and changing the negative. In sticking with the assertive versus aggressive example, take an honest look at yourself and examine how you would react to the following situations.

☆ *A Quiet Evening at Home*
You planned a quiet evening at home to watch a television special you have been waiting for over one month to see. You prepared a hot cup of cocoa and sat down on your favorite recliner to watch the show. Shortly after getting comfortable, you receive a call from a friend who only calls you when she needs something. She asks if you can watch her kids while she runs some errands for a few hours.

How do you respond to this request? Here are some examples of non-assertive, aggressive and assertive responses to her request:

> *Non-assertive:* "Well, I was going to watch this television show, but (sigh) okay, bring them over. I guess I can catch it on a re-run."

> *Aggressive:* "No way! I have plans of my own and I'm tired of you only calling when you need me to baby-sit."

Assertive: "I'd love to help you out, but I have plans for tonight. My neighbor's daughter babysits regularly in the area and may be able to help you. Would you like me to get you her phone number?" or "I'd love to help out, but I already have plans for tonight. I'd be happy to watch the kids tomorrow evening."

The non-assertive response places you in a less-than-desirable position and gives your friend permission to continue to use you. If this decision is a burden to you, it can generate feelings of resentment. You can feel used and unappreciated, and the resentment can grow. As a result, your self-esteem may suffer and you may find that you are unhappy with yourself and your actions.

While the aggressive response may give you the peaceful evening at home that you wanted, it positions you as a bully and may hurt your friend. This may change the way she views you and your relationship.

The assertive answers are the winners. You get to follow through with your plans of a relaxing evening at home, and you have also offered your friend good alternative solutions to her problem. Whether she chooses to use those alternatives is up to her, but you can feel good knowing that you have given them to her as viable options that serve both of you well.

☆ *Exciting Plans After Work*

You have plans to enjoy dinner and a show with some friends after work tonight. You have been planning this outing for a few weeks and you are very excited about it. As quitting time nears, your boss tells you he has to give a presentation at 10 a.m. the next day and needs you to stay and type it for him.

How do you respond to this request? Here are some examples of non-assertive, aggressive and assertive responses to his request:

Non-assertive: "Sure, I'll get it done for you. I'll just make a phone call and cancel my plans for the evening."

Aggressive: "No. My quitting time is 5 p.m., and if you want me to stay later than that you need to let me know by noon. I have a life too, you know."

Assertive: "Actually, I have plans for this evening that I made a while ago, but I'll be happy to come in an hour earlier tomorrow to help you out. If you leave it on my desk tonight, I'll have it ready for you when you arrive in the morning. That will still give us time to make any changes you want before the meeting."

The non-assertive response places you in a win-lose situation. Your boss wins—you lose. You will not be able to go to your concert and you will disappoint yourself and your friends. You might also grow to resent your boss for "making" you stay and work. This resentment will continue to fester, eroding your already fragile self-respect.

The aggressive response will label you as uncooperative, and it may spoil your chances for advancement in the company. This may be especially true if you have a demanding supervisor. While it may offer you a short-term victory of allowing you to go through with your plans, your long-term position in the company will probably suffer.

The assertive response offers a win-win solution. It allows you to proceed with your plans, while effectively supporting your organization and making your boss happy. Your supervisor will appreciate and respect the fact that you are willing to arrive early to have the work finished for him.

APPLYING INNOVATION AND ADVENTURE TO YOUR FAMILY

Up to this point, you have looked at your individual plan for change from both personal and professional perspectives. Now, take a look at how this idea of change could affect your life as a parent. When you have a child, you tend to raise that child very close to the way your parents raised you. Even people who say things like, "I'll never do that to my child," usually do those things they swore off. It is normal for us to react in a familiar way, so we may continue the cycle demonstrated to us by our parents. The problem is that not everything your parents did was right. Times change and so do child-rearing principles.

The advent of computerization for the masses has changed some aspects of childhood forever. Parents who have open minds and are receptive to change within their own lives will be better able to adapt to the differences in the lives of their children. What used to be good when you were a child may not be good anymore.

People who resist change are likely to have certain characteristics in common. For example, those who happily embrace change enjoy figuring out different ways of doing things and learning more about other people and how they do things. They tend to be more low-key and easy-going and, therefore, find it easy to get along well with different types of people. On the other hand, people who are afraid of change like to do everything in a consistent and predictable manner. They are often more comfortable listening, instead of talking or telling others what to do. If you asked people who are afraid of change how they preferred to do things and interact with others, some of the responses might be:

- "I like it when things go smoothly and there is not a lot of change."
- "I enjoy working together with others on projects and just being one of the group."
- "I like tried-and-true methods of doing things."
- "I enjoy praise when it's sincere. It doesn't have to be loud; quiet recognition and appreciation are fine."

Unexpected changes can be difficult for all of us. We must learn to handle these situations without stress. Do not shy away from changes; instead, strive to meet them head-on. In time, each change will become a little easier and less stressful.

If you fear change, you are more likely to take care of things yourself, rather than trust someone else to do it your way. It is important that you learn to delegate tasks to get the desired results. Realize that others might do things differently than you would, but they are still capable. Be open to change. You will find that you have fewer burdens, and you will begin to enjoy giving others the chance to experience success in a job well done.

We all like things to go smoothly. Often we try to avoid confrontations by remaining quiet and unassuming. In learning to deal with change, however, we must learn to be more assertive. You will learn soon that people will work more effectively and more willingly with or for someone who is self-assured enough to lead the way and who projects an image of confidence.

Finally, you must learn acceptance. Change is inevitable; you will lose if you try to fight it. By accepting change as a part of life, you can experience the opportunity to learn, grow and discover new and different things.

In both my practice and my life, I have observed that some people need to be forced to change, but once they do change, they become avid advocates of the process. Below is an example of someone who was forced to embrace change but benefited in the end.

☆ *Larry*

Larry is an example of an individual who needed to be convinced of the need for change. His mind was closed, and he did not take kindly to learning new processes or exploring new ideas. Larry was a professional printer who began his career when type was set by hand. Over the years, the printing industry went through a series of drastic changes until the company Larry worked for finally shifted to being completely computerized. In order to keep his job, Larry had to learn each new process as it came along. He changed, even though he resisted it. As a result, he also experienced new elements in his personal life, becoming more open to change, which allowed him to bring about differences in his private life.

Now that Larry knows more about computers, he is able to email his grandchildren who live in another state. Instead of a monthly phone call, he emails a few times a week. He is able to see pictures of his grandkids online and print them out to show his friends. It is clear that, although Larry was forced to change, it benefited him and his family in the end. As a result, Larry will probably be more open to change in the future.

Below is a poem by an anonymous author that sums up this "Embracing Change" section very well.

The Comfort Zone

I used to have a comfort zone where I knew I couldn't fail,
The same four walls of busy work were really more like a jail.

I longed so much to do the things I'd never done before,
But I stayed inside my comfort zone and paced the same old floor.

I said it didn't matter that I wasn't doing much,
I said I didn't care for things like diamonds or furs and such.

I claimed to be so busy with the things inside my zone,
But deep inside I longed for something special of my own.

I couldn't let my life go by just watching others win,
I held my breath and stepped outside to let the change begin.

I took a step and with new strength I'd never felt before,
I kissed my comfort zone good bye and closed and locked the door.

If you are in a comfort zone afraid to venture out,
Remember that all winners were at one time filled with doubt.

A step or two and words of praise can make your dreams come true.
Greet your future with a smile, **success is there for you!**
— Author Unknown

Repeat the last line of this poem to yourself several times: "Success is there for you!" You can begin right now to develop a plan that will put you on the path to success.

IMPROVING YOUR INNOVATION AND ADVENTURE

Now that you have learned the importance of innovation and adventure, I want you to document a plan for trying new things and embracing change. On the following chart, in the left column, list some innovative ideas you might have or some adventures you might like to try. In the right column, write down how you can achieve that goal. For example, you might have always wanted to paint your bedroom a bold color with fancy stencil work. In this case, some ways you can achieve this goal are by going to a hardware store and getting paint samples, or by going on the Internet and searching for designs that inspire you. Another example is if you have always wanted to ride a roller coaster, but were afraid to try. One way of achieving this adventure is to go to a nearby amusement park. Open your mind and be adventurous...the possibilities are endless.

My Individual Plan for Innovation and Adventure

Innovative Idea/Adventure I Want to Try:

Example: Take a road trip.

_____

_____

_____

_____

_____

_____

_____

Ways I Can Achieve This:

Go online and print out maps; invite friends

SUMMARY OF CHAPTER TWO

In this chapter, you organized your plan for change and success by continuing to work on your emotional health. By working on your emotional health, you are getting more equipped to be a life-coach for your children.

This chapter taught you that an important asset of discovering who you are is to think and act innovatively. Through an assessment of your adventure profile, you found out how open you are to new ideas and actions. You learned how to bring out your innovative side with the use of relaxation and affirmations.

This chapter discussed the fact that, although change is good and necessary, not everything about old ways is bad. You learned to pick and choose what aspects of your life you feel need to be changed. You learned about the importance of taking risks, making decisions in a timely manner and embracing change. Finally, you finished by documenting your individual plan for innovation and adventure.

☆ Try a new activity.

☆ Decide on a life change I can make.

☆ Repeat my positive affirmations.

☆ Practice asserting myself.

☆ Embrace change.

Chapter Three

ASSESSING YOUR LEADERSHIP SKILLS
Documenting Your Leadership Plan

CHAPTER OBJECTIVES

- Learn what it means to be a leader.

- Learn about the qualities common to all leaders.

- Learn how to incorporate leadership qualities into your family life.

- Assess your current leadership skills.

- Learn ways to practice your leadership skills.

- Document your leadership plan.

*"If your actions inspire others to dream more, learn more,
do more and become more, you are a leader."*
— *John Quincy Adams*

In the previous two chapters, you examined your lifestyle, discovered areas that you felt needed to be changed and worked on those changes in order to work toward the ultimate goal of success. In this chapter, you will continue your journey toward self-improvement and success by working on your leadership skills. Remember that creating and documenting your goals is the third step on the Pyramid of Success. Enhancing your leadership skills is an important goal you should set. By enhancing your leadership skills, you can help both your professional life and your family life. You can advance in your job, because you will show people how capable you are and be granted more responsibility. At home, you will be able to guide your family with strength and purpose, without being dictatorial. You will also be an excellent role model for your children to emulate.

In this chapter, you will learn what it means to be a leader. You will learn about the qualities that are common to all leaders and how to incorporate those qualities into your family life. You will assess your current leadership skills and learn how to practice using those skills. Finally, you will create and document your own individual leadership plan.

WHAT IS A LEADER?

Every unit, whether it is an organization, job or family, must have a leader to be successful. In a family, the leadership role most often belongs to the parents. As children grow in an effective family unit, they are given opportunities that will allow them to assume more duties and responsibilities over time. If they have parents as good role models, they will have no trouble stepping into demanding situations that may arise in their future, because they will have spent years as a member of a team with one or both parents positioned as team leader(s). This will make the transition from childhood to adulthood much easier.

Leadership is the ability to influence others to work toward desired goals and objectives. The primary function of a leader is to show others the way through words and actions. While there are many sources of social power, it is generally accepted that effective leaders in our culture are not dictatorial in nature, but they are looked up to and respected. Some people are natural leaders who others gravitate toward for guidance, while others must work at being a leader and strive to learn leadership qualities.

Every company values employees who can lead. If you show your employer that you are a respected and confident leader, your chances for quick advancement will increase tremendously. If you display excellent leadership qualities at home, you will be a role model for your children, which will help them later in life. Once you have mastered the skills of becoming a leader in the workplace or at home, it will be a simple transition to use these skills in other situations.

Being a leader is not always easy. There are times when you must make unpopular decisions and disagree with your friends, family or associates. Knowing, however, that your children are observing and learning from your example should make it easier. You will be setting standards and examples that your children can follow when faced with peer pressure.

Good leaders do not make decisions based solely on personal preferences. Rather, they gather solid facts, accurate intelligence and sound reasons for making decisions. They consider what is best for the majority. Good leaders are open to different opinions and opportunities. They are not afraid to change their stance about something when new information comes along or if someone suggests a better alternative. The following is an example of such a leader.

☆ *A Real-Life Example of Leadership: Matthew*
Several years ago, I was asked by a member of a local school board to sit in on a meeting that was open to the public. He wanted me to

observe one member in particular, Matthew, who was resisting change by being obstinate and holding up a major decision that had to be made.

The intermediate school was outdated and in need of major repairs. The school district had given authorization to either repair the building or tear it down and build a new one. The school board was given the power to make this decision. This issue caused many heated debates at Board meetings, as members of each side were ardent in defense of their own views. The Board had received several bids from contractors to do the job, but it was coming down to the wire. The government grant money was in jeopardy of being rescinded if they did not act soon.

Studies were conducted showing that, without a doubt, it would be more economical and beneficial to build a new school rather than repair the old one. The problem was that many of the parents had sentimental ties to the old building and wanted to repair it instead of build a new school. Matthew initially agreed with the parents' views and supported repairs to the old complex. As a result, he had become the leader for that group, and they looked to him to uphold their position. It now appeared that no amount of persuasion or information could convince Matthew to vote for building the new school.

I attended the meeting and observed the debate and conflict within the room. After the meeting, I met privately with Matthew. He admitted that the plan to build the new school made more sense, but said, "The parents are depending on me to stick to my guns, and I don't want to let them down."

It took many hours and several pots of coffee, but I finally convinced Matthew that, because he was looked to as the leader of the group, he had the power to bring the facts to the parents. I told him that he should calmly and rationally explain that, although he was originally in agreement with their views, he had come to the understanding that it would be in the best interest of both parents and children to vote for the new building. While I agreed with him that it would not be easy, I made it clear that he could put out the fires by being a true leader and doing what was best for the community.

Matthew called a meeting with his group to discuss the pros and cons of keeping the old building. He explained that he had changed his mind on the proposal, and then presented his reasons for the change. He then urged the parents to examine the facts in a non-biased way and follow him in efforts to bring harmony to the assembly. Although there were still a few who grumbled and remained dissatisfied, most saw that he was right and followed his lead.

Matthew performed well as their representative when he exhibited his true leadership abilities. He recognized what was best for the community and convinced others to see the facts and make the best decision. As a result, the children of that community received the opportunity to go to school in a modern and safe building.

COMMON QUALITIES OF LEADERS

What is it that makes people gravitate toward certain individuals and look to them for leadership? Is it a force or magnetism that pulls them? Is it due to attitude, personality or knowledge? Actually, it is a combination of traits and talents that all leaders have in common.

The following are eleven leadership qualities common to all leaders:

1) Knowledge and confidence
2) Effective communication of knowledge
3) Approachability
4) Comfort in leadership positions
5) Loyalty
6) Organization
7) Fairness
8) Remaining calm during disputes
9) Effective delegation skills
10) Willingness to give credit or take blame
11) Humor

These leadership qualities are followed by examples of people who either exhibited these qualities or could have used these qualities to be a more effective leader. Later in this chapter, you will learn how to incorporate these leadership qualities into your family life.

Leadership Quality 1: Knowledge and confidence

To be an expert leader, you must be knowledgeable of every phase of an operation for which you are responsible. This is because employees at work and family members at home must have confidence in their leader's ability to make effective decisions.

When a question is asked, leaders must be prepared to respond with an authoritative answer or clear position. Leaders must find a solution based on their knowledge and experience, then demonstrate an effective resolution process and a commitment to their choice. Others are depending on your leadership, so you cannot expect them to provide you with the knowledge you need—you must seek it out on your own.

As the leader, you must project trust and confidence and demonstrate ethics at all times. Providing false information or poor judgment will yield negative results, and the truth will come to light at some point. As a leader, it is vital that you are credible and trustworthy.

While you are not expected to know everything, you are expected to get answers. Do not be afraid to say, "I don't know, but I'll find out for you." By admitting that you do not have the answer, but offering to get it, you will gain respect. After all, **truth has power.** The following is an example of what can happen if you are dishonest and claim to have all of the answers.

☆ *A Real-Life Example of Knowledge and Confidence: Melanie*

Melanie had a problem admitting to her son that there were some things she did not know. It started when her son, Timmy, was quite young and into the "why" and "what's that" stage. When he would ask a question that Melanie did not know the answer to, she would make one up. She rationalized that he was too young to know the difference, and it was fun to see him believe everything she told him. As Timmy got older, however, he began to question the answers he received. Unfortunately, making up answers had now become a habit for Melanie.

Timmy finally discovered that not all of Melanie's answers were correct. In fact, some of them just did not make sense. When

Timmy went to school, he repeated the information his mother had given him to some friends and they laughed at him for being so wrong. In time, Timmy began to mistrust what his mother told him. He lost his confidence in Melanie and stopped asking her questions. It got to the point where Timmy did not believe much of anything his mother told him. Melanie had lost the respect and admiration of her son. This all could have been avoided if Melanie would have taken the time to find the correct and honest answers for her son when he was younger, rather than making things up.

Trust is too precious to ruin with lies. If you do not know the answer to something, admit to it and then take the time to find the answer. Others will respect you as a leader for seeking out truth and knowledge.

Leadership Quality 2: Effective communication of knowledge

Have you ever taken a course with a teacher who was extremely knowledgeable in her field, but when the class was over, you felt as though you had not learned a thing? Have you ever asked for an explanation from someone and, after a lengthy answer, you did not know any more than before you asked the question? Being knowledgeable and being able to communicate that knowledge are two very different things.

In order to communicate your knowledge, you must first have patience. You must remember that if someone knew the answer, he would not have asked you in the first place. Never make people feel like they are stupid for asking questions. If you do, it will not only intimidate them and keep them from asking questions in the future, but it will make others lose respect for you. Never be too busy to give explanations.

While certain information is basic to you, it may not be easy for others. Keep your reply simple and avoid using a lot of technical terms, unless you are sure others will know the meaning of those terms. Answer the question that was asked. Offering more explanation than is necessary will only cause confusion. In other words, if someone asks you what time it is, do not give a speech about how the watch was made.

Remember that if others do a good job, it is going to reflect well on you. Therefore, it is to your advantage to see that they understand and do the job correctly. Another advantage of giving a good explanation is that others will truly understand and learn from you, so that the next time the situation arises, they will remember what you said and know what to do. In the long run, it saves you time to explain it right the first time. The following is an example of what can happen when someone is extremely knowledgeable in his field but does not know how to communicate that knowledge.

☆ *A Real-Life Example of Effective Communication of Knowledge: Eli*

Eli was one of the top people in the field of public relations. He owned a company and had many prestigious clients. When Laura had the opportunity to attend a lecture by Eli, she was thrilled. This was the field she had decided to enter as a profession, and she was excited to listen to an expert in the field and learn from his experience.

Unfortunately, she was extremely disappointed with his lecture. Eli's talk was full of industry terms that were unfamiliar to most in the audience. Questions that could have been answered in a few sentences were long and boring, and often lost the original thought. Laura had very limited funds and felt that the lecture was a waste of her money. She had a negative view of Eli after that lecture.

Had Eli considered the knowledge level of his audience and simplified both his talk and the answers to questions, he would have been much more effective as a speaker and teacher. Eli could learn from his experience by asking the audience to evaluate his lectures; this would allow him to know what was good about his speech and what areas he should change.

Leadership Quality 3: Approachability

As a leader, your workers and/or your family must know that they can come to you with a question or problem. Your workers depend on you to give them information, settle problems and relay any grievances through the proper channels. The same situation is true of your family; they must know that they can come to you at all times.

There are different ways to be approachable. Some people use an "open door" policy. This means that individuals know they can approach you at any time. Others use scheduled periods of time to be reached. For instance, let everyone know that you will be available any time between 1 p.m. and 3 p.m. This allows you to do your work, uninterrupted, for the remainder of the day. If you choose to schedule your open time, it is vital that you stick to your word and are available at the time you set. You should also make it clear that you expect to be informed at any time in case of an emergency, and explain in detail what constitutes an emergency.

Make sure you choose a method of approachability that suits you best. Whichever method you choose, be sure that all persons involved are aware of it. People like a leader who is available, approachable and helpful. The following is an example of how important it is to choose a style of approachability that works for you.

☆ *A Real-Life Example of Approachability: Nathan*

Nathan was a friendly guy. When he became a manager, he thought he would do well with an open door policy. To his dismay, he discovered that he was working late most nights to catch up on the work that he could not get done during the day. People were in and out of his office all day with questions and concerns. Each time he began to concentrate on the pile of papers on his desk, another employee wandered in and wanted to talk. After a few weeks of this, he found that, unless he wanted to live in his office, he had to change his policy.

Nathan called a meeting and informed everyone of the change in his policy. He said that, unless it was an emergency, his office would be open only between the hours of 2 p.m. and 4 p.m. It took a few days for his employees to become familiar with the new time limits, but a gentle reminder from Nathan got everyone on the new schedule. Nathan was then able to keep up with his work, while still being approachable and available to his employees.

Leadership Quality 4: Comfort in leadership positions

Being a leader is not all wine and roses. There are some people who simply do not like the responsibility of leadership. There are times when you must come off as the "bad guy." Friendships frequently suffer when one friend becomes a leader. If you are not willing to put up with any of these things, then being a leader is not for you. You have to make that decision; no one can make it for you.

There are many people who are happy to continue with what they do and have no desire to reach higher. All they want is to go to work, do their job, go home and get their paycheck. There is not anything wrong with that. It would be a mistake to take a leadership position if you do not really want one. It would make you and those around you unhappy, and you would probably not do the best job. Occasionally, management will observe a worker who performs duties excellently and, as a means of reward, will promote that worker to supervisor. If the employee, however, is not interested in a supervisory position, everyone would benefit if she would turn down the promotion.

As a supervisor, there will come a time when an employee needs to be disciplined or when management needs you to pass along unpleasant information, such as bad news regarding pay increases or vacations. These are all things that might make the leader appear as the "bad guy." As a result, you may have to reprimand a friend, be excluded from get-togethers or notice a pause in conversation when you approach. There comes a point when friendship must give way to supervision. If you are not willing to draw the line between friendship and supervision or put up with these pressures, then you should rethink your position as a leader. There are few things worse than getting up every day and going to a job you hate—you suffer, the job suffers and those you work with suffer.

You may, however, be a person who thrives on the pressures and responsibilities that go along with leadership. In this case, you would probably make a great leader. Evaluate your current position and then decide if you would be comfortable in a higher leadership position. The following is an example of a person who was ready and eager to be in a leadership role. As a result, she thrived in her new position.

☆ *A Real-Life Example of Comfort in a Leadership Position: Christine*

Christine had been working for her company for five years and was beginning to feel restless. She knew every aspect of her job and had trained a number of new employees. Christine felt that she was at a standstill. She knew her job so well that there was no longer any challenge involved. She was beginning to feel that she wanted to move on to something bigger and better.

One day, everything changed. Christine was called into the office of the top official of her company. She was told that her immediate supervisor was taking an early retirement and that he had recommended her for his position. Because of his recommendation, management had been watching her carefully for the past several months. They liked what they saw and decided that she was the best person for the job.

Christine became a supervisor and handled her new responsibilities well. She was able to maintain a friendly relationship with the other employees and, because of her knowledge of departmental duties, she was able to help solve many problems that arose.

As a result of her new position, Christine became a much happier person and fulfilled her duties with much success. She was perfect leadership material and was finally utilizing her full potential. Christine put her leadership qualities to good use and worked successfully to make everyone happy.

Leadership Quality 5: Loyalty

The people you lead, whether they are your family, your employees or a committee, expect you to stick by them. They expect you to represent them and their best interests. At work, however, your company depends on you to look after company interests and uphold company rules. Sometimes you might feel torn between your loyalty to your employees and your loyalty to your company. This is not easy, but a good leader can handle it. You must be able to separate your two loyalties and fulfill both roles while satisfying both parties. This takes a person with an even temperament, effective communication skills and the ability to see both sides of an issue. A leader who can do this is invaluable, and will be rewarded by both employee loyalty and company recognition. The following is an example of a leader who was loyal to both the company and his employees.

☆ *A Real-Life Example of Loyalty: Frank*

Frank was the supervisor for the shipping room employees at a small manufacturing plant. Everything seemed to be going well until the company decided to stagger lunch breaks, rather than have everyone go at the same time. These employees, for the most part, had worked together for a number of years and had developed friendships. Everyone had particular friends they wanted to eat with and enjoyed the camaraderie that existed when the whole group ate together. It was such an important issue to the workers that they threatened to walk out over it.

Frank had his hands full; the workers were threatening a walkout and management was depending on him to settle things amicably. He called a meeting during which he explained the company's reasoning behind the change. The economy was not great at the present time and, in order to meet costs, they could not afford to have all of the work and machinery shut down for one hour each day. They did not want to take away something the employees enjoyed, but it was a simple matter of economics.

The employees understood the situation as Frank described it, but they were still opposed to the idea presented by management. Frank asked if anyone had any suggestions on how to remedy the situation. A hand went up in the rear of the room and John, a man who was looked to as a leader by the others in the department, offered a solution.

"Maybe," he said, "a few men, a skeleton crew, could keep the machinery running and handle the work until the rest return from lunch. The men who would remain to work would be on an alternating schedule, so that the same people wouldn't have to do it regularly. That way, the department can continue to run, while the majority of workers would still be able to have lunch together."

After some discussion, the workers of the department agreed that they could accept such a plan. Frank presented the plan as outlined by John to management and they also accepted the solution. While it was not the ideal situation for everyone involved, it was a fair compromise that benefited both the employees and the management.

This is a clear example of two people who used their leadership qualities effectively. Frank used his skills to approach employees in a proper manner, while John used his leadership position as unofficial spokesperson to offer a compromise. The two men proved their loyalty to the company by finding a solution to provide continuous operation, which was necessary to meet rising costs. They also proved their loyalty to their fellow employees by recognizing legitimate grievances, listening to their views and offering a workable compromise. This compromise aided in increasing company loyalty for all employees.

Leadership Quality 6: Organization

Organization is a building block to success. To be an effective leader, you must be organized. You must always have a plan for each day—a flexible plan, but a plan nevertheless. Know what you want to accomplish. Set a time for each project, but be reasonable and be sure to factor in interruptions. Keep it loose, but keep it organized.

One of the most important aspects of being organized is to set priorities. Decide what needs to be done and in what order. You will be surprised at what a difference it makes when you are not jumping from one project to the next, or when you do not have six different things going on at the same time. Your work will go more smoothly, you will not feel so hassled and you will accomplish a lot more with less anxiety. You will also discover that working with a schedule makes both your personal and professional life easier. The following is an example of someone who took charge and decided to organize her life.

☆ *A Real-Life Example of Organization: Jeanne*

Jeanne was a stay-at-home mom. She was married and had two small children. Her life was hectic, to say the least. Things piled up around the house, because she never had the time to clean up and clear out the unnecessary items. Her desk was piled high with letters she had to respond to, bills she had to pay and coupons she had to sort. She was experiencing anxiety, and knew she had to gain control. The problem was she simply did not have the time or energy to devote to organizing her life.

Jeanne made a decision that saved her sanity. Out of desperation, she enlisted the help of a professional organizer. The organizer came into Jeanne's home and helped her eliminate the clutter. She then showed Jeanne how to organize, such as designating a place for every type of item. For instance, boxes for toys were put in places that were convenient for the children. All clothing was hung up and not thrown over the backs of chairs. Dishes were dried and put away, not left to dry on the counter.

Jeanne and her family had a meeting and everyone agreed to follow the new guidelines. It did not take long for Jeanne's home to go from hazard to happy. Due to some simple organization, her home and her mind were free from clutter, and her productivity showed a marked increase.

Leadership Quality 7: Fairness

A good leader is a fair leader. Others may disagree with your decisions, but people will learn that they can count on you to be a fair arbitrator and not show favoritism. Do your best to see that work is equally divided, and never let misunderstandings fester. Make your decisions known, as well as your reasons for making those decisions—and stick to those decisions. Do not allow yourself to be swayed by the loudest argument. In general, do your best to be fair in all of your dealings. Being fair is not always easy, but it is always right. The following is an example of a leader who made a difficult, but fair, decision.

☆ *A Real-Life Example of Fairness: Sanford*

The company Sanford worked for was sending him on an all-expenses-paid trip to act as their representative at a national convention. He was told that he could take one other person from his department with him to serve as an alternate. He was advised that the person he chose to take should be able to represent the company in a knowledgeable manner.

Sanford had a dilemma. His best friend Jim worked in his department and would expect to be chosen for the trip. Sanford knew they would have a wonderful time if they went together, but he also knew that Jim was new to the company and still had a lot to learn. Bob, on the other hand, would make an excellent representative. Although he and Sanford were not especially close, Bob was knowledgeable and represented the company well.

After careful consideration, Sanford asked Bob to go to the convention with him. Sanford called Jim into his office and privately explained to him that, although he knew they would have a good time traveling together, he knew Jim was not yet ready to answer difficult questions about the company. In fairness to the company and to the employees, he had to choose the person who was most qualified for the job. Jim understood and was glad that Sanford had taken the time to explain his reasoning to him. Sanford saved a friendship and made the best choice for the company by acting fairly.

Leadership Quality 8: Remaining calm during disputes

The number one factor for staying in control during a dispute is to keep a tight reign on your temper and avoid engaging in a shouting match. If you begin to shout and argue, you have lost control of the situation. You have put yourself in a position of defense and have made yourself vulnerable. In addition, you might have lost the respect of those for whom you are expected to set a good example.

One of the most effective tools a leader can possess is the ability to remain calm and in control. There are several ways to do this. If you find yourself losing your temper, you can try doing the following:

- Acknowledge the other person's feelings (e.g., "I can appreciate the way you feel, and I'm sorry you feel that way.").
- Suggest discussing the matter at a later time when both parties are calmer.
- Grip the sides of a chair, pencil, notebook or any other object that will help you release the tension, instead of blowing up at the person confronting you.
- Calmly excuse yourself and leave the room; e.g., "I'll be right back; there's something I need to take care of." Take a minute to calm down, use positive affirmations and then return to the room.

Your attitude reveals many aspects of your true self. Remember, cooler heads always prevail. The following is an example of someone who remained calm in a difficult situation.

☆ *A Real-Life Example of Remaining Calm During a Dispute: Sylvia*

When Sylvia signed on as a volunteer for her local school board, she was warned to watch out for Jacki, who was a known troublemaker. Sylvia tried to heed the warning, and went out of her way to avoid any confrontation with the infamous Jacki. Unfortunately, no matter what she did, Jacki tried to use it as an excuse to start an argument with her.

One day, when both women were at the snack table, Sylvia accidentally spilled some coffee on Jacki's blouse. Jacki blew up and accused Sylvia of everything from spilling the coffee on purpose to trying to manipulate the rest of the board members. Sylvia remained calm and tried to reason with Jacki, but Jacki continued to rant. As a last resort, Sylvia calmly said, "I cannot discuss this with you when you are so upset. Once you've calmed down, I'll be happy to talk to you about what's bothering you." With that, she left the sputtering Jacki and went back to the meeting.

By remaining calm and not letting Jacki's comments personally affect her, Sylvia was able to gain control of the situation. Thus, she gained the respect of the other board members.

Leadership Quality 9: Effective delegation skills

There are some leaders who try to do everything alone, because they are afraid that either it will not be done to their satisfaction or that they will be perceived as incapable if they do not do it themselves. Do not try to be a superhero. Getting the work done well and on time can only be a credit to you if you use good delegation skills. Proper delegation is an art form. The following are a few basics you can use to begin delegating.

Give some thought to whom you will delegate responsibilities. The first person you meet is not always the answer. Each project will have certain requirements. Think about the person who will best fill the role. If the task requires a lot of detail work, then choose a person who is very detail-oriented. If the task requires a lot of social contact, then choose a person who works well with others.

Once you choose the proper person, make sure you do the following:

- Make sure that person understands his role. Be certain he understands the role's expectations. Ask if there is anything else he needs to know before starting the project.
- Be certain to set the rules.
- Let that person know you will support him.

- Offer to help, if needed, but allow that person to do the project himself.
- Give any insight you have as to who will or will not be cooperative.
- Let the deadline for the final report be known, and set one or two dates for a progress check. Be definite in times and duties.
- Let that person know he will receive recognition if the job is completed correctly.

Once you learn to delegate some of your responsibilities, you will feel a huge weight lifted off your shoulders. The following is an example of a mother who had to learn to delegate her responsibilities to other members of her family.

☆ *A Real-Life Example of Effective Delegation Skills: The Millers*

Sylvia Miller was a full-time mom, head of the PTA and very involved in local charities. She was always busy picking up the kids from school and taking them to soccer practice and ballet lessons. When she was not playing the role of chauffeur, she was running PTA meetings or volunteering at local charities. Sylvia began to feel overwhelmed; it seemed as though there were not enough hours in the day to get everything done. When she got home from her busy day, she still had laundry and other chores to do around the house. She thought about asking her husband to help, but she was worried that he would be too tired after coming home from work. She thought about asking the kids to help out, but she was worried they could not do as good a job and might turn all of the clothes pink when attempting to do the laundry.

One morning, the kids were telling her of all the activities they had for the day and when they needed her to pick them up. Then her husband asked her to pick up his shirts at the drycleaners. All of a sudden, Sylvia got completely overwhelmed and shouted, "Stop! I'm not a superhero—I can't do it all!" Her family was stunned; they had never seen her react this way. They had always assumed that she could handle everything.

Sylvia gained her composure and said to her family, "I'm sorry. I've just been feeling very overwhelmed lately and could use some help around here." The Miller family talked it out and decided to delegate responsibilities. Sylvia agreed to teach her son how to do the laundry, and he agreed to do it on the weekends. Sylvia's daughter agreed to take the trash out every night. Sylvia's husband agreed to pick up the kids from their after-school activities on his way home from work. This freed up much of Sylvia's schedule so that she did not feel like everything was on her shoulders.

It was hard at first, because Sylvia had to relinquish some of her control. At first, some of the laundry turned colors or shrunk, but Sylvia showed her son the proper way to do it and he eventually learned. Sylvia was worried that her husband would forget where and when to pick up the kids, but he got the hang of it and would call her if he had any questions.

By delegating her responsibilities and trusting her family, Sylvia felt a huge sense of relief. She no longer felt overwhelmed. As a result, she was a calmer, more easy-going person.

Leadership Quality 10: Willingness to give credit or take blame

Give credit where credit is due; that is the fair thing to do. If others see that their efforts are recognized, they will be much more willing to go out of their way to do a good job for you again.

On the other side of the coin, if a project fails, do not always blame others for everything. You are the leader, and some of the responsibility must fall with you. It is up to you to choose the right people for the job, follow-up with their progress and see that the work is done properly. If a project fails, do not beat yourself up over it, but acknowledge your responsibility and be willing to take some of the blame.

By giving credit where credit is due and taking the blame when things go wrong, you are showing that you are a true and responsible leader, and others will respect you more for it. The following is an example of someone who did not take responsibility for his actions and tried to place blame on others.

☆ *A Real-Life Example of Willingness to Give Credit or Take Blame: Shawn*

Shawn was given the task of preparing a proposal to obtain more work from an important client. He was going on vacation in a few weeks, so he enlisted the help of Alex, a fairly new employee. Shawn did the preliminary work before going on vacation and then turned the project over to Alex. When Shawn returned from vacation, he scanned Alex's work quickly and then sent the proposal to the client. The client rejected the proposal because of several errors in cost figures, and the work went to a competitor.

Shawn was called into his manager's office who proclaimed his disappointment in the careless work that was sent to the client. Rather than apologize, Shawn began to offer excuses such as, "They wanted this in a rush, and I didn't have time to check it as thoroughly as usual." He tried to shift the blame by saying, "Alex did that part of it and never told me he was having a problem. It wasn't my fault. I did my part and everyone else let me down."

Shawn would have gladly taken credit if the proposal had gone well. Since it did not, however, he avoided taking blame for a failure that could have been avoided if he had done his work properly. As a result, Shawn was not only reprimanded by his manager, but he also lost the respect of his co-workers.

If Shawn had taken the blame and faced up to his mistake, he might still have been reprimanded for not being thorough, but he would have gained respect in the eyes of his co-workers and manager for admitting his faults and not blaming others. Remember, if you drop the ball, do not blame others.

Leadership Quality 11: Humor

All leaders make mistakes from time to time. You should never be so serious that you cannot laugh at yourself every once in a while. Everyone makes mistakes, and sometimes those mistakes are really stupid. Laughing at yourself is a great tension-breaker; it puts everyone at ease and makes it easier for others when they make errors. Presenting yourself as perfect only sets you up for failure. The following is an example of someone who used humor to diffuse the tension of an awkward situation.

☆ *A Real-Life Example of Humor: Miguel*

Miguel had prepared all day for his meeting with the management team to discuss his possible promotion. He was excited and nervous about the meeting. He went in and sat down. Just as he was pouring himself a glass of water, his glass tipped over, spilling the water all over the table. Miguel got very nervous, but then realized that he was human. His bosses would not have called him in there if they didn't respect his work. Miguel thought of a quick come-back line.

"Anyone else want a glass of water—I'll try not to spill it on you. It's a good thing I'm not applying for a job as a server, huh?" The management team all laughed and everything seemed okay after that.

Miguel had confidence in himself and realized that he could diffuse a potentially awkward situation by using humor. The meeting went very well, and Miguel was later awarded the promotion.

YOUR PERSONAL ASSESSMENT

In order to decide which leadership skills you already possess and which skills you still need to develop, you are now going to fill out a questionnaire to determine your leadership potential. On the following chart, you will find ten true or false statements. When you are done responding to the statements, you will assess your responses and initiate specific changes for personal improvement. Each of us is unique in our feelings and observations, so the best results are obtained when the assessment is completed separately by all of the adults in the family. Remember, there are no right or wrong answers—just be honest with yourself.

Please circle true or false for the following statements:		
1. I feel confident expressing my opinions.	true	false
2. People often look to me for guidance.	true	false
3. I could be described as a risk-taker.	true	false
4. I enjoy making decisions.	true	false
5. I do as much as possible to help others.	true	false
6. I admire people who are respected and confident leaders.	true	false
7. I work well as part of a team.	true	false

8. I am comfortable speaking in public.	true	false
9. I listen to and consider the opinions of others.	true	false
10. People say I am easy to talk to.	true	false

Leadership Statement 1: I feel confident expressing my opinions.

A good leader exhibits confidence in her opinions. If you know a subject well, whether it is related to your career, your family or an organization, you should be ready to say what you are thinking without hesitation. If you feel that you are not prepared to share your views, then you may need to become more familiar with the topic.

You should practice a few positive affirmations (you can use the ones you created earlier or create new ones) and repeat them often throughout the day. The affirmations will help you believe in yourself, and will give you the self-confidence to let others know your opinions. The goal here is not only to be confident, but also to exude that confidence. **When you believe in yourself, others will believe in you too.**

Leadership Statement 2: People often look to me for guidance.

If people view you as someone who can guide them in the right direction, your leadership abilities are already apparent. When people are natural leaders, others can sense this quality about them. If you are a natural leader, follow up on it and use this to your advantage.

If you are not a natural leader and need to develop your leadership skills, you should examine past experiences to see what you could have done differently. You can then coach yourself to correct any qualities that might hinder you in your efforts. Eventually, you can become a leader who people look to for guidance.

Leadership Statement 3: I could be described as a risk-taker.

A good leader must be willing to take risks. Risk-taking is not easy; it can be challenging and even frightening. It might be scary to take risks, because it could leave you vulnerable to failure or ridicule. In seeking success, however, you must exercise personal strength and confidence. You must want success enough to take risks. Everyone makes mistakes from time to time. If you do make a mistake, admit it, learn from it and move on. Through life-coaching, you can eradicate your fears and move ahead in life.

Leadership Statement 4: I enjoy making decisions.

Leaders make decisions. It is as simple as that. They do not push decisions onto others, and they do not blame others when things go wrong. Good or bad, the outcome rests with them. If you are uncomfortable with this, then you may need to rethink your position as a leader. While it is easy to live with the rewards of success, the tough part is living with the negative outcomes that may accompany certain decisions. You must learn to live through both the good and bad outcomes that go with making decisions—that is your job as a leader. Study some past decisions that you have made and contemplate what was good about those decisions and what you could have done differently.

Leadership Statement 5: I do as much as possible to help others.

People depend on leaders, so it is important that leaders do not let them down. As a leader, you should be ready and willing to provide any assistance that is within your power. Sometimes this assistance is simply to steer people in the right direction; other times it may require active participation on your part to create solutions.

Have you helped others in the past? Have you been there for people when they needed you most? If not, think about a situation in the past where you could have helped someone. Figure out what you could have done to be more helpful, and make the decision to be more receptive to helping others in the future.

Leadership Statement 6: I admire people who are respected and confident leaders.

Who do you consider to be a hero? From childhood on, we select characters and people that we look up to and want to emulate. It can be anyone from fictional characters to real-life examples. We admire people for many reasons—money, fame, character, beauty, integrity, etc.

As we grow up, we look to our leaders to fulfill our hero representation. If you have found a heroic leader, then you can model yourself after that person. Heroes and leaders are real and vibrant, and if you are elevated to this level, you need to honor it.

Leadership Statement 7: I work well as part of a team.

No leader can stand alone, since leadership is granted by those who are being led. Therefore, leaders must be able to work well with others and be effective team builders. Leaders should never ask others to perform actions they would not want to do themselves. When leaders are one with their team, others will go the extra mile for them; the team will do this not because they have to, but because they want to.

If you have an aversion to working as part of a team, try to figure out why this is so. Consider past experiences that you have had as a team member and discover why you dislike teamwork. Once you have done this, you can then work to change your outlook.

Leadership Statement 8: I am comfortable speaking in public.

Speaking in public should be easy and enjoyable for you if you have self-confidence, know what you are talking about and are comfortable in your leadership role. Statistics show that people who are comfortable in almost any other situation still have a fear of public speaking. If you have this common fear, there are classes and self-help groups to get you over the anxiety of giving a speech. Each time you speak and express your opinion, speaking in public will become easier for you.

Exercise your outgoing side by becoming an effective extrovert. You can do this by speaking in public. As your own life-coach, you can study your fear of public speaking and decide exactly what aspect you fear most. You can help yourself become a better, more confident public speaker by doing things such as taking a public speaking class, taking deep breaths and meditating in order to relax.

Leadership Statement 9: I listen to and consider the opinions of others.

Good leaders value the opinions of others. Leaders should never feel that their decisions represent the only path. They should be open to all voices. This does not mean leaders should be swayed by every person who provides input in the decision-making process, but it does mean that considering all angles will yield the best solution to any problem. Leaders should be focused on the final outcome rather than on their own agenda. There is no such thing as too much learning; something can be gained from every idea, especially those that differ from your own. If you open your ears and mind to others' thoughts and opinions, you will become a more effective leader.

Leadership Statement 10: People say I am easy to talk to.

People will see you in a much more favorable light if they know they can speak to you freely. If you brush them off or make yourself unavailable when they need to talk to you, they will not want you to lead them. If possible, they will find someone else to lead them. If you truly want to be a leader, then you must make yourself accessible to others. If people are comfortable with you, they will want you to lead them.

APPLYING LEADERSHIP SKILLS TO YOUR FAMILY

Our main discussion thus far has centered on you and the development of your leadership role. We are now going to see how your development as a leader can affect your family. Every group needs leadership, and a family is no different. Without proper guidance, this central unit will fall apart.

Raising a child in today's world can be extremely difficult. Your children look to you for guidance. Even if they seem to rebel against your authority at times, they still need your guidance and leadership and will appreciate it later in life. If you remember that you are a role model, your family members will take their cues from you regarding what is right and what is wrong. By providing them with the guidance of a good leader, you will be helping to create a happy and successful family. You will see your children follow in your footsteps to success.

By excelling as a leader, you bring values and ideals into your family that your children will benefit from for the rest of their lives. The leadership qualities mentioned earlier in the chapter can be transferred to family life easily and will enhance your relationship with your children. Let us take a look at the leadership qualities again, this time in relation to your family.

Leadership Quality 1: Knowledge and confidence

By gaining knowledge about different subjects and learning with your children as they learn, you will be more confident in answering their questions. By maintaining a confident manner, your family will perceive you as a person who believes in what you say, and this will build their trust in you. They will also learn to have faith in their own ideas and not be afraid to voice their opinions.

Leadership Quality 2: Effective communication of knowledge

When explaining something to your children or teaching them how to do something, be sure to be clear and concise. Remember that your children are learning from you. Just because you know how to do something well does not mean your children will catch on right away. Be patient and take your time when explaining things.

Leadership Quality 3: Approachability

Your family members need to know that you are there for them if they need you. You need to assess the situation. Sometimes they must wait for your attention. They can't expect you to always drop what you're doing, but they should always know they can always interrupt you in an emergency. Perpetual excuses, such as "I'm busy now," or "Can't it wait until this television show is over?" can leave your children feeling unimportant. It may make them feel like they cannot count on you for support. They need your attention now—not later. Make sure your children know that you are there for them and that you want to help them in any way you can.

Leadership Quality 4: Comfort in leadership positions

You must be willing to take both the good and the bad as a leader. When your children succeed and make accomplishments in their life, you can pat yourself on the back for having a hand in that success. There are times, however, when you must play the disciplinarian or be the "bad guy." You must feel comfortable in your role as a leader in your family. You must display confidence and know that the decisions you make for your family (as hard as they may be) are for their own good.

Leadership Quality 5: Loyalty

One of the most important ways to build trust in your family is to show that you are loyal to them. Make them your first priority. Make sure they know that your job, your volunteer commitments and the errands you have to run all come after your commitment to them. Sometimes you might have to make decisions that seem like you are siding with someone else. When this happens, let your children know that the decisions you make are for their own good and that they are still your number one priority.

Leadership Quality 6: Organization

Be an example to your children. Show them that by being organized, everything is handled more easily and efficiently. Create game plans and schedules. Organize your paperwork so that documents are easy to find. Organize your kitchen so that cooking is clean and orderly. By watching your organized style, your children will learn how much easier life is when they are organized.

Leadership Quality 7: Fairness

Your children will look to you to help them when problems arise, whether their problems are at school, during play or within the family. They will count on you to take an impartial view and not play favorites. Do not show favoritism to one child over another. Recognize that each child is different and that they all have their strengths. Show fairness when assigning chores by developing a method in which each person does an equal share, including you and your spouse. Be fair in all of your dealings.

Leadership Quality 8: Remaining calm during disputes

By remaining calm in the midst of confusion, you retain control of your family and their respective tempers. You can exercise your authority in a way that helps everyone settle down and discuss problems in a mature manner. This can bring about a solution that will be agreeable to everyone.

Leadership Quality 9: Effective delegation skills

Your family needs to know what is expected of them. Each family member should have specific chores to do. By delegating household responsibilities, you take pressure off yourself and teach your children about responsibility and work ethic.

Make sure the chores you assign fit the person. For example, it makes no sense to have your five-year-old daughter wash dishes, while your twelve-year-old son picks up toys from the floor. Be sure that each person has chores that are age- and skill-appropriate. Giving children responsibilities that they are not capable of performing properly will only frustrate and anger them, causing upheaval within the family. If more than one child is capable of performing the same chore, perhaps a rotating schedule can be worked out.

Leadership Quality 10: Willingness to give credit or take blame

Everyone will work harder and more effectively if they are recognized for their efforts. There are many ways to do this. Give credit for things well done during the family dinner hour. Have a weekly family meeting to praise your children for the good things they have done. Another idea is to post a notice on the family bulletin board. It is not important what method you use to give credit and appreciate your family, but it is important that you recognize and praise your children's accomplishments.

Set a good example by showing that the blame for any situation should lay with the person responsible. If you continually place blame on other people, your children will think this is the right way to react. Show them that responsible adults admit their mistakes and accept the consequences of their actions. Your children will not think less of you if you admit you make mistakes; in fact, they will feel more comfortable with you because they will know you are human too.

Leadership Quality 11: Humor

You are a leader, but this does not mean you will always make perfect choices. Learn to laugh at your mistakes. You will not only show your children that it is okay to make mistakes, but you will lighten the atmosphere and create family harmony.

IMPROVING YOUR LEADERSHIP SKILLS

So far in this chapter, you have learned what leadership entails and how to be an effective leader. It is now time to practice your leadership skills, because just reading about becoming a leader does not make you one. You need to jump in, get wet and develop and practice your talents. The following are some ways to practice your leadership skills.

Charities are always in need of help. Sign up for a charity and practice being a leader by taking charge of an area of the organization. By volunteering, you will not only be developing your leadership skills, but you will also be helping out a worthy cause.

Another excellent way to get leadership experience is on a civic level. Almost every town has some sort of festival or large event that is held annually. Normally, there are plenty of worker bees, but no one wants to take on the role of queen bee. Having a lead role can actually be the least demanding job, if you use your leadership abilities correctly. You need to employ each skill listed above, especially delegation, organization and standing firm in your decisions. If done properly, the event will run smoothly, and each person will know what her responsibilities are and how to follow through with them. This experience will be invaluable to you.

Do you belong to any large organizations? Do they hold annual conventions? This is your opportunity to demonstrate your expertise as a leader. Offer your services to the committee planning the convention. Speak up at the meetings and make your opinions known in a confident manner.

The more often you exercise your leadership skills, the more they will become second nature to you. These are only a few ways for you to practice your leadership skills. Think of other ways you can practice your leadership skills and try those methods out. In the next section, you will be documenting your own leadership plan.

Positive Inspiration: The more you lead, the more you will want to lead. Being a leader takes practice and patience. Remember that you were put into a leadership position because you have demonstrated the ability to do the job. If this is a position you want and you feel that you can handle all that goes with it, then by all means grab it and go for it. You are a fair leader, a respected leader, a confident leader, an approachable leader, a calm leader and an organized leader. You are a leader who has good delegating skills and is not afraid to use them. You are a leader who will give credit when credit is due and take blame when appropriate. You do not take life so seriously that you cannot laugh at yourself. You realize that you are human and subject to error, as are the people you lead. Others enjoy having you as their leader.

Document Your Leadership Plan

Give serious consideration to how you can develop and document your leadership plan. What steps do you need to take to make your plan work? Do you feel like you are not strong enough to assume a leadership role? Perhaps you can take an assertiveness training workshop at a local community college. Do you feel like you are too high-strung and aggressive to lead your family? Perhaps you can enroll in a yoga class that can help you learn to relax.

On the following chart, list at least at least five places (e.g., your place of employment, civic organizations, etc.) where you might try your hand at a leadership role. Next to each place, write down how you can assume a leadership role there. Within the next three months, volunteer to lead an upcoming project in at least one of these places. After six months, assess how much you have moved ahead and how much more of a leadership role you have assumed. You will be proud of yourself for the progress you have made and how far you have come.

My Individual Leadership Plan

Places I Can Assume a Leadership Role:

Example: *Volunteer at the PTA.*

_____

_____

_____

_____

_____

_____

_____

_____

How I Can Lead at These Places:

Head a sub-committee.

_____

_____

_____

_____

_____

_____

_____

_____

_____

SUMMARY OF CHAPTER THREE

In this chapter, you learned what it means to be a leader. You learned the qualities that are common to all leaders and you read examples of how different people put these leadership qualities into action. You then learned how to incorporate these leadership qualities into your family life. You assessed your current leadership skills, and the assessment you completed helped you realize the areas you need to improve upon to prepare for leadership roles.

Career and family go hand in hand, and the same leadership qualities used on the job can be used in the home. Therefore, you practiced some leadership skills and learned how to apply them to your own family.

Finally, you created and documented your own individual leadership plan by seeking out ways you can hone your leadership skills and assume more responsibilities. By following the suggestions in this chapter, both you and your family will benefit from the happier, more self-assured person you become. The positive changes in your life will affect your role within the family, giving you the advantage of influencing your children in a positive manner while leading them in their search for success.

> ☆ Be knowledgeable, communicate my knowledge well and display confidence in my knowledge.
> ☆ Be loyal, be fair and be approachable.
> ☆ Remain calm, be organized and delegate responsibility.
> ☆ Be responsible by giving credit and taking blame.
> ☆ Be comfortable as a leader and laugh at myself.

Chapter Four

USING YOUR PROFESSIONAL AND LIFE EXPERIENCES TO SET FAMILY SUCCESS GOALS
Mixing Business With Pleasure

CHAPTER OBJECTIVES

- Learn about the "business" of raising a family.
- Learn the traits of successful people and how to incorporate them into your family.
- Learn the secrets of successful managers and how to incorporate them into your family.
- Learn how to combine management skills with love.
- Assess your child's success skills.
- Create a positive family environment through life-coaching.
- Review how to achieve overall success in your family.
- Design a success plan for you and your family.

"It is easier to rule a kingdom than to regulate a family."
—*Japanese proverb*

In this chapter, you continue on your journey toward self-improvement by learning how to use management skills in your family life. You will learn that raising a family is a lot like running a business. I will teach you the traits of successful people and the secrets of successful managers, so that you can use these in both your professional and personal life. You may notice that some of the traits and secrets of successful managers are similar to the leadership traits you learned about in the last chapter. In this chapter, however, we will be looking at these traits from a different angle.

Next, you will assess your family's success skills in order to identify areas in which you can bring about positive changes. I will then show you how to create a positive family environment through coaching. Finally, you will design a success plan that can be used to lead your family to harmony and success.

THE "BUSINESS" OF RAISING A FAMILY: YOUR MOST IMPORTANT MERGER

When two companies merge, they do so hoping to build a better, more productive business by combining the best skills of both companies. In a family, the personalities, talents and competence of each member is merged under parental leadership. The difference between running a family and running a business is that you must lead your family with love.

Success, whether in business or family, is not achieved without compromise. Many individuals feel that if they follow a certain formula and faithfully do certain things, everything will run smoothly and life will be wonderful. By believing this false illusion, people may get frustrated and give up when they meet resistance. It is important to remember that there are no formulas for parenting—there are merely guidelines that will set you on the right path and help ease your way through problems.

No one likes to deal with unpleasant situations, but every problem, no matter how big or small, can and should be used as a learning experience. Once you meet the problem head on and find a solution, you will know how to handle similar situations in the future. Remember, no problem is insurmountable, and all families encounter problems from time to time. It is how these problems are tackled that determines the outcome. You can either cause the problem to escalate into a major issue, or find a resolution to the problem that satisfies everyone. The way you deal with a problem will help determine the resolution.

In preparing yourself through successful personal life-coaching, by setting goals and developing your own life-plan changes, you now will know the proper way to address issues and problems that might arise in your family. Life-coaching will not eliminate your problems, but it will arm you with the proper tools to meet obstacles head on. It will also build your confidence and self-esteem, so that you can successfully and responsibly lead your family.

☆ An Example of the Importance of Compromise: The Rogers Family

The Rogers family consisted of Ted, his wife Mary Lou, and their fifteen-year-old daughter, Missy. It was the typical family with the usual parent-child skirmishes.

Ever since Missy entered high school, she began to stay late after school with her friends and come home after dark. When Missy's parents questioned her about this, Missy became obstinate and accused them of trying to prohibit her time with her friends. Missy said all she was doing was spending time with her friends at school, talking and hanging out.

This may have seemed like a minor problem to some families, but for the Rogers it was a big problem. The family had always been very close, and now this closeness was being threatened. Each time something was said to Missy about not coming home on time, she would reply, "You don't understand. I just want to spend time with my friends. Can't you understand that?"

Ted decided to call a family conference. He proposed one possible solution that met everyone's approval: Missy's friends could come over to the house on specific days after school. The refrigerator would be stocked with soft drinks and snacks. The game room would be off limits to everyone except Missy and her friends between the hours of 3 p.m. and 5 p.m.. They would have the freedom to talk and snack for a two-hour period, without interference.

This solution worked out well for this particular family. Other problems can be solved in a similar manner by using discussion, compromise and understanding.

USING COMMUNICATION SKILLS AT WORK AND HOME

How you say something is equally as important as what you say. If you use your communication skills properly, you can be a very constructive force. If you use them improperly, your influence will prove to be destructive instead. **Communication is the lifeblood of socialization.** A person who is a good communicator can expect to both move ahead in business and be an effective and positive influence at home. The example you set for your family will provide a role model for your children to follow in their search for success and happiness.

A communicator has it within his power to be either a positive and helpful influence or a negative influence that destroys initiative and self-esteem. The same principles that apply to the workplace can be transferred to the home to help promote family harmony.

I was once called into a company to observe a manager and give him advice. He was well liked by management because of his work ethic. In addition, he knew the product inside out, was loyal and had worked for the company for many years. The problem was that he had difficulty communicating with the employees he managed.

Through several meetings with him, it became apparent that he was having the same difficulty at home. It seemed as though every time he asked his children to help with anything, it turned into an argument. After several observations and counseling sessions where we worked on his communication skills, we came up with the following list of life-coaching tips that proved to be helpful both at work and in his home. The following tips can help you as well.

Life-Coaching Tips:

1) Study the situation carefully.
2) Opinion or fact?
3) Be willing to assume some of the blame.
4) Do not analyze inappropriate behavior—deal with it.
5) Balance criticism with praise.
6) Do not personalize your criticism.
7) Build goodwill.
8) Avoid generalities.
9) Avoid absolutes.

Tip 1: Study the situation carefully.

Before you jump in with advice, you should know what is actually happening.

In the home: You come home from a long day at work to find your daughter in front of the television with an open textbook in her hands. You immediately tell her she must turn off the television and study in her room without distractions. Her attempts at, "But mom…" are ignored as you continue to lecture on the bad habit of having the television turned on while trying to do homework. It is only after your lengthy monologue that she has the opportunity to tell you that she was doing her homework. Watching that particular show was given as an assignment in her history class, and a paper based on the show was to be written the next day.

On the job: You notice that Gladys, a new employee, is taking an especially long time filing. You stop by her desk and explain your method of filing in great detail and how much faster that method is. You find out later that her immediate superior told her to take her time learning a new system he had put into place.

Tip 2: Opinion or fact?

We all have strong opinions about some topics and, at times, we allow those opinions to be confused in our minds with facts. Before criticizing, listen carefully to the facts and be sure that what you are stating is a fact, not merely your opinion.

In the home: Your teenage son wants to attend his first rock concert. Although you have never been to such an event, you have formed the opinion that there is nothing good about these concerts and you refuse to allow him to attend. You discover later that this particular concert was sponsored by reputable members of the community and was well-organized and chaperoned. You have refused permission to your son based on your opinion, an opinion that you considered to be fact.

On the job: For five years, you performed a particular task at work. Now your duties have changed and someone else has been given that assignment. You watch for several days to see how he will handle the job. It seems to be going well, but it is not how you did it. You approach him and tell him that he is not doing it correctly and proceed to show him the right way. You have criticized based on your opinion, but you have made that opinion a fact in your mind.

Tip 3: Be willing to assume some of the blame.

Avoid "you" comments, such as, "You never ask for directions." Instead, say something along the lines of, "Let's make sure we have all the directions right before we leave." When you say "you," you are placing blame, which will always result in a defensive reaction.

In the home: Instead of telling your child, "You always leave your room such a mess," try to take a different approach. "We need to talk about your room. Maybe I didn't explain clearly enough how to keep it in order." This takes the accusation out of your remark and gives the impression that you are not placing blame entirely on her shoulders.

On the job: Customers are complaining about the abrupt manner in which your secretary answers the telephone. There are two ways to handle this: You can do it yourself by saying, "I may not have made myself clear on the way I would like to have my phone answered. Let's sit down and go over the procedure." Another way is to have a speaker who specializes in telephone etiquette come to the company and give a talk to all the employees. His helpful suggestions can incorporate the problems you are having without actually confronting the individual. Either way, you are showing your willingness to confront the problem without casting your secretary in a bad light.

Tip 4: Do not analyze inappropriate behavior—deal with it.

Your goal should be to deal with other people in such a way that you will bring about the desired behavior and exercise your authority with the least embarrassment and discomfort to the other party.

In the home: If Carla neglects her homework nightly by watching television or talking on the telephone, telling her that she is avoiding the problem and that she is shirking her responsibility will do no good. It is up to you to take charge. Turn off the television and allow no calls until the homework is completed, even if it means you will also miss a favorite program. The most important thing is to stick to the rules. By coming up with a solution-based approach, you are able to change the inappropriate behavior.

On the job: You have an employee who is chronically late. Telling him in front of his peers that he is lazy and inconsiderate will humiliate and anger him. Instead, take steps to deal with him privately. Give him ultimatums informing him of the consequences he will face if he continues to disregard the time. Then, as above, follow through. It does no good to make threats that are never carried through.

Tip 5: Balance criticism with praise.

Constant criticism will result in low self-esteem and an antagonistic attitude. By interjecting praise, people will understand that you recognize their skills and strong points, and your advice will be taken as an attempt to help them do better.

In the home: Your daughter, Marsha, is learning to sew. For her first project, she has chosen a pattern that is more complicated than she can handle. Instead of saying, "You'll never be able to make that," you can say, "You learn so easily that I know you could make this, but why not try something a little simpler for your first project and save this for later?" In this way, you have 1) told her that she learns things quickly, 2) given her your faith that she will be able to handle the pattern and 3) assured her that she can make the pattern she chose at a later date.

On the job: You feel fortunate that you have a secretary who is skilled in office procedure, making your job easier. You have noticed, however, that her telephone skills are not always polished. You feel that this reflects badly on you and the company. You might approach her with, "I rely on your help in running this office. You save me a lot of time and aggravation daily, and I also appreciate how well you relate to people. I'd like to help sharpen your telephone skills even more. The local phone company is offering a seminar on telephone etiquette and professionalism. I'd like to send you to that seminar and have you give a report on it at our next staff meeting so others can benefit from it as well." You have boosted her confidence by letting her know that she is valuable to you, and you have given her the responsibility of relaying what she will learn to others.

Tip 6: Do not personalize your criticism.

Keep personal observations out of any criticism. It will put your impartiality at risk, in addition to causing hurt and anger.

In the home: Bette's friend is having a party and Bette has not received an invitation. Instead of saying "Don't be such a baby! You always take offense at nothing," try something like, "It may have been an oversight. Why not call her and tell her that you haven't received an invitation and didn't know if it was an oversight or if she had to limit the number of guests?" Not only are you not placing blame on Bette's poor behavior traits, but you are also giving her an option of finding out the reason why she had not been invited.

On the job: Jim and Joe were both up for the same promotion. Jim got the job, and since then, Joe has been telling anyone who will listen that it is because of Jim's friendship with the supervisors that he was promoted. When word gets to you, the manager, you call Joe into your office. Rather than telling him that he is being mean-spirited and childish, it would be better to say something like, "Your talk about Jim is very unfair. Both of you were given equal consideration, but Jim had slightly more experience than you did. I'm sure that when the next opportunity comes along, you will again be considered. In the meantime, I would suggest that you prepare yourself by taking some classes and becoming more involved in the operation of the company." You are letting Joe know that he was definitely in the running for the position and will be considered again. You are also giving him helpful ideas on how to increase his chances in the future.

Tip 7: Build goodwill.

The words you choose can make the difference between constructive and destructive criticism. The way in which your advice is interpreted will reflect your skills as a communicator.

In the home: Bobby has a terrible time remembering to pick up his toys. They are scattered all over the house, and it takes nagging on your part to get them put away. You get tired of telling him the same thing over and over and finally say, "I'm constantly picking up after you. I'm tired of you being so messy." You are essentially telling Bobby that you are giving up on him. A better approach might be, "Your toys are all over the house. Let's find a place where you can keep them, and then you'll know just where to put them when you're through playing." Working together will get the job done and still keep Bobby's self-esteem intact.

On the job: You notice an employee who is taking much too long to file. Her system seems to be haphazard and is holding her back. You could say to her, "You're doing that all wrong," but a better way would be, "I've found a way to file that is much faster. Would you like me to show it to you?" In this way, you are not telling her that she is wrong, only that you can help her do a better job.

Tip 8: Avoid generalities.

It is impossible for anyone to respond to a generality. When offering criticism, be specific about what you are criticizing.

In the home: "John, you are so inconsiderate of your sister's feelings" will not be understood or accepted as well as, "John, I want you to stop teasing your sister about her weight. She is trying very hard to lose weight and needs your support." Saying this lets John know exactly why you are upset and what you expect from him.

On the job: "You are being careless" is not as good as, "I need you to double check all outgoing correspondence for spelling errors. Several typos have been caught lately and it puts our company in a bad light." The other party will know exactly what the problem is, why it is a problem and what you expect him to do about it.

Tip 9: Avoid absolutes.

Never say "never," and never say "always." These absolute terms will seldom get the results you desire.

In the home: "You never help with the dishes" is sure to provide ammunition for the listener to respond with, "I certainly do. Don't you remember last Sunday when we had company and I helped clear the table?" "You always whine about taking out the trash" is sure to be answered by, "I take the trash out every day. You only notice the few times that I complain."

On the job: "You never answer the telephone when Nancy is on her break" is sure to elicit a defensive response. Why not suggest a compromise to assure that each of you will have an equal share of telephone duties?

THE TRAITS OF SUCCESSFUL PEOPLE

Studies show that successful people exhibit ten common traits that, when used together, can propel individuals to achieve their dreams. By working hard and being the best you can be in business, you can more naturally bring these attributes to your family. Below, you will find each success trait followed by ways to integrate the traits into your family. You will then find a life-coaching tip you can use to strengthen your skills in that area. The traits successful people exhibit are:

1) Positive thinking
2) Documenting goals
3) Taking action
4) Continuous learning
5) Practicing hard work and persistence
6) Attention to details
7) Remaining focused on your time and money
8) Daring to be different
9) Perfecting the art of communication
10) Taking responsibility for your actions

Success Trait 1: Positive thinking

The power of positive thinking is overwhelming. You cannot fake it. You may speak in a positive manner, but that is just giving lip service to an idea. Your innermost thoughts will always come through and affect others. If you get into the habit of thinking positively, you will find that it results in a positive outcome.

Incorporating this trait into your family: A team that takes the field with negative thoughts such as, "This other team is so much better than we are. We don't have a chance," probably will not win. A good coach teaches his team to think positively. The coach will give the team members a winning attitude, so they are ready to take on the opposing team. The team with a positive attitude will have a greater chance of taking home the win. Even if they do not win, the coach will have the good sense to use it as a learning tool rather than a defeat. This is the same attitude you need to use with your family.

Be a good coach and a good cheerleader for your children. Erase the word "can't" from your vocabulary. Use your life-coaching skills to guide your children in a positive direction. If your children know you support them and encourage them to reach for their dreams, their chance of realizing those dreams will increase dramatically. **Remember, a positive attitude is a winning attitude.**

> **Life-coaching tip:** When you find yourself entertaining negative thoughts about a particular situation, stop immediately. Search diligently for a positive aspect of the situation and grab onto it, no matter how insignificant it may seem. Work it through in your mind until the negativity disappears. You will then begin to see how to resolve and learn from the problem.

Success Trait 2: Documenting goals

In order to be effective, goals must be documented; they must be written in a specific, precise manner. You might think this is a waste of time since you know what you want to achieve, but goals that are documented are more concrete. By documenting your goals, you become more likely to remain focused on them. Be very specific when documenting your goals. It does no good to say, "I want to make a lot of money this year." Instead, you should write, "I want to make $75,000 this year."

It is equally as important to document ways of achieving a goal. At the end of Chapter One, you created an individual plan for change in which you documented some things you would like to change about yourself. You also documented how you are going to make those changes happen. At the end of Chapter Two, you documented your individual plan for success by writing down some goals and how you are going to achieve them. At the end of Chapter Three, you developed and documented a leadership plan in which you identified ways you could take on a leadership role. All of these action plans are examples of having definitive goals and methods for achieving those goals.

Incorporating this trait into your family: Help your children by working with them to set their own definitive goals. Begin by explaining to them exactly what a goal is: an objective or purpose toward which an endeavor is directed. Teach them the right way to set a goal and how to go about developing a plan for the realization of that goal. Set both personal goals and family goals. Develop long-term and short-term goals, and plan them together as a family project. Write these goals down and refer to them often for inspiration. Help your children understand that goals are just that—goals. There are times when goals must be changed. The main idea is to have a goal and then do whatever is possible to attain it. Working with goals will help your children through every phase of their lives.

When teaching your children how to document their goals, encourage them to keep an ongoing journal of situations they deal with on a daily basis, such as peer pressure. Have them document ways they handled various situations, how they felt, etc. You might also consider role-playing with your children. Pose various scenarios and ask them how they would deal with those situations. Encourage an open dialogue, and have them write down the solutions you both brainstorm.

Life-coaching tip: When confronted with a new idea, sit down with a pen and paper. At the top of the paper, write down the idea and mark it as a goal. List all of the pros and cons of that goal. If you decide that the pros outweigh the cons, then list the steps necessary to see the idea through to completion.

Success Trait 3: Taking action

You can write down hundreds of goals, but if you never act on them, you will never see results. Look at your goals and study your plans. Decide today to take whatever action is necessary to begin your journey toward success.

Incorporating this trait into your family: Let your family in on the progress you are making toward reaching your goals. Show a real interest in your children's goals and ask about the progress they are making. Children are like little human camcorders. They record everything they see you do. Your job is to see that what they do record will be useful to them throughout their lives. Set a good example by showing your children you are an action-taker, and they will take your lead.

Life-coaching tip: Never procrastinate. Begin immediately to act on the steps outlined in your plan. The sooner you act, the more likely you are to achieve your goals.

Success Trait 4: Continuous learning

There is no such thing as having too much knowledge. Keep learning in every way possible. Take courses, attend seminars, take training classes and join organizations that feature educational speakers. Learn to rely on your own knowledge, so you do not have to be dependent upon others when making important decisions.

Incorporating this trait into your family: Very few children actually embrace the idea of going to school, and those who do often deny it because of peer pressure. Show your children that learning is a lifetime process. Show them that learning can be fun. Avail yourself of every opportunity to increase your knowledge, and encourage your family to do the same. Make learning fun for your children. Discover your children's individual interests, and then make them aware of newspaper articles, websites or museums that address their interests. Match their enthusiasm by asking questions and listening to the answers. More can be said through proper listening than through talking. Master the art of being a good listener. Most children will be eager to tell you about their learning experiences.

Life-coaching tip: Make it a priority to take at least one course each year. It may be something you always wanted to know more about, such as oil painting; or it may be a training course to help with your career, such as website design. No matter what you to choose to learn, it will be advantageous to you throughout your life.

Success Trait 5: Practicing hard work and persistence

Every goal, every plan and every expectation is guaranteed to hit rough spots along the way. The easy answer is to quit and pursue something simpler. You must remember, however, that anything worthwhile usually does not come easily. **Work hard for what you want and never stop trying. Believe, every minute, that you can achieve your dreams.** What you accomplish depends on you—no one else. If you work hard and persist, the results will be that much sweeter when they arrive.

Incorporating this trait into your family: Be an example to your children and show them that persistence and hard work go hand-in-hand. Show them they must work hard and pursue their goals in order to succeed.

Imagine two friends, Henry and Walter, who both wanted a bicycle. Henry had an indulgent uncle who just gave him a bicycle, while Walter had parents who did not believe in handing him everything on a silver platter. To get his bike, Walter mowed lawns and ran errands until he saved enough money. Knowing the hard work he put in to earn it, Walter appreciated his bicycle much more than Henry and, as a result, took better care of it. Instead of giving in to their son's every wish and handing him a bike, Walter's parents taught him a valuable life lesson about hard work and persistence.

Life-coaching tip: When you encounter a problem that seems to be overwhelming, do not give up. Roll up your sleeves, work hard and stick with it. You will be amazed at the results you can achieve.

Success Trait 6: Attention to details

If someone fails, it usually is not the big things that trip her up, but rather, a lack of attention to details. The overlooking of details can become the stumbling block to success. Strive to become a detail-orientated person. Be familiar with every aspect of a project. If you are aware of the details of a project, you can keep control of the situation and head off any problems before they pop up. Do not do careless work, and do not accept careless work from others.

Incorporating this trait into your family: Teach your children to be detail-oriented. Show them that no job is too small to matter. Explain to them that being well-informed of the details of a project helps avoid unpleasant surprises. Show them, by example, that when you pay close attention to detail in any plan or project, you are rewarded with positive results.

> **Life-coaching tip:** Examine all angles of any project. It will not take long for this skill to become a life habit.

Success Trait 7: Remaining focused on your time and your money

Time and money are the two things people will always try to take away from you some way or another. Learn to be frugal with your time in business dealings. Give of it, but only to the point that it does not interfere with your work. As a successful person, you will be asked to give your time to many different causes. Choose one and use your time for that special cause. The same is true of money. By all means donate, but be selective. You cannot give to everybody, so limit yourself to one or two charities that you really believe in.

Incorporating this trait into your family: Spend quality time with your family. Your children not only need your words, but also your physical involvement. Do not be afraid to sit down and help your children plan for success. This will show your children that you are interested in them, and will make them feel they are not alone. Be available to your children; show them through your words and actions that you care and are there for them. Help your children understand that time is valuable, and that you choose to spend that commodity with them. Whether at work or at play, your children should be aware of time and learn to use it wisely.

The same is true of money—teach your children the value of money. Show them how to allocate their funds by dividing it into spending money and saving money. Teach them the importance of donating a portion of their money to others less fortunate than themselves. If your children grow up with these good habits, they will have them throughout their lives.

> **Life-coaching tip:** Become a person who leads a well-rounded life. Allow time for work, play and personal fulfillment.

Success Trait 8: Daring to be different

It takes confidence and courage to attempt something new and innovative. A good leader will accept challenges and reach for the horizon. Become a leader and embrace change.

Incorporating this trait into your family: Instill in your children the idea of daring to be different. If their friends are involved in illegal or immoral activities, teach them to have the confidence and courage to back away and follow their own path. Teach them the importance of having their own thoughts and ideas; they need to understand that being different is not a bad thing and that they should embrace differences.

> **Life-coaching tip:** Accept challenges and do your best to meet them. Never back away from a new idea or venture unless you are convinced it will be harmful or illegal. Keep a journal of your new experiences, so you can look back and remember how you felt during those experiences.

Success Trait 9: Perfecting the art of communication

More problems are caused by misunderstandings than anything else. Learn to understand others and use effective communication to motivate. **Communication is a two-way street; know when to listen and when to speak.**

Incorporating this trait into your family: To be an effective life-coach and parent, you need to become an expert in communication. Children, particularly teenagers, have a wide communication gap that can result in misunderstandings and family confrontations. Forget the "I am the parent, you are the child. I will speak and you will listen" attitude. Too often, parents jump to conclusions only to find that many of their problems could have been avoided if they had only listened to their children. Do not get caught in that trap. Be willing to listen to all sides of a situation before making a decision. This example will show your children the value of listening and the effects of good communication.

> **Life-coaching tip:** Pay close attention to people you consider to be good communicators. Make note of what they do. Study how they speak *and* how they listen. Learn how to improve your own communication skills by observing good communicators.

Success Trait 10: Taking responsibility for your actions

This is, perhaps, one of the most important success traits you can possess. The other nine traits depend upon this one. **Be dependable and honest, and show people they can count on you.** Give credit where credit is due, and do not blame others if things do not go as expected. Josiah Stamp once said, "It is easy to dodge our responsibilities, but we cannot dodge the consequences of our responsibilities." The bottom line is that we all must take responsibility for our actions.

Incorporating this trait into your family: Set an example for your children by acknowledging the good work of others, and do not take credit for other people's work. Admit when you are at fault; do not blame others for things that go wrong in your life. This sets a terrible example for your children and gives them the idea that they can do and say whatever they please. Explain to your children that by not taking responsibility for their actions, they will lose the respect of those around them. This lesson in responsibility will be invaluable to your children, not only in their business lives, but also in their personal lives.

> **Life-coaching tip:** Responsibility and leadership go hand-in-hand. Together, they can make you a powerful figure who leads a life others will want to emulate.

Shared Secrets of Successful Managers

Successful managers did not become successful by accident. They have developed "tricks of the trade" that have helped them succeed in the business world. Below, you will find twelve secrets of successful managers, followed by ways to integrate these success secrets into your family. The secrets are as follows:

1) Admit there are things you do not know.
2) Develop potential.
3) Influence thinking.
4) Foster the right attitude.
5) Recognize individual differences.
6) Reach objectives through creativity.
7) Be a boss, not a buddy.
8) Set the standards.
9) Train your people well.
10) Address issues as they arise.
11) Recognize everyone's contributions.
12) Use cooperation, not manipulation.

Management Secret 1: Admit there are things you do not know.

Strong, effective managers are not afraid to say, "I don't know." They do not dodge issues and pretend to know more than they actually do. By admitting there are some things they do not know, they show their emotional maturity, sense of self-worth and sense of credibility.

Good managers compliment employees who ask questions. If they do not know the answer to a question, they will encourage employees to find the answer by steering them toward specific resources. This allows both the manager and the employee the opportunity to grow and learn from their experiences. It also fosters a positive relationship between the two.

Incorporating this success secret into your family: It is important for your children to understand that you, as a parent, do not know the answers to all questions. If you set yourself up in your children's eyes as all-knowing, the day will come when you will fall from that pedestal and their confidence in your abilities will be shattered. Never be afraid to say the words, "I don't know" to your children. If you do not know the answers to their questions, urge them to find the answers by guiding them to proper sources of information. Follow up on what they discovered, so that you can both learn by looking over the information together. By doing this, you will show your children you think their questions are valid and that you are interested in knowing the results of their search. At the same time, your children will learn more by researching the question themselves than they will by simply receiving an answer from you.

Management Secret 2: Develop potential.

Good managers do more than solve problems; they allow others the opportunity to resolve their own problems. They do not underestimate their employees' potential for success, and they do not set limitations or quotas for their employees.

Incorporating this success secret into your family: As you work with your children, do not limit them. Instead, encourage them to go beyond their dreams. Give them the opportunity to seek answers to their questions. Be there for them as a guide and let them know you are behind them. Let them reach for the stars, and offer support no matter how far-fetched their ideas may seem. Support them in reaching for their goals.

Management Secret 3: Influence thinking.

As project leaders, effective managers are often able to develop their employees' skills by influencing the way they think. In doing this, they are able to have their employees step back and look at the big picture in order to gain a new perspective. This helps employees see how their role impacts the outcome of the entire project.

Success often calls for risk, so managers must encourage their team to be innovative in their thinking and try new methods that go against the odds. Good managers think outside of the box and encourage their employees to do the same. Good managers are not deterred by the fear that an idea is too extreme, but instead examine every aspect of an issue and choose their solution wisely.

Incorporating this success secret into your family: Children can sometimes come up with plans and schemes that sound outlandish. While you, as an adult, recognize that these plans may not work, you need to allow your children freedom to pursue their dreams, within reason. Praise your children when their efforts are successful and praise them for trying when their efforts fail. After all, just having a unique idea and the courage to see it through deserves your praise.

In influencing your children's thinking, you should try not to stifle their creativity. In fact, you should let them know that it is through the ideas of dreamers that some of the world's greatest achievements have been realized.

Much of what you accomplish in life is due to your self-esteem and faith in your abilities. The encouragement you give to your children is key. By encouraging your children to pursue their dreams, they will eventually realize that anything is possible. Through this influence, they will accomplish more goals and will feel better about themselves.

Management Secret 4: Foster the right attitude.

Effective managers work toward developing a team spirit among employees. They watch out for those who try to undermine efforts and establish a "them against us" attitude. Good managers show how teamwork leads companies to success by their own attitude and effort. Promoting teamwork ensures a healthy atmosphere.

Incorporating this success secret into your family: Parents and children should work as a team. Through your own attitude and actions, show your children that working together will accomplish more than one person working alone. Remember, every member of the family is an integral part of the whole and, by acting as a team, each person will help the others accomplish their goals. What might be a huge task for one person will probably be easy when a team tackles it.

When everyone's opinion cannot be realistically addressed, the parents must work together and act as team leaders. Discourage one parent from siding with the child against the other parent. Encourage the children to respect both parents' authority. Although the parents are the leaders, give children the opportunity to be an integral part of the team when possible.

Management Secret 5: Recognize individual differences.

A wise manager realizes that each employee has a unique personality and must be treated as an individual. Workers will react in a favorable manner if they know you understand their differences and treat them as people rather than numbers. You will also benefit by recognizing their strengths and weaknesses, because you can appropriately assign work. In this way, you will get the best results from each employee.

Incorporating this success secret into your family: It does not matter if a family consists of two members or twelve members; each member is unique and should be treated as such. You need to take the time to get to know your children, their likes and dislikes and where their strengths lie. If one of your children loves science and gets excited by testing theories, you cannot expect your second child to demonstrate the same excitement. Your second child may excel in sports. One talent is not better than another—they are different, but of equal value. Lead your children and teach them to be cheerleaders for the rest of the family by treating everyone's differences with respect.

Management Secret 6: Reach objectives through creativity.

Successful managers understand their environment and the conditions that exist, and they use this understanding to their advantage. This allows them to discover creative means to reach objectives. When faced with a problem, they ask themselves, "How can I use this situation to my advantage?" By approaching a problem from this angle, they imagine many possibilities and will discover a unique, individualized solution.

Incorporating this success secret into your family: Do not allow your family to get locked into thinking that there is only one way to reach a goal or solve a problem. Encourage creativity through the use of activities like family meetings and brainstorming sessions. Teach them to always consider a variety of solutions and not to take "no" for an answer until absolutely all other avenues have been thoroughly explored. By learning at home that there are several answers to every question, they will learn to approach life with an optimistic attitude, and will develop a drive that will take them as far as they want to go.

Management Secret 7: Be a boss, not a buddy.

Successful managers realize that they cannot pal around with their friends on the job—it just does not work. There is an invisible line they recognize and respect. There are times when managers must discipline an employee or even terminate someone's employment. This would be even more difficult to do if they were, for example, socializing with that person the night before. Wise managers realize that in order for them to exercise authority in the workplace, there must be a certain degree of distance between themselves and their employees.

Incorporating this success secret into your family: You have had your childhood—now it is time for you to be an adult and a parent. Children need rules and boundaries; they need someone to look to for guidance. As their parent, you are the one to guide them. They do not need you to be their friend; they have plenty of friends in their own age group. What they need from you is a positive adult role model. This is not to say you cannot do things together and enjoy each other's company. You must, however, remain an example to your children and continue to influence them in a positive manner. As hard as they will try to push the boundaries, you must be firm. Just as in business situations, you cannot be your child's best buddy all day and then a disciplinarian in the evening.

Management Secret 8: Set the standards.

Effective managers set high, but reasonable, standards and present them to their employees in a positive manner. These standards instill motivation, confidence and self-assurance. Wise managers realize they must follow their own rules. Organizational standards should be viewed as a covenant between a company and its employees, and if managers want their employees to follow the rules and standards, they must set the example. The norms and guidelines established set the tone for business, and are the basis for sensitive decision-making.

Incorporating this success secret into your family: You are the leader. You set and follow the standards to which your family subscribes. Children need guidelines, but they also need to see you observing the rules set down for the family. They may rebel at times, but it is really a relief to them to have the safety of clear rules they know they must follow. No matter how they act on the outside, there is comfort for them to be able to say, "No, I'm not permitted to do that," rather than to be torn over every difficult decision.

A major point here is that you must *not* say "These are the rules I have made and you will follow them, because I am the parent." There are times when rules do need to be set, but it can be done with an explanation of the consequences. Standards need to be understood and agreed to by family members just like they are in business. Discussion among family members is necessary, and compromise should also be an option. Most rules should not be so rigid that they cannot be adjusted. As your family grows and matures, standards need to be readjusted. Having standards to follow will give your children a solid base from which to make intelligent, well-thought-out decisions.

Management Secret 9: Train your people well.

There are three reasons why people fail to do their job. These reasons are:

1) The individual does not know what the job is.
2) The individual does not know how to do the job.
3) Someone or something interferes with the individual's desire or ability to do the job.

Successful managers address and correct the above issues. First, they clarify the job and what it entails. They set expectations their employees fully understand. Effective managers know that the best way to do this and avoid misunderstandings is to provide employees with a written job description. They discuss the job with their employees to verify that they understand exactly what is expected of them.

The next thing successful managers do is see that their employees receive proper training for the job. They ensure that effective classroom training or on-the-job coaching is received, so that employees are prepared to accomplish the assigned tasks.

Incorporating this success secret into your family: Everyone should have responsibilities and be accountable for them. It is up to you to see that family members understand what is expected of them and have the proper training to perform their roles. For example, you cannot tell your son he is responsible for cleaning the bathroom, and then leave him on his own without showing him how it is done.

Be sure to provide proper training and supervision for your children when you give them a job to do. Do not leave them to flounder and then show your disappointment if the job is not done to your satisfaction. Show them what they need to do and then answer any questions they may have. Give them the support they need. When your children do a good job, pile on the praise and show them you are proud of the work they have done.

Management Secret 10: Address issues as they arise.

A problem that is not addressed is a problem that will continue to grow. Successful managers confront problems immediately. The purpose of confronting employees is not always to impose punishment, but to give a positive voice to the actions you want them to accomplish in the future. There is nothing to be gained from anger or embarrassment; therefore, effective managers handle situations tactfully and avoid negative confrontation. Below are some tips that successful managers use when confronting employees:

- Do not confront employees when you are angry. Anger solves nothing and only causes an escalation of the problem. Anger on your part will cause employees to resort to defensive, angry behavior as well. Work to remain calm and in charge of the situation.
- Correct the behavior immediately. Do not give the behavior a chance to repeat and develop into a larger problem.
- Correct the behavior privately. **Praise in public—criticize in private.** Never embarrass employees by reprimanding them in front of others.
- Be specific. Do not use generalities, but instead zero in on the specific behaviors you perceive to be the problem. Other issues can be discussed at a later time.
- Be prepared and have the facts ready. Have exact dates and times that the behavior occurred. Have your facts in writing and be ready to confront the person with specific information.
- Be clear. Make certain the employee knows what you are concerned about, why it concerns you and how you feel about the behavior. Do not give conflicting signals.

- Provide redirection. When you express your displeasure about an employee's behavior, give some positive direction on how to avoid that particular behavior in the future. Identify the problem and help provide some solutions.
- Do not belabor the issue. Once the meeting is over, as long as the behavior does not occur again, the only reference to the issue should be compliments when the desired behavior is achieved. After all, the goal is to fix the problem and move on.

Incorporating this success secret into your family: Each of the above tips can be incorporated into your interaction with your family. Remember, however, that situations are neither black nor white. To ensure your children's cooperation, you must include them in the discussion about undesirable behaviors. Listen to them to discover why they acted the way they did. Again, remain calm and initiate an open, two-way conversation. Come to an agreement with your children on suitable resolutions to problems. Then, just as with employees, provide positive reinforcement when your children behave properly.

Management Secret 11: Recognize everyone's contributions.

Organizations are made up of a variety of people doing many different things. No one can effectively produce good work without the cooperation of others. Effective managers know that it is a mistake to recognize and applaud only the "star" performers in the company. Successful managers are committed to teamwork, and work to develop team spirit among their employees. When accolades are called for, they give them appropriately to the team and not just to individuals. All workers, regardless of the job, are proud of their performance and need to be recognized for their accomplishments.

A good manager works with each employee to develop objectives and goals. A good manager also frequently reviews performance and provides recognition for progress toward the accomplishment of goals. The recognition need not be lavish; it can be a simple thank you to let employees know that their progress is noticed and appreciated.

Incorporating this success secret into your family: See that family members receive regular praise for whatever accomplishments they have made for the month. Some may have achieved difficult goals, while others may have only moved a small step ahead. Regardless of the amount of progress your children have made, they should be complimented and recognized for their performance. As a parent, your approval is paramount to your children. Recognition provides the incentive people need to reach further and accomplish more. When your children see that they have pleased you, they will be proud of what they have done and will strive to move ahead even more.

Management Secret 12: Use cooperation, not manipulation.

Successful managers use cooperation to influence people to perform properly and produce good work. The use of fear and rewards is a manipulative tool that can be a detriment to organizations. Those who use fear will threaten employees with dire consequences, such as, "Do the work properly or you will lose your job" or, "Produce as expected or be humiliated in front of your peers." Managers who only use rewards to get desired results may be successful, but only for a short time. Without long-term meaning and fulfillment, the reward system loses effectiveness.

Employees with positive attitudes will produce higher quality work; therefore, effective managers provide the necessary means to develop positive attitudes among their employees. There are many ways to influence motivation and create positive attitudes. For example, you can impact attitude through environmental changes, such as painting the office space or rearranging the furniture for a more ergonomic effect. You can also increase morale by throwing simple celebrations, such as weekly pizza lunches or recognition meetings.

Incorporating this success secret into your family: As in business, families do not respond well to manipulation. They do, however, respond to a united and positive family attitude. To engage this attitude, you should try to make your home one in which your family will want to spend time and bring their friends. Make it warm, welcome, bright, cheery, clean and inviting. You should introduce new ideas into the environment, such as playing games as a family or reading to younger children.

Just as in business, fear and rewards are not good motivational methods for families. Fear will ultimately lead to rebellion, and physical punishment rarely changes undesirable behavior. Children do need to learn right from wrong and, at times, punishment is necessary to teach that lesson; however, never use physical punishment, as it is neither positive nor effective. When deciding on an appropriate punishment, keep in mind the differences in your children and use a non-violent method that will be effective for them. Be selective in your methods of punishment. Some children are so sensitive that just knowing they have displeased you will bring about a change in behavior.

Rewards will lose meaning and effectiveness if they are used as the only means of behavior modification. Use praise and verbal rewards often and liberally, reserving rewards for special occasions. If your children do well, make sure you tell them and reinforce that positive behavior; this will encourage them to repeat the positive behavior in the future.

COMBINE MANAGEMENT SKILLS WITH LOVE

Now that you have learned some traits of successful people and secrets of successful managers, you can start to incorporate them into your family life. The important difference, however, is that you must use love when leading your family.

As parents, the most important thing you can give your children is love. Fortunately, for most parents, this is a natural emotion and not one that must be learned. Anyone can give children basic care, but parents provide the *emotional* security necessary for children to grow up and become loving, well-balanced individuals.

Supplying your children with an abundance of material possessions may make you feel you are doing your job well, but this is not what children need. Some of the happiest, most successful individuals grew up in poverty, but in homes where they were surrounded by love.

One of the greatest challenges will be applying the necessary discipline in your family, while continuing to maintain an aura of unconditional love. Discipline is often difficult to administer, but you do your children no favors by allowing them to do whatever they please, whenever they please. Discipline, after all, is intended to help mold children and lead them to success. If they grow up spoiled and self-centered, they will be in for great disappointment and will be unable to cope with adversity.

We must work to keep the lines of communication open. When your children misbehave or break the rules, they must know why they are being punished and what they have done to disappoint you. Remember, different situations call for different degrees of discipline. The punishment must be fair and suited to the infraction. Though you are the adult, your children should be treated with fairness and respect at all times.

An important element in effectively combining love with management skills is openness. If you feel that your child has begun to spend too much time with the wrong crowd, your approach should be "I'm worried about you because...." Avoid the accusatory approach, such as "You're wrong" or worse, "I forbid you to see them anymore." Taking that approach is a sure way to push your children in the direction you do not want them to go.

Your children need to feel that—in any situation, and at all times no matter what the problem—they can talk with you. They must know that you are an ally who will stand by them through good times and bad.

In business, you need to approach situations with authority and confidence, and as an effective manager, you need to provide guidance and leadership. These are the same qualities demonstrated in effective parenting with one extremely important addition—love. Love given is love returned. Love, however, does not mean giving in to your children's every demand. Your children might resent the family rules and your involvement in their lives at first, but you must remain the parent and allow love to govern your actions.

There are contemporary television commercials that illustrate these points very well. In one commercial, several children with angry voices say things like, "You looked in my room when I wasn't there!" or, "You made me tell you who I was going out with and what time I would be home!" or, "You checked up on me at school to make sure I was doing my work." At the end of the commercial, the children all say, "Thank you." Those parents showed their love by showing their concern and doing something about it. The children may not have been pleased with the actions of their parents directly at that moment, but as time moved along they grew to appreciate it, because they knew it was done with love.

As a parent, if you love your children and guide them effectively, they will love you in return. Watch as your children grow into happy, well-adjusted and successful adults. Provide them with examples of how loving, responsible parents should act. As a result, you can watch with satisfaction as they repeat your loving behavior with their own families. To be a parent is joy. To see your children grow up to be happy, responsible and successful adults is bliss.

AN ASSESSMENT OF YOUR SUCCESS SKILLS

The first assessment to make is of you and your readiness for success. In order to decide which success skills you already possess and which skills you need to develop, fill out the following questionnaire.

Below, you will find eleven true or false statements. When you are done responding to the statements, you will assess your responses in order to initiate specific changes for personal improvement. Each of us is unique in our feelings and observations, so the best results are obtained when the assessment is completed separately by all of the adults in the family. Remember, there are no right or wrong answers—just be honest with yourself.

Please circle true or false for the following statements:		
1. I enjoy new experiences.	true	false
2. I am receptive to new ideas and ways of doing things.	true	false
3. I am achievement-oriented.	true	false

4. I am action-oriented.	true	false
5. I am a goal-setter.	true	false
6. I focus on maximizing my potential.	true	false
7. I am committed to lifetime learning.	true	false
8. I am detail-oriented.	true	false
9. I am considered to be a good communicator.	true	false
10. I believe in the value of teamwork.	true	false
11. I would rate my self-esteem in the normal to high range.	true	false

Look at your assessment and make note of the statements you responded to with "false." These are areas you need to work on to develop your success potential to its fullest.

A successful individual enjoys new experiences and is receptive to new ideas and new ways of managing old problems. A successful person does not stand still, but continuously moves ahead looking to achieve. She sets goals and takes action. She is committed to lifelong learning in order to maximize potential. She is detail-oriented, a good communicator and works well within a team.

Success can only be achieved if a person's self-esteem is intact. An individual must think highly of himself before he can expect the respect of others. When he exudes self-confidence, he becomes a leader, not a follower. People want to follow a leader who has obvious self-confidence. If you practice the above listed traits, your self-esteem will increase. Each time you accomplish a project successfully, it will compel you to try even more new ideas.

No matter how nice it would be, success is not going to fall into your lap—you have to want it badly enough to work for it. With hard work, persistence and a positive attitude, it will surely come your way.

AN ASSESSMENT OF YOUR CHILD'S SUCCESS SKILLS

The next assessment to make is of your child's readiness for success. In order to decide which success skills your child already possesses and which he still needs to develop, fill out the following eight true or false statements about your child. When you are done, you will assess the responses in order to initiate specific changes you can help your child make.

Please circle true or false for the following statements:		
1. My child is open and excited to try new experiences.	true	false
2. My child is intrigued by new ideas and is willing to experiment.	true	false
3. My child sets goals and works diligently to achieve them.	true	false
4. The idea of learning excites my child.	true	false
5. My child communicates effectively.	true	false
6. My child works well individually and as part of a team.	true	false
7. My child generally feels good about himself.	true	false
8. My child is comfortable in the role of leader.	true	false

Look at your assessment and make note of the statements about your child that you responded to with "false." These are areas your child might need help working on in order to fully develop his success potential. Now, go through each of the statements above and learn why each trait is important and how you can help your child become successful. Each trait will be followed by an example.

Success Statement 1: My child is open and excited to try new experiences.

Successful people, both adults and children, are the sum of many experiences. Each experience, whether good or bad, supports individual growth and the knowledge that is necessary for personal success. As you learn from trial and error, each new experience teaches you a lesson that is a useful step on the climb up the Pyramid of Success. To remain with the familiar and comfortable is confining. Success does not come from confinement or stagnation, but from willingness to listen to new and different ideas and experiment with them. Remember, no experience is a wasted one. The following is an example of a child whose parents encouraged him to try new things, which led to positive results later in life.

☆ *A Real-Life Example of Openness to New Experiences: Bill*
Bill was a child who liked the familiar. When he had the chance to try something new or different, he usually balked; he preferred to remain in his comfort zone. When Bill was the right age for scouting, his parents tried to get him involved. He attended the scout meetings, but did not want to go camping. He had never done it before, so he just assumed he would not enjoy it.

Bill's parents explained to him the importance of experiencing new things. They encouraged him to try camping and promised him that if he did not enjoy it, he would not have to do it again. Bill went camping with his troop later that month and learned about living outdoors. He was surprised to find that he enjoyed the experience and was eager to do it again. Growing up, he continued to go on several outdoor adventures and enjoyed them thoroughly.

When Bill was an adult, he worked as a salesperson. He heard of an opening in a larger company, which would mean a major jump in salary for him. The job he was applying for was a sales position for an outdoor equipment company. One of the job requirements was to have basic knowledge about the outdoors and camping. The combination of Bill's sales abilities and his knowledge of the outdoors got him the job. As a result, he is making more money and working in a position he loves. This shows how valuable it was for Bill's parents to encourage him to try new things.

Success Statement 2: My child is intrigued by new ideas and is willing to experiment.

As a parent and life-coach to your children, you should encourage their participation in activities that will provide them with information for the future. Some children fear that experimentation will result in failure, viewing failure as a strictly negative thing. Therefore, they stick with the status quo and do not try new things. It is up to you to teach your children by word and example that important life lessons can be learned from successes as well as failures—everything is a learning experience. The following is an example of a father who taught his son that every experiment is a valuable lesson learned, regardless of whether or not he is successful.

☆ *A Real-Life Example of Willingness to Experiment: Willy*

Frank arrived home from work to find his son, Willy, very upset. He was sitting in the yard, surrounded by various small, metal parts and the motor from his old erector set. The following is the exchange that took place between Willy and Frank.

> *Frank:* "Hi there son. What're you up to?"
> *Willy:* "Nothin'."
> *Frank:* "Well, it looks like you're in the middle of a project. Anything I can do to help?"
> *Willy:* (wiping a tear from his face) "No. I was trying to hook this motor up to my old merry-go-round toy to see if I could get it to work again, but I guess I just don't know enough about anything to do it right."
> *Frank:* (tinkering with a gear) "Maybe this will help."
> *Willy:* "No. That would mess up the turning." Frank continued to ask about different methods of doing the job, and Willy was able to tell him, each time, why that particular part would not be right.
> *Frank:* "By trying all of these different things, look how much you have learned. Maybe your original idea didn't pan out, but you sure learned a lot today. I'm very proud of you for trying to fix the toy. I'm even prouder that you learned quite a bit on your own

about what will and will not work." Frank went on to explain to his son that he was successful, because of what he learned that day and continued, "Tomorrow is Saturday. Let's work on this together and see what we can do. We're already ahead, because of the time you put into it today."

Frank helped his son understand that it was the knowledge he gained that was important. He also suggested working on the project together, giving encouragement and time to his son. He showed Willy that he enjoyed spending time with him and solving problems with him. He avoided treating the situation as a failure, thus giving Willy incentive to try again.

Success Statement 3: My child sets goals and works diligently to achieve them.

Without goals, we would drift through life in an aimless fashion. Goals allow us to know where we want to go and develop a path for getting there. A young child can begin with minor goals, such as earning an "A" on a test or making the cheerleading squad. As she matures, goals will become larger and more meaningful. The foundation of finding the necessary means to achieve goals should be established early in life. Proper planning can help both you and your children achieve goals. The following is an example of a father who worked with his daughter to set a goal, follow through and achieve that goal.

☆ *A Real-Life Example of Setting and Working Toward a Goal: Shelli*

Jim walked into his living room to find his young daughter, Shelli, very upset. When he asked what was wrong, she told him about an upcoming competition at school. In three months, the five best math students would have the opportunity to compete on a local television show with students from other schools. The winners would receive special prizes and recognition. Shelli wanted desperately to be chosen, but her math skills were average at best.

Jim wanted to help Shelli reach her goal. He sat with her, and they made a chart together. At the top of the paper, they wrote down the goal: to be chosen in three months for the math team.

Under this goal, they listed ways for Shelli to prepare, such as studying math for one hour each evening, visiting the library to get different math books and forming a study group with friends.

Shelli stuck to her plan, and Jim helped her if she had any questions. Jim was there to cheer his daughter on to victory in the tournament. Shelli was so pleased at the outcome of her goal-setting, that she began to do that same type of exercise for future goals. She had learned a valuable lesson about setting goals and working hard to achieve them.

Success Statement 4: The idea of learning excites my child.

Knowledge is power. When you satisfy a thirst for knowledge, you arm yourself for life's challenges. Good learning habits will provide your child not only with information, but also with the self-confidence necessary to be successful. The following is an example of a child who wanted to learn and whose parents encouraged her thirst for knowledge.

☆ *A Real-Life Example of Interest in Learning: Pam*

When Pam was five years old, she was able to read simple words. This ability to read fueled her desire to continue reading, regularly escalating her level of difficulty. Pam was an inquisitive child and an answer of "because" to her questions was never enough to satisfy her; she wanted facts. The library was a source of wonder, and she could study there for hours at a time.

Pam's parents encouraged her quest for information. They provided books and other tools to learn about a variety of subjects that were of interest to her. Pam's thirst for knowledge led to excellent grades in school, which led to excellent grades in college. When she was ready to join the workforce, she had no trouble getting the job of her dreams.

Pam proved to be an inquisitive person who craved knowledge, and this was a great advantage for her. If, however, her parents had not encouraged her, she may have lost her desire. The combination of Pam's thirst for knowledge, along with encouragement from her parents, led her to a successful life.

Success Statement 5: My child communicates effectively.

Skilled communicators have the ability to share their ideas in such a way as to ensure that others understand them. Developing the skills to critically construct our thoughts and communicate them effectively is the cornerstone of this trait. It is important that you teach your children how to communicate their ideas and thoughts. Teach them by word and by example. The following is an example of a child whose parents helped her learn valuable communication skills.

☆ *A Real-Life Example of Effective Communication: Kristen*

As a child, it was obvious that Kristen was very bright. She was also a very quiet child. Kristen was a wonderful writer and got excellent grades on her book reports, but she seemed to have difficulty expressing her ideas to others.

One day in the 4th grade, she had to give an oral presentation on her report. She stood up in front of the class and could not get her points across. She started mumbling and eventually clammed up. Kristen's teacher, who knew that Kristen was an excellent student and was concerned about her performance, called her parents. They had a meeting and the teacher told them about Kristen's trouble presenting her report. Kristen's parents sat down with her that evening and talked about what had happened earlier that day. Kristen explained to them that she got nervous when she had to speak in front of the class. She knew the information in the report well but was afraid that she would not get her point across.

Over the next several weeks, Kristen's parents worked with her to practice her presentation skills. First, she practiced presenting the report to her parents. Then, she practiced in front of her parents, siblings and grandparents. Pretty soon, Kristen felt comfortable presenting to a larger group of people.

For her next oral presentation, Kristen felt confident in her communication skills. As a result, she got up in front of the class and presented with confidence. Kristen received an "A" on her presentation. More importantly, she learned valuable communication skills to use throughout her life.

Success Statement 6: My child works well individually and as part of a team.

Like many adults, some children prefer to work alone. Children need to learn to be able to work as a member of a team in order to make their mark in today's society. People will work better and more willingly with a team player than with a loner. It takes a team to build success. While it is a valuable tool to be able to work alone and be autonomous, it is even more important to understand that there are times when it takes more than one person to do a job. The following is an example of a child whose mother taught her the importance of working as a team and valuing her teammates.

☆ *A Real-Life Example of Working Well in a Team: Olivia*
Olivia was at the top of her 8th grade class. The school was asked to choose a team to compete against several other schools in a knowledge competition. Five students were chosen, one of whom was Olivia; she was chosen as the team captain. Olivia secretly felt that the four other students were unnecessary and that she could handle the competition alone. When practicing for the competition with her teammates, she would jump in with every answer before consulting with them.

Olivia's mother, who came to pick her up from practice, noticed Olivia's behavior. Later that evening, Olivia's mother explained to her the importance of teamwork. She explained that every member brings value to a team and that she must respect and utilize the other members of her team. Olivia seemed to understand and promised her mother that she would make an effort to be a better teammate.

On the day of the competition, Olivia knew many of the answers, but still consulted with her team before blurting them out. Finally, it came down to a tie-breaking question. The moderator asked the question and Olivia was confident that she knew the answer. She was about to blurt out the answer, but remembered what her mother told her about working as a team. As a result, she conferred with her teammates. Three of the other team members thought that the answer was something different from Olivia's. Although hesitant, Olivia decided to go with the majority and give her teammates' answer, rather than her own. The answer she gave was correct, which resulted in a win for Olivia and her team.

By observing her child and taking the time to teach her an important lesson in teamwork, Olivia's mother armed her with skills she could utilize and carry with her throughout her life.

Success Statement 7: My child generally feels good about himself.

Having self-confidence is the first step toward success. If your children have doubts about their abilities or any other facet of their life, you can help them gain the confidence they need to succeed. First, you can help them by exhibiting your own self-confidence. If they see that you are confident, they will learn by example. You can also help them through encouragement and positive reinforcement. If your children do not feel strong in a particular area of their life, help them improve it.

For example, if they do not feel confident in giving presentations, have them practice speaking aloud in front of you. Always let them know that you have confidence in their abilities and that you are there to back them up in their endeavors. The following is an example of a mother who noticed her daughter's lack of self-confidence and worked hard to build it up and help her daughter make positive changes in her life.

☆ *A Real-Life Example of Feeling Good About Yourself: Bonnie*
Rhoda came home from a PTA meeting and sat down to talk to her daughter, Bonnie. The following is the conversation that ensued.

> *Rhoda:* "I heard tonight that tryouts are coming up for the high school play. You'll be trying out, won't you?"
> *Bonnie:* "Nah, I would never get a part, so why bother trying out?"
> *Rhoda:* "How can you be so sure? You should at least try out."
> *Bonnie:* "Forget it mom. I'm too fat for any of the parts, and if I try out the kids will just laugh at me."

Rhoda was astonished. She knew that Bonnie would love to be in the play, but her weight was destroying her sense of self-confidence. Her child was hurting and she wanted to help her.

The next day, Rhoda and Bonnie sat down together and made a plan. Bonnie really wanted to lose weight and she committed herself to do so. They used a notebook to outline their strategy. First, they went to the doctor to make sure that her weight was not due to a medical problem. Second, they visited a nutritionist who developed a sensible, healthy plan for Bonnie. Third, Rhoda gave Bonnie a membership to a local gym as an early birthday gift. They designed a program especially for Bonnie, taking into consideration her age and what goals she wanted to achieve.

Her mother worked with her and followed the nutrition plan herself, joining the gym so they could work out together. Six months later, Bonnie had achieved her goal, lost weight and had confidence in herself. She felt like she was on top of the world and could do anything. Later that month, Rhoda proudly sat in the audience and applauded loudly as her daughter shined on stage.

Rhoda helped her daughter by paying attention and noticing her lack of self-confidence. She discovered the root of her daughter's issues and helped her make improvements in that area. She encouraged her along the way and even led by example. As a result, her daughter made positive changes in her life and developed self-confidence.

Success Statement 8: My child is comfortable in the role of leader.

If your children grow up with your support and have knowledge and self-confidence, they can naturally assume leadership roles. If you encourage your children to lead in small ways when they are young, their leadership skills will grow while they do. The following is an example of parents who encouraged their children to assume leadership roles when they were very young.

☆ *A Real-Life Example of Comfort in the Role of Leader: Todd*
The Mitchell family had a long-standing tradition in which, each week, one family member would decide on a fun activity for the entire family. The person who decided the activity would have to

gather all of the information and make the arrangements for the outing.

Todd was the youngest in the family. He became very comfortable planning and leading his family when it was his turn. By the time he reached high school, he felt very comfortable in a leadership role. He held a position as a class officer, arranged for class field trips and headed several community service projects. Due to his parents' teaching and preparation, Todd was well on his way to becoming a successful leader.

CREATING A POSITIVE FAMILY ENVIRONMENT THROUGH COACHING

Now that you have completed an assessment of your child's success skills, it is time to help them make any necessary changes in order to succeed in the future. There are several ways to create a warm and safe environment for your children. Below are some tips on ways to foster a positive environment for your children:

1) Reserve judgment.
2) Communicate.
3) Establish a warm, neutral tone.
4) Focus on the desired goal.
5) Strive for personal development and success.
6) Adapt to your children's needs.
7) Be flexible.
8) Establish clear boundaries.

Tip 1: Reserve judgment.
Some parents seem to have a natural tendency to use the "my way or the highway" method of thinking. They tend to forget the struggles they had as young people to find their own way, such as wearing their own style of clothing and listening to their own music.

Children are young people who need to be judged on their inner-person, rather than their external appearances. Parents must let their children know they are loved and respected, no matter what they wear or what kind of music they listen to. Jumping to conclusions is unfair to your children and unfair to you as the family leader. Your children should learn from you to reserve their own judgments until all of the facts are known.

Tip 2: Communicate.

There is nothing as frustrating as explaining something to someone who is not paying attention to a word you are saying. Let your children know that you are listening to them. Pay attention to them, and give verbal cues that you are listening, such as saying things like, "Yes, I understand" or, "That's very interesting."

Another good way to communicate with your children is to give them non-verbal cues, such as nodding your head or raising your eyebrows in interest. Listening to your children is another way to express how much you care. Even if you do not always agree with your children, give them the consideration that you expect from others; let them know that you understand and respect their opinions.

Tip 3: Establish a warm, neutral tone.

You should never assert your authority as a parent by shouting or belittling. This will only serve to alienate your children, and may result in them cutting all lines of communication with you. By assuming a warm and neutral tone in both words and actions, you will be able to maintain a firm position without building a wall between you and your children.

Be sure to listen to your children and respect their opinions, even if you do not agree with them. Through your actions, you will show your children that you are willing to listen to their side of the story. Your children will learn from you that the way to get results is by understanding and reasoning with others, rather than shouting or using aggressive behavior. They will also respect your opinions more, because they know you respect *their* opinions.

Tip 4: Focus on the desired goal.

When working to solve problems in your family, you should evaluate the situation and identify the objectives you would like to meet. Take steps to prevent conversation from turning into a blaming match. Stay focused on the topic of discussion and work toward resolving differences in a calm and rational manner.

Tip 5: Strive for personal development and change.

By demonstrating mature, adult behavior, you are being an exceptional role model for your children, and they will develop positive traits just by watching your example. Your efforts will help prepare your children for success by teaching them how to react in different situations.

Tip 6: Adapt to your children's needs.

Your children have their own needs, which may not always coincide with your own. While your schedule may be demanding, your children have needs which may require you to be more flexible. For example, say you have a tradition of getting together on the first Friday of every month with your college buddies for a night of pizza and poker. One of these nights, however, your daughter is singing in her school chorus. As much as you would like to go out with your friends, this is clearly a time when you should bow to the needs of your child and provide her with the support and encouragement she needs.

Tip 7: Be flexible.

There is no set of rules that can cover every possible situation or instance that may arise. Try not to get caught up in how things "should" be done. Recognize the individual differences in every event or situation. Use what you have learned as guidelines, but be flexible.

For example, if you have two sons who go out often with irresponsible friends, stay out late, and do not get their school work done, you may want to instill a curfew upon them. If, however, you also have a young daughter whose friend only throws parties where parents are present, calls home if she is going to be late, and excels in school, it may not always be necessary to give her a curfew.

Though it may seem unfair to your sons, keep in mind the difference between your children, and base decisions upon individuals, rather than sticking to harsh rules that punish both good and bad behavior.

Tip 8: Establish clear boundaries.

Children will quickly learn how far they can push your limits, and will try to get away with as much as they can—this is why it is important to set clear boundaries. In the end, they will appreciate it, because it gives them a sense of safety and lets them know that you care. Embrace your role as a parent in a loving way. This will provide your children with a model for success they can emulate throughout life.

OVERALL SUCCESS IN YOUR FAMILY

Social reformer Booker T. Washington once said, "I have learned that success is to be measured not so much by the position that one has reached in life, as by the obstacles which he has overcome while trying to succeed." When you are able to climb over what is thrown into your path and still reach your goal, you will truly find success.

This chapter has discussed what success is and what it means to you. You learned that success means something different to each person. The same is true for families; members of the same family may have differing views on what constitutes success. You learned the traits of successful people as well as the secrets of successful managers. You learned how to incorporate those traits and secrets of the trade into your own family by incorporating love.

Families have particular criteria for success. Below is a summary of elements that are unique to family success:

- Unconditional love exists among family members.
- There is a presence of strong, but fair, adult leadership.
- All family members' opinions are taken seriously, regardless of age.
- All family members are given the opportunity to learn.
- Independence is encouraged, while interdependence is maintained.
- All family members have the fundamental knowledge that they are not alone.

- Family members love and support each other.

Much of the success of your family will be the direct result of you and of your leadership. This is a big responsibility, but with proper preparation through personal life-coaching, and the love you have for your children, you will be up to the task.

Siblings will have differences, and children will occasionally rebel against parental authority; by utilizing your own skills and following the advice in this book, those times should pass quickly without any permanent damage. Your life-coaching skills will come into play and you will be a positive role model for your children.

IMPROVING YOUR SUCCESS

In Chapter One, you learned the equation for individual success:

Emotional health + Social health + Spiritual health = SUCCESS

You thought about what it means for you and began to think about your own model for success. Remember, no two people want or need the same things to make them feel successful.

In this chapter, we assessed you and your child's success skills. Now, you are going to organize and document your plan for family success. To design a plan to suit you, you must think again about what it is you want for you and your family. This is important, because you cannot move forward effectively until you have figured out what you want and need.

Sit in a quiet place with no distractions. On the following page, document your plan for success by writing a list of successes you would like your family to achieve. Next to each success definition, list what you need to do, as the leader, in order to achieve that success. Feel free to write down multiple ways of achieving that success.

For example, say your success goal is to bring your family closer together and get some bonding time. A way you can achieve this success is by organizing a family game night. Get each family member involved and work as a team. You will enjoy the activity that much more because you all planned it together. Another example is if you want to let your children know that you love them unconditionally. A way to achieve this is to make a point of telling them that you love them at least once a day.

When making your list, develop an order of priority. Take it one step at a time and do not take on too much. Never attempt to tackle more than one change at a time. Good luck and have fun marking your road to success!

A Success Plan for Me and My Family

Success I/We Would Like to Achieve:

Example: Make my children aware that I love them.

_____

_____

_____

_____

_____

_____

_____

_____

_____

_____

_____

Ways I/We Can Achieve This Success:

Say "I love you" at least once per day.

_____

_____

_____

_____

_____

_____

_____

_____

_____

_____

_____

SUMMARY OF CHAPTER FOUR

In this chapter, you learned how to merge business skills with love in order to bring about family harmony and success. Common traits of successful people were discussed, as well as secrets of successful managers. You then learned how to incorporate these secrets into your family life.

You conducted two assessments: one to measure your readiness for success, and one to measure your child's readiness for success. By looking at the results, you identified areas you need to work on in order to achieve success. Children cannot thrive in an environment that is cold and uninviting, nor one that is stifling to the imagination. In this chapter, you learned how to make a positive environment available to your child. Finally, you documented a success plan for you and your family.

> ☆ Be a positive role model to my children.
>
> ☆ Be a manager in my home.
>
> ☆ Provide a warm environment for change in my family.
>
> ☆ Provide my children with unconditional love.
>
> ☆ Keep a positive attitude.

Part Two

THE FIRST ACTION GOAL

Putting Your Goals into Action With Your Children and Integrating Those Goals into Your Lives

Chapter Five

DISCOVERING THE WONDERFUL COMPLEXITIES OF YOUR CHILD

Learn Why Each Child is Special

CHAPTER OBJECTIVES

- Learn why each child is special and different.

- Learn how to look at your children objectively and be a fair judge and critic.

- Learn about extreme parenting—using, not abusing, parental authority.

- Complete a personality assessment about your children.

- Learn the importance of recognizing your children's passions and allowing them to have their own dreams.

- Learn how to understand your children's limits and support their strengths.

- Complete worksheets with your individual children on how each of you view your strengths and limitations.

"*The parents exist to teach the child, but also they must learn what the child has to teach them; and the child has a very great deal to teach them.*"
— *Arnold Bennett*

In Part One of this book, you planned, organized and documented your goals. Now that you have done this, you are ready to turn these goals into action and are well on your way to the top of the Pyramid of Success.

In Part Two of this book, you will begin working with your children. When children partake in their own life plans, it helps them build self-esteem, teaches them communication and social skills, increases their confidence in their abilities, allows them more control over their life choices and instills in them the skills they need to flourish throughout their lives. You will start this process and put your goals into action while also integrating them into your children's lives. You will learn about your children and have them partake in their own goal-setting, making them active decision-makers. Both you and your children will perform tasks to enhance your children's interests and involvement in the family and their own success, and put those interests into action.

In this chapter, you will begin to put the skills you learned in the first four chapters into action, with the ultimate goal of being a life-coach to your children and achieving success. You will look at your children from the outside in, develop a personality profile of them and learn how to recognize their passions. You will read real-life examples from my clinical practice of people who have successfully used these life-coaching methods to improve their lives. At the end of this chapter, you will create a balance sheet tailored to your child's strengths and areas for improvement. Your child will also create her own personal balance sheet to assess her strengths and areas for improvement. She will include ways to build upon her strengths, and ways to make necessary improvements. She will also include ways that you, as a parent, can help her achieve her goals. You will then learn how to communicate with your child, discuss this exercise and come up with ways that you and your child can help make her goals a reality. You will ultimately facilitate parent-child teamwork by discussing these exercises and understanding ways that you and your children can make their life goals a reality.

WHY EACH CHILD IS SPECIAL AND DIFFERENT

It is often said that no two people are alike. Unfortunately, most people forget this saying when it comes to their children and expect their children to think, act and react in the same manner. Parents, in an effort to increase their children's self-esteem, will repeatedly tell their children that they are unique individuals and that no one else is like them. Yet, somehow, these same parents are surprised when their children differ from their siblings and have different outlooks on life. These parents will declare that they do not understand why their children are so different after being brought up the same way in the same household.

As you learned in previous chapters, treating employees as individuals is a key factor in effective management—the same principle applies to families. In your role as parent, it is your responsibility to recognize each child as an individual. It is essential you do not compare your children to other people's children. Remember that every child is special and deserves to be treated as an individual.

☆ *A Real-Life Example of Individuality: James and Jude*

James and Jude were identical twins. From the moment they were born, they were treated equally. As a toddler, Jude was more aggressive and demanded a greater share of attention. James, on the other hand, took things in stride and had a more even disposition. In elementary school, Jude became very familiar with detention and required parental visits with teachers and the principal. During high school, Jude was the star quarterback of the football team, while James excelled in debate and chess. Even though James and Jude looked the same and grew up in the same household, they were very different from each other. This individuality gave each of them their own personality, needs and reactions.

☆ *A Real-Life Example of Individuality: Stephanie*

Stephanie was an only child and was envious of her friends who came from families with many children. She always wished for brothers or sisters with whom she could play. When Stephanie became a mother, she was overjoyed to have two sons who were born only one year apart, and she had visions of her sons being best buddies and sharing the same friends and interests.

Stephanie's hopes plummeted when she realized how very different her boys were in temperament, as well as most other aspects of their lives. Each son gravitated to groups that were suited to their own likes and dislikes. Her older son ran with a crowd that was always testing authority and pushing the limits. He ignored curfews, experimented with drugs and caused Stephanie and her husband a great deal of anxiety. Stephanie's younger son did his share of pushing limits as well, but never went too far. His group of friends had a completely different outlook and their interests were channeled in diverse directions. In addition, they got better grades in school. Stephanie was very upset because she thought her two sons would never be close, as they seemed to have nothing in common.

Despite her disappointment, however, she continued to nurture both sons and show them unconditional love. The unconditional love that Stephanie and her husband had given to both sons proved to be the basis for family unity and success. Her older son went on to become a local councilman and her younger son became a teacher. Her sons continue to be very different individuals, but they have become close friends. Although they seldom have the same point of view on any given subject, they respect each other's views and value their relationship.

Looking at Your Children Objectively

Step back and take a look at your children and how they behave on a daily basis. Keep in mind that all children have good and bad days (just as adults do); therefore, it is necessary to make your observations over several weeks in order to observe a pattern of behaviors in a number of different situations.

Consider how you would handle a situation where one of your employees suddenly started to act unprofessionally and was rude to others. You would probably carefully monitor him to find the reason for the disturbing behavior. There are many potential causes for these problems, ranging from the attitude and treatment of co-workers, to personal problems, to your management style. As a manager, you would make every effort to resolve the problem so that the organization prospers.

If you found that the employee's problem had to do with another co-worker, perhaps you could counsel all concerned or rearrange workstations and break times to keep the two apart. If a personal problem seemed to be the reason, a quiet offer to listen might be appreciated. If you found the problem concerned your management style, perhaps you could take a look at your style and make some changes to create harmony. The point is, adults do not often react the same way to stimuli or events; this is why it is so important to be flexible and adjust your management style for different employees.

Look at your children in a similar way. If you notice behavior that you feel needs to be addressed, you should check out these influencing sources: friends, personal issues and your parenting style. Pay attention to your children and their friends. Are they being bullied or do others take advantage of them? Are they included in plans and events? What is their position in their group? Do they get involved? Are they leaders or followers?

There are times when the best way to settle social problems for your children is to encourage them to develop new friendships and find new interests. Perhaps finding groups with similar likes and interests may make them more comfortable. Additionally, if your children are finding it difficult to fit in, you may want to consider assertiveness training.

If you feel that your child is struggling with a personal problem, choose a quiet time when the two of you can talk without interruption. Gently remind him that you are there to listen—without judgment—to whatever he would like to discuss. While your child may not want to talk the first time you approach him, this will provide an opportunity to build up trust. As a result, it will set the stage, establishing that you are there no matter what. It may take time, but your child will understand that you want to listen and help.

Being a Fair Judge and Critic

To judge and compare one child to another is not fair. To criticize a child because she looks, thinks or acts differently than other children is not fair. All children should feel they are important. If you give one child more attention, or treat one child better than his sibling, then the other child might get into trouble in order to gain your attention. He may also build up resentment toward the sibling, and this resentment may never be resolved. The child to whom you are paying more attention may also suffer. He might feel pressure caused by your high expectations. He may crave his sibling's friendship and not understand the resentment that he is receiving instead. As a result, he may do something rebellious just to prove that he is not always perfect. As parents, we need to be equally receptive to each of our children's accomplishments and needs, no matter how large or small. **Take the steps necessary to ensure that each of your children knows that he is special.**

When talking to your children, avoid judgmental words and phrases that may impact how they view themselves. Words are considered to be judgmental if they convey a sense of good or bad, better or worse. It is every child's right to have a positive self-image, which is often enhanced by a sense of feeling capable, loved, valuable, competent and unique.

☆ *A Real-Life Example of Being a Fair Critic: Paula and Marlene*

Sisters Paula and Marlene were born two years apart and attended the same high school. Paula was an extremely creative person. She loved to have her hands in one project or another and participate in the annual school play. Marlene, on the other hand, leaned more toward scholarly pursuits and did not care much for extracurricular activities.

Their school was sponsoring a trip to an amusement park in a neighboring state and both girls wanted to go. The trip would be costly, especially if both children went. Their father, Harry, did not want to deny them this opportunity. He made a deal with them: "Bring home a report card with at least five A's and you can go. Anything less and you can't go on the trip." He considered this to be a fair proposal.

Harry failed to take into consideration the differences between his daughters. To bring home the grades he required to go on the trip was no problem for Marlene, but was a major problem for Paula. Harry's solution may have appeared sound on the surface, but he should have taken a closer look. While Harry thought that he was treating his daughters equally by asking the same thing of each, he was actually being unfair to Paula who would have to work twice as hard to reach that goal. A better choice might have been to ask Paula to get two A's on her report card, or ask Marlene to do extra chores around the house or join a club at school.

☆ A Real-Life Example of Being a Fair Critic: Lawrence and Cliff

Lawrence was a neat boy who kept his room fairly clean and his clothes hung up. He enjoyed reading and could spend all day buried in a book. His brother Cliff, on the other hand, had a room that defied description, with clothing covering every inch of the floor. Cliff had many friends and spent all his spare time with them. Loud and energetic, you always knew when he was close by. The one thorn in Cliff's life was from the question frequently asked by his parents: "Why can't you be more like Lawrence?"

The answer to his parents' question is easy; though his parents didn't see it. The reason why Cliff cannot be more like Lawrence is because he is *not* Lawrence; he is his own unique person. While Lawrence may be easier to bring up, they must not ignore Cliff's special qualities that make him who he is. They undoubtedly love Cliff, but they need to learn to appreciate him, rather than try to make him more like Lawrence.

EXTREME PARENTING: USING, NOT ABUSING, YOUR PARENTAL AUTHORITY

A good way to begin understanding your children is to examine your own method of parenting. It is important *not* to implement one stringent, extreme method of parenting. In this section, you will read about three styles of extreme parenting: authoritative parenting, permissive parenting and vigilant parenting. As you read, note if you use any of these parenting styles. To parent in any of these ways is an abuse of parental power. **The authority you have as a parent should not to be taken lightly**. You should use your authority in the best possible way to help your children become successful, mature adults. Make that your goal and stick to it.

Authoritative Parenting

Parents are automatically given "authority" over their children. How parents use or abuse this authority is often a determining factor in how children view themselves and the world around them. An authoritative parent takes absolute and total control over their children's lives; there are no excuses for deviations from the rules. Children must tow the line exactly as defined by their parents. When parents are too authoritative and barely allow their children to breathe without their permission, children can become stifled. This can lead to damaged self-esteem and lack of assertiveness.

☆ *A Real-Life Example of Authoritative Parenting: Sandra*
Marge was very fond of telling everyone what a wonderfully obedient girl her daughter, Sandra, was. She would say things like, "I never have to tell her twice to do her homework, to clean her room or to do the dishes. She obeys me immediately. I'm so lucky to have such a good child."

Sandra's 4th grade teacher, Miss Connors, saw Sandra in a different light. What she observed was a nine-year-old girl who seldom ran and played in the schoolyard with her classmates. Sandra would become visibly upset if her clothing became dirty or torn, and even a mild reprimand would cause her to tremble and stutter. She was a timid child who always appeared to be nervous and anxious.

Miss Connors' concern for this frail child led her to arrange a meeting between Marge, Sandra and myself, the school psychologist. At first, Marge balked, stating that her family had no need for a psychologist, especially Sandra who was so well-behaved. She was finally convinced that the meeting was in Sandra's best interests, so she agreed.

During our first session, Marge immediately began to tell me what an exceptionally well-behaved child Sandra was. While her mother was speaking, Sandra sat quietly. I asked Marge if Sandra had always been such a good child. "More or less," she said, "when she was much younger, she broke a lot of the rules, but that doesn't happen anymore." I asked her what kind of rules Sandra used to break. "Oh, you know…being loud, touching knickknacks, running in the house, getting her clothes dirty, that sort of thing," she said. I asked her what would happen when Sandra broke these rules. She said, "Well, after a few spankings and other punishments, she found out that I don't tolerate that kind of behavior and she settled down."

Next, I turned my attention to Sandra and asked her what she did for fun. She thought about it for several minutes and finally said, "After my homework is finished I'm allowed to watch television. Sometimes I help momma in the kitchen when she makes dinner, or I play with my dolls." I asked her if she ever had friends over to play. "No… Momma says they mess things up too much." I proceeded to ask Sandra if she ever went to her friends' houses to play or for sleepovers. "No…Momma says she would worry about me. And besides, she says they get wild and noisy and she doesn't want me to get like that."

The problem in this family was obvious. Marge wielded absolute authority over Sandra and controlled her every action. Yes, she had a model child, but at what cost? The nature of a child is to laugh, play and occasionally get loud and messy. Sandra was not given a chance to be a normal child, nor was she able to discover or express her creativity.

Growing up in such an environment could result in two scenarios. The first is that she could be successful in a career, but unsuccessful in life, having developed a complex in her early years as a result of always trying to live up to her mother's expectations. The second scenario is that once she was out from under her mother's thumb, she could throw away her inhibitions and restrictions and become involved in detrimental activities. She could use this new freedom to indulge in things she knew her mother would never approve of.

It took many sessions and a lot of hard work to break through Marge's resistance to therapy. She was convinced she was doing what was best for Sandra and that her method of parenting was the right one. I had to work extensively with her until she understood that she was stifling her daughter and setting her up for problems later in life. As her mother's control loosened, Sandra began to enjoy life as a normal child.

Permissive Parenting

Permissiveness and total authority are at two opposite ends of the parenting spectrum. While authoritarian parents practice absolute control over their children, permissive parents abdicate the parental role by giving total control to their children. Their lives are dedicated to ensuring that their children have their every whim satisfied. Parents often think they are helping their children have a good life by being permissive; the word "no" does not exist in their vocabulary.

Children of permissive parents know exactly what they can get away with. They are aware that all they have to do is turn on the tears or throw a temper tantrum and their parents will give in. Children of permissive parents become masters in the art of manipulation. Permissive parents allow their children to dictate every aspect of family life, from what the family eats, to bedtime, to what they do for relaxation.

In their quest to ensure the happiness of their children, permissive parents neglect to set guidelines, establish rules or review the consequences of breaking the rules. It is not easy to stand by while children cry or plead to get their way; however, by giving in, you are not helping your children succeed later in life. **Children need to learn that the world does not revolve around them and their desires.** If they learn about accountability and appropriate behavior at an early age, they will be able to handle the reality of adulthood much more effectively.

☆ *A Real-Life Example of Permissive Parenting: Nolan*
Nolan was in the 7th grade and caused his teachers a great deal of stress. He would talk during class, chew gum and make fun of classmates. When he first began 6th grade, his teachers would call Nolan's house to speak to his parents about his unruly behavior. It became apparent after a few futile efforts that Nolan could not do

anything wrong in his parents' eyes. When his teachers explained Nolan's behavioral problems at school, his parents would immediately come to his defense and would hear none of what the teachers had to say.

When Nolan entered the 7th grade, he had a reputation of being a troublemaker, and his parents had a reputation of giving in to his every whim. It got to the point where none of the teachers wanted Nolan in their class. One day, his homeroom teacher got fed up with his behavior. After attempting one more time to get through to his parents without success, she decided to enlist the help of a psychologist, and that is where I came in.

I called a meeting with Nolan and his parents. The first words out of their mouths were, "Our son is a good boy. We don't know why you would call us here in the first place." I calmly explained to his parents that every teacher in the school who had Nolan in her class had some issues with Nolan's behavior. He was unruly and had developed a reputation of being the class troublemaker. Nolan's parents could not believe what they were hearing. They were very defensive and did not want to admit that their son was anything less than perfect.

In an effort to make his parents understand their son's behavior, I invited them to sit in the back of one of Nolan's classes and observe. Sure enough, Nolan was self-assured and thought he could get away with anything. He started throwing spitballs and talking back to the teacher. Nolan's parents could not believe their eyes and ears. They were shocked.

I met with Nolan's parents after to discuss how they were feeling. His father said, "I had no idea he was so much trouble. I always thought he was a good boy." His mother said, "Where did we go wrong?" I explained to them that while it was good that they showed Nolan unconditional love and support, they were actually hurting him in the long run by protecting him and not admitting that he had faults. I explained to them the importance of not letting Nolan get away with everything. "I guess I was afraid he wouldn't love us if we didn't give him what he wanted. You see, Nolan is adopted and we've always wanted to give him what he's wanted so that he would accept and love us," his father said.

After several meetings and a lot of hard work by Nolan and his parents, everyone began to notice a difference in Nolan's behavior. His parents made an effort to not let him get away with everything. Once they did this, Nolan realized he could not manipulate his way out of every situation. As a result, he began to make more of an effort to behave properly, both in school and at home. Nolan's behavior did not change overnight, but it did change. This change will help him later in life when his parents will no longer be able to come to his defense. It took a while for Nolan's parents to get used to the idea of standing up to their son. They had to learn that by parenting their son, he would not love them any less; in fact, he will probably be grateful to them later in life.

Vigilant Parenting

The vigilant parent is an extension of the permissive parent. Parents naturally want to protect their children from harm, but vigilant parents take protection to the extreme. They rush in to help with every small hurt, throwing a cloak of protection over their children. Vigilant parents often do not allow their children to play with other children for fear that they will catch an illness or get hurt. Vigilant parents may not allow their children to go swimming because of a fear of drowning, or they may insist that their children dress warmer when there is a slight breeze in order to avoid catching a cold. These are only a few examples of actions taken by vigilant parents.

What is going to happen to the children of vigilant parents when they peek out from under that protective cloak and step into real life? What will happen when the parents are no longer there to protect their children? Their children might be unprepared and unable to cope with reality as an adult.

All children get bumps and bruises—it is part of the learning process of growing up. Parents should be available for guidance, but children need to learn about life on their own at times so they will be equipped to live it fully.

☆ *A Real-Life Example of Vigilant Parenting: Lauren*
Lauren's mother, Jeanie, brought her to my private practice after the guidance counselor at school suggested that they visit a family psychologist. I met with Lauren and her mother on a beautiful spring

day. The first thing I noticed was that Lauren was wearing a heavy coat and the temperature was about 70 degrees. The next thing I noticed was Lauren's mother handing her a wet wipe to clean her hands the minute she walked in.

Although I had some idea, I asked Lauren and her mother the reason for their visit. Jeanie answered, "Lauren's guidance counselor at school was concerned that she is withdrawn and is not exerting herself enough. She's worried that she won't get into a good college if she doesn't start participating in school activities. She also said that she thinks Lauren is a loner." I asked Lauren how she felt about this, and she immediately looked at her mother for the answer. Her mother cut in, "She's only in the 10th grade. She doesn't have to worry about college yet. She's got excellent grades. I don't want her participating in sports or staying after school in clubs. It's dangerous. These kids at Lauren's school are trouble, and she does not need friends like that."

I asked Lauren if she was interested in any of these extracurricular activities. Lauren hesitantly stated, "I sort of do, but I know it's not good for me and I might get hurt. My mom is right; I need to focus on my grades. I don't need a bunch of friends anyway." It became clear to me that Jeanie's over-protectiveness was the problem. It did not allow Lauren to have a social life, and it also stopped her from participating in activities she might enjoy and that might help her in the future.

After a few weeks of therapy, and some resistance by Jeanie, she slowly began to realize that she needed to let Lauren live her life. She needed to let her be a normal 10th grader. It was hard for Jeanie to let go and face her fears of something happening to her daughter. It also took Lauren some time to get used to the idea of going out and participating in activities that were forbidden for so long. Eventually, they got used to the idea and worked together to overcome their fears. Lauren agreed to always let her mother know what activities she was participating in and to call if she was going to be coming home late. This alleviated Jeanie's constant worrying, knowing that Lauren was safe. Jeanie allowed Lauren to participate in more activities and recognized the need for her to interact with friends and schoolmates. Jeanie's willingness to change and conquer her irrational fears will ultimately help Lauren later in life.

AN ASSESSMENT OF YOUR CHILD'S PERSONALITY

The best way to understand your children is to look at them from a variety of angles. Below is a personality questionnaire to complete about your child. It will help you develop a better and more accurate assessment of your child. Through the use of a personality profile, you will learn how to help your children with their approach to real issues, as well as adjustments you may need to make to your parenting methods in order for your children to grow into happy and successful adults. When you are done with the questionnaire, you will review your answers in order to develop a personality profile for your child.

Please circle always, usually, seldom or never for the following statements:

1. My child is even-tempered.

   Always   Usually   Seldom   Never

2. My child is well liked by other children.

   Always   Usually   Seldom   Never

3. My child can amuse himself for long periods of time.

   Always   Usually   Seldom   Never

4. My child needs constant reassurance.

   Always   Usually   Seldom   Never

5. My child prefers the company of adults.

   Always   Usually   Seldom   Never

6. My child is comfortable making decisions.

   Always   Usually   Seldom   Never

7. My child has nightmares.

Always   Usually   Seldom   Never

8. My child is a good student.

Always   Usually   Seldom   Never

9. My child works well in a team.

Always   Usually   Seldom   Never

10. My child prefers the role of leader.

Always   Usually   Seldom   Never

11. My child does household chores without complaint.

Always   Usually   Seldom   Never

12. My child shows good judgment.

Always   Usually   Seldom   Never

13. My child is impulsive in his actions.

Always   Usually   Seldom   Never

14. My child reacts defensively to criticism.

Always   Usually   Seldom   Never

15. My child seems to live in a fantasy world.

Always   Usually   Seldom   Never

16. My child sees projects through to the end.

Always   Usually   Seldom   Never

17. My child has definite goals.

Always   Usually   Seldom   Never

18. My child makes friends easily.

    Always   Usually   Seldom   Never

19. My child is neat and tidy.

    Always   Usually   Seldom   Never

20. My child's feelings are easily hurt.

    Always   Usually   Seldom   Never

Statement 1: My child is even-tempered.

The ideal responses to this statement are usually or always. No one, neither child nor adult, is always in a good mood. If your children are seldom or never happy and are always losing their temper, you need to find the reason for this behavior. Is too much expected of them at their age? Do they receive outward signs of love, such as words and actions, often enough to properly influence their behavior? Do you give them your time, or do you brush them off in favor of things you consider to be more important? Do you exemplify a happy, well-balanced life? Does their temper resemble yours? Once you pinpoint the causes of your children's behavior and actions, you will be able to take the necessary steps to remedy problem situations that may exist.

Statement 2: My child is well liked by other children.

Always or usually are ideal responses to this statement, while seldom or never need to be looked into further. While there may be several reasons for this, the most probable cause is some form of bullying. Children who are bullies will have a problem dealing with peers. This is also true of children who practice another form of bullying, which is insisting on getting their own way and never allowing others to have a say. If these children do not get their way, they might run home in tears or lash out physically at other children. If this is a trend in your children's actions, you may be giving in to them too much. You could be practicing a form of permissive parenting. If children achieve complete domination in the home, then it is natural for them to think this power extends outside of the home as well.

If you see this bullying trait in your children, you must regain control and assume your parental duties. If this behavior pattern is already well established, the change will not be easy to accomplish. You may need to be prepared for tears and tantrums. With time, however, your children will become more well adjusted.

Your children may also not be well liked if they suffer from poor self-esteem. Sometimes children can be very cruel to one another. If they do not dress or act like "the crowd," they may not be accepted or liked by others. If this is the case with any of your children, you should work hard to build their self-esteem. Assure them that they are a good person and they should continue to do their best in every situation. Supply them with unconditional love and support. Be there to listen if they need you. If your children feel loved and appreciated at home, they will begin to develop the confidence that will extend to other areas of their life.

Statement 3: My child can amuse himself for long periods of time.

The ideal response here is usually, as this denotes self-acceptance and satisfaction. If your children always prefer to be alone, there may be an underlying problem, such as feelings of inadequacy or not being able to interact well with others. If this is the case, you should work with them to build their social skills. Give them enough self-confidence to know that others will want to spend time with them.

If your children seldom or never amuse themselves, they may be suffering from low self-esteem and consider the company of others to be better than their own. If this is the case, you should spend time building their individual confidence and finding ways to demonstrate that you think they are very special and have unique qualities. In addition, you should expose your children to different opportunities or hobbies.

Statement 4: My child needs constant reassurance.

The ideal responses to this statement are seldom or never. Of course everyone needs reassurance at one time or another, but if you responded with always or usually, then your child may have a poor self-image. If this is the case, then you should work hard to increase their self-esteem. If your children's grades are poor, help them with schoolwork and projects or hire a tutor. Make sure that in your efforts to help your children, you are not doing the work for them; this will send your children the absolute wrong message. Instead, work *with* your children to achieve success.

Your children may also have issues with their appearance. If this is the case, first reassure your children that they are beautiful, inside and out. If your children want to make changes to improve how they look, help them do so in a healthy way. If they have a weight issue, go to a doctor to see if there is an underlying health issue, such as an underactive thyroid. If no health conditions exist, have your doctor help you determine a healthy goal weight. Then, work with your children to achieve this goal in a healthy way. For example, help them to eat properly by keeping lots of healthy foods around the house. Set up reasonable daily exercise regimens, and make sure your children do not do any extreme form of dieting. Instead, remind them that a slow and steady health regimen is the best solution.

If your children are unhappy about a certain feature, such as hairstyle or clothing, then work with them, within reason, to make some changes. Take them to a salon where they can get a hairstyle that makes them feel good. Teach them how to build a wardrobe of pieces that go well together. There are many other ways you can help improve your children's personal outlook to make for happier personal recognition and self-confidence. The key here is to identify what is causing your children's low self-confidence and then work from the inside out. While you can help increase their confidence by making changes to their outer self, it is important to work on their inner self as well.

Statement 5: My child prefers the company of adults.

The ideal response here is seldom. Healthy children enjoy being with other children their own age. If your children do not prefer being with other children, then find out why. Are they being bullied? Do adults spoil them so much that they don't want to be around children? Even highly intelligent children who are interested in adult conversation need to spend the majority of their time with peers and should take pleasure from doing typical, childlike things.

Statement 6: My child is comfortable making decisions.

The ideal response here is usually or always. In order to be successful and happy, children must know that what they think matters. They need to have confidence in their decisions. If each time they make a decision, they are ridiculed or ignored, they will eventually stop making decisions altogether.

If your response was either seldom or never, then you really need to listen to your children and work with them to give them more decision-making opportunities. If your child makes an unhealthy decision, explain why he should re-think the decision—do not simply reject ideas without giving reasons for doing so. Let your children know that their voices are heard and that you have confidence in their decision-making abilities. After all, you are trying to prepare your children to be successful adults who will need to have the courage to make difficult decisions, as well as the confidence to stand by these decisions.

Statement 7: My child has nightmares.

The ideal responses here are seldom or never. Nightmares are caused by any number of influences and are not uncommon for children; however, they should not be the norm for healthy children. If they begin to occur frequently and become routine, bring your child to a physician to determine if there is a physical cause for these dreams. If no obvious physical cause exists, then you should start to search for other sources on your own.

Try to discover if your children feel threatened in any way. Look to friends, school or even yourself, especially if major changes have occurred within your family. Question whether a particular event, such as a death in the family or personal loss, has been so upsetting that it triggers these nightmares. Do your children watch too many scary television shows or movies? If so, eliminate these shows, as they may contain disturbing scenes which can affect their entire day. Do your best to uncover the reason, and then try to resolve the issue. If it happens to be an event that has caused the onset of these dreams, then talk soothingly and reassuringly to ease your children's fears. If the problem continues, make an appointment with a psychologist who specializes in working with children. There are instances in which a professional can get to the root of a problem when family members cannot. If needed, you should be ready to accept this level of help.

Statement 8: My child is a good student.

This response is not as easy to analyze as some of the others. Not everyone is capable of bringing home perfect report cards. It does not make someone a bad student if her grades are not all A's. As long as your children are doing their best work, and are happy and well adjusted in school, then they are on the right track. Even if your children do not get the best of grades, you may have responded to this statement with always or usually, simply because they show consistent signs of hard work and improvement.

In supporting your children, it is important for them to know that if a problem occurs, they can count on you for help. Offer your support and encourage them to improve, but also let them know that as long as they are giving their best effort, you will be satisfied with their results. If grades are consistently poor and show no signs of improvement, your children may need parental or private tutoring, or special classes. Whatever the remedy, it will result in happier children.

Statement 9: My child works well in a team.

To be successful in life, you must be willing to be a team player. If your children always or usually enjoy being part of a team, they will have a foundation for situations later in life that require cooperation.

To seldom or never work well in a team may indicate a lack of self-esteem. It may also indicate the total opposite, which is total self-absorption and insistence on making all decisions and garnering all of the attention. Since this is not the way a team works, these children will either choose to work alone or with people who allow them to dominate the team.

Improving this situation requires you to encourage team participation. When your children participate well in a team, applaud their efforts. As parents, you need to show that you are proud of your children when they cooperate and work well within a team.

Statement 10: My child prefers the role of leader.

A leader is a person who understands the principles involved in being in charge. If your children usually prefer this role, they are preparing for the future in a very positive way. If your children always prefer this role, you should make sure they understand the concept of teamwork and what it means to be a leader. They must be able to be a leader *and* work as part of a team.

Some people, both adults and children, do not enjoy being in a leadership role. They prefer to be part of the crew and let the captain make the difficult decisions. This is fine; however, these individuals may not rise to the very top of their profession. If they are afraid of taking risks and do not want to take blame if things go wrong, then they are not equipped to be a leader. Respected and confident leaders are risk-takers who assume responsibility and accept the consequences of their actions. In order to strengthen your children's leadership qualities, put them in charge of some household duties. Make them feel a sense of empowerment at home. They may discover that they enjoy being in a leadership role after all. Once their confidence begins to develop inside the home, they may be more inclined to take on a leadership role outside the home.

Statement 11: My child does household chores without complaint.

Most people do not look forward to completing assigned chores. Children usually prefer to be with friends or involved in activities that hold their interest; therefore, they will complain from time to time about the chores they must do at home. If they usually or always do assigned jobs without making a fuss, it shows they understand their part in helping the family to function as a unit. Through accomplishment of chores, they are learning a valuable lesson; there is a time for work and a time for play, and others depend on them to perform their duties.

If your children constantly complain about their assigned chores, perhaps you have given them work beyond their capability, or an amount that is too much for them to accomplish at their age. When making assignments, review your expectations with a realistic view. If changes are called for, institute them and never be afraid to admit that you made a mistake.

Statement 12: My child shows good judgment.

If your children are usually or always able to think for themselves and value their own opinions, they probably have a good sense of self-esteem. Be careful, however, if your children are easily swayed by the opinions of others, or if they enter into activities that they know are wrong just to be "one of the gang."

You can reinforce your children's capacity for good judgment by demonstrating your own moral evaluation of issues, and encourage them to do what they feel is right. Teach them to be a leader who strives for good, and not a follower who goes along with the wrong course of action. As a parent and family leader, you can help by asking their opinion on certain matters at home. You should then take time to discuss the reasons why they chose that particular response. As you finish these discussions, always show respect for their thoughts; even if you do not agree with them. This demonstrates that it is good to think and act independently.

Statement 13: My child is impulsive in his actions.

Spontaneity can be a good thing, as lack of planning sometimes adds a great deal of fun to an occasion. If, however, your children always act in an impulsive manner, then they need to learn that a key ingredient for success is proper planning.

If your children seldom act on impulse, but instead plan things out and think before they act, they are probably on the right track. You should, however, promote occasional spur-of-the-moment acts, and allow them to indulge their need to be spontaneous. While it is good to think before acting and weigh the results and consequences, to never act impulsively generates a serious and unbending attitude. Additionally, a lack of impulsiveness could constitute a fear of risk and failure. Encourage your children to take sporadic risks, and make them aware that failure is not the end of the world.

Statement 14: My child reacts defensively to criticism.

The ideal response here would be seldom. While it would be unnatural to never react defensively, if your child is usually or always defensive, you should take a look at your parenting style.

Are you always criticizing their faults without praising good points? Are you seldom, or never, satisfied with the work that they do?

If your children feel they never do anything right, they may become immediately defensive. It can get to the point where the simplest statement, such as, "You forgot to put away the dishes" can be blown out of proportion. They may think they can never do anything to please you and, therefore, may not even try. This attitude can lead to major problems in adult life.

As a parent and an adult, you need to try to overlook things that do not meet your expectations completely. Instead of saying, "You didn't dust the coffee table," try saying, "You did a great job of helping me to clean the living room. I appreciate your help. If you can dust this table for me, we'll be all finished in here." We all like to hear what we have done well, instead of what we did not do well. Try to temper your criticism with praise.

Statement 15: My child seems to live in a fantasy world.

How much time? What kind of fantasies? While seldom or never may be the best answer here, dreams and fantasies are an important part of who we are. Fantasizing and dreaming are not necessarily bad things to do. A child may dream of becoming a doctor when he grows up, so he spends a lot of time pretending. Another might imitate her favorite superhero, using an old curtain as a cape to save the world from villains. Some children without siblings invent brothers and sisters as playmates. None of these activities are necessarily harmful. It is a problem, however, if fantasy takes over and children spend most of their time occupied with the fantasy.

If your children live exclusively in a world that is not reality-based, it is time to discover why. Find out what is lacking in their life that makes them want to avoid reality. If the answer is not clear, seek professional help, but try hard not to be overly judgmental or angry.

Statement 16: My child sees projects through to the end.

If your children usually or always follow through when they start a project, they have the ability to focus on the job at hand and understand the importance of following through. This is a vital part of success in adulthood.

If they jump from one unfinished endeavor to the next, however, you may have answered seldom or never. You should then help them understand how important it is to see a project through to its completion. If your children lose interest in a project, or if you think the project has become too challenging, make time to work with them. Working together will communicate that you care enough to help them succeed and that their endeavor is meaningful.

Statement 17: My child has definite goals.

The ideal response to this statement would be always or usually. Goals are not just for adults; children of any age can and should have goals. Children in grade school may have a goal of winning a spelling bee, and in high school, a goal might be to earn an athletic letter from the track team. Commitment to achieving goals demands hard work; through this commitment, goals may be realized. If setting definite goals becomes an internal norm for your children, then they are on the path to developing a life-long habit that will see them through many challenges and obstacles.

On the other hand, if you notice that your children do not set goals and instead seem to float from one idea to another without any real focus, you need to step in and help. Take the time to teach the value of goals. Talk about their vision for the future—three months, six months or a year down the road. Help them outline a plan that will detail each necessary step in order to achieve their goals. Monitor their progress and show an interest and desire for them to achieve their goals.

Statement 18: My child makes friends easily.

Do your children always have a wide circle of friends? If so, they probably have a good personality and show a natural interest in others. Making friends easily is a valuable tool that can be used throughout life. It can lead to success in both business and personal situations. Additionally, friends establish a strong framework that can establish them as a leader and prepare them for the future.

If you think your children may have a problem in this area, try to discover the reason. Is it a demonstration of inadequate feelings around peers? You should strive to help your children develop positive self-esteem. Many people prefer to have a few good friends rather than a full circle of acquaintances. This is fine, as long as they have no trouble accepting the friends they have chosen.

Encourage your children to make friends, but let them work at their own pace—do not push too hard. Do not make them feel any less special if they do not have a lot of friends. Support your children and show an interest in their activities, but do not intrude on them. Be available if called upon to listen and advise. Create a safe environment and make your children's friends welcome in your home.

Statement 19: My child is neat and tidy.

If this is usually or always the case, then your children probably have a good sense of responsibility and like order in their surroundings. Chaos results in a mess, and no one can focus on important issues while in a chaotic environment. Disorder may also contribute to stress.

Help your children get into the habit of keeping themselves neat and clean. Show them the value of picking up after themselves and keeping their area free from clutter. They will soon discover how stress-free and conducive a well-organized area is to producing good work, and they will want to continue along that path.

If, however, your children seem to be obsessive about cleanliness and compulsive in their actions to be neat and tidy, this may indicate a problem. If you notice that your children's obsession with cleanliness is interfering with daily life, seek professional help for them.

Statement 20: My child's feelings are easily hurt.

The ideal responses here are seldom or never. If your children's feelings are easily hurt, what could be some reasons for this? Are they very sensitive to criticism or joking? Have they been hurt in the past, causing them to be defensive?

Take steps to help your children understand that constructive criticism can improve their performance. After all, each of us needs to learn to laugh and not take ourselves too seriously. Try to teach, by example, that everyone does things from time to time that cause amusement to others. These situations may be embarrassing, but the embarrassment will vanish quickly if they can learn to find the humor in the situations.

Being sensitive to the needs of others is an excellent quality for one to hold. Being oversensitive to your own feelings, however, can cause a lifetime of misery. As a parent, be sparing in your criticism and more lavish in your praise. Help your children learn how to take comments as they were meant to be taken, and not to look into every statement too seriously.

Recognizing Your Children's Passions

Childhood interests will change as your children mature, but it is a mistake to ignore interests because you assume they will not last. You should encourage your children to improve their skills and to learn everything available about a topic that they find fascinating. This knowledge will not go to waste. If the interest lags as your children grow older, they will always have the learning experience to support them. A childhood interest that continues to grow may even lead to a lifelong career.

Talk to your children and become aware of their interests and passions. As long as those interests are healthy and safe, support and encourage them. Your children will appreciate that you are listening to them and understand their desire to explore their true passions.

The example below illustrates the need to listen to your children's interests and desires, rather than assume you know what they like. The following examples illustrate how childhood interests can lead to successful careers later in life.

☆ *A Real-Life Example of Recognizing Your Children's Passions: Dan and His Family*

The holidays were over and Dan was puzzled. He thought his gift to the family this year was the best ever and could not understand why it fell flat. He and his wife, Suzanne, were avid skiers. Their children, Zane, who was eight years old, and Maggie, who was ten, were finally old enough to join them on a vacation at their favorite ski lodge. Instead of spending a lot on individual gifts, Dan used the money to go on the trip. The disappointment began on Christmas morning when Zane was upset because he did not get the bicycle he hoped for. In addition, Maggie pouted all morning because the computer she wanted was not under the tree.

Dan was sure that everything would be all right once the kids saw the resort and realized what a great time they would have. Once again, he was wrong. Maggie tried the beginners' slope twice, and after that stayed in the lodge and watched television. Zane spent the majority of his time in the game room. Dan and Suzanne could not fully enjoy themselves because they were concerned about their children. All in all, the vacation was a bust.

Dan had been certain that he had come up with the perfect gift, but it turned out to be a disaster. Dan's biggest error was not listening to his children or making an effort to understand their true passions. He assumed that because he and Suzanne were avid skiers, their children would naturally take to the slopes as well. If he had paid attention, he would have discovered that Zane felt left out of his group of friends because they spent almost all of their free time riding bicycles. Maggie spent as much time as possible on the family computer. She loved learning all about the different programs and how they worked. She wanted a computer of her own so she would not have to share the one used by the entire family. In addition, she needed one for her schoolwork. She had even picked out the place in her room where she could set it up and work on it as long as she liked. Instead of feeling that her interests were understood and respected, she felt ignored.

Although his intentions were good, the better choice for Dan would have been to listen to his children. If he could not afford the gifts they wanted this year, then he could have explained why and let them know when they could look forward to them. He should have put off a family skiing trip until the children showed some interest in the sport.

☆ A Real-Life Example of Recognizing Your Children's Passions: Emory

As a gift for his eighth birthday, Emory's grandfather bought him an erector set. That gift was the beginning of a lifelong love for building and construction. Emory always had one project or another underway. He read every book he could get on the topic, and he apprenticed at a construction firm while in college, learning the trade literally from the ground up.

Today, Emory runs a successful construction business. His company has constructed almost all of the major buildings in his community and the surrounding areas for the past twenty-five years. From the very beginning, his family made it easy for him to follow his dream. Without the family support he received, his budding ambition may have withered away. He could have wound up in a job he did not enjoy. Instead, he wakes up each morning excited to go to a job he loves.

☆ *A Real-Life Example of Recognizing Your Children's Passions: Della*

When six-year-old Della received a doll for her birthday, she immediately changed the doll's hairstyle. In fact, she did that to every doll she ever owned. As she got older, her styling improved and she even insisted on certain hairstyles for herself. As a teen, she gave her friends haircuts and creatively colored and styled their hair. She had a knack for knowing just how to twist a strand and where to place a pin.

Della's parents were both engineers and had high hopes that Della would go to college and follow in their footsteps, but Della had other ideas. She convinced her parents to allow her to attend beauty school. She promised them that if, after a year, she found that this career was not for her, she would then go back to college and study engineering.

Della loved what she did and was good at it. As a result, she was able to build up her clientele. Within three years, she owned her own shop and had three assistants working for her. Della's parents' willingness to allow her to follow her dream helped her achieve success and love her life's work.

☆ *A Real-Life Example of Recognizing Your Children's Passions: Samantha*

Samantha is a well-known attorney in a large city. Early on, she got hooked on television shows that featured lawyers in principal roles. She loved them and would often try to guess the strategy that would be used before it was revealed on the show. An avid reader, she began to concentrate on stories involving attorneys as key figures. The more she read about the law, the more she wanted to know.

Her parents supported this passion by encouraging her to go to law school. Samantha even worked nights and weekends to help pay for her education. Both Samantha and her parents' dedication were rewarded. Today, she has a thriving law practice.

Allowing Your Children to Have Their Own Dreams

Each of us holds dreams that are extremely personal and potentially mark our future. As a parent, it is unfair to negate your children's dreams in order to satisfy your own. You run the risk of disappointing your children by stifling their dreams. As a result, you may drive a wedge between you and your children with your self-motivated actions.

There are instances when the passion of the parent influences the child as well, and they share their enthusiasm equally. If that does not happen, do not let it ruin your relationship with your child. Each of our children is entitled to their own hopes and dreams and should be given the opportunity to explore the world wherever their interests lie.

Allow your children to pursue their dreams. Do not live your life vicariously through your children. Encourage their dreams and passions. Be confident and happy that you played a role in their success by allowing them to have their own dreams.

☆ *A Real-Life Example of Allowing Children to Have Dreams: Annabelle and Rochelle*

On a cool November day, Annabelle brought her thirteen-year-old daughter, Rochelle, to meet with me for counseling. Annabelle was somewhat nervous, but Rochelle was quiet and subdued. I asked Annabelle why she felt that her daughter needed counseling. "Two reasons," she answered, "her dancing and her attitude." I asked her to explain what she meant.

Through probing and the use of pointed, specific questions, I was able to ascertain that Annabelle had aspirations of becoming a ballet dancer for as long as she could remember. She wanted desperately to become a member of a dance troupe, perhaps one day even be featured as a lead dancer. Due to family financial circumstances, however, she had to discontinue her lessons. By the time she was able to afford them, it was too late.

Annabelle was thrilled when she became a mother. She wanted her daughter, Rochelle, to have all the opportunities that she had missed. Rochelle, however, did not share her mother's enthusiasm for ballet. She attended the classes that her mother dragged her to, week after week, but her efforts were only half-hearted; it was obvious that she was only going through the motions.

"For the past six months," Annabelle said, " Rochelle has been spending more time at the local animal shelter, where she volunteers, than she has on her ballet." She went on to relate that she had tried to dissuade Rochelle from volunteering, because it took time away from dancing. Annabelle now found that Rochelle was skipping dance classes to be with the animals.

Rochelle's version of the story was short and to the point. "Ballet is okay, but I don't love it like my mother does. I went to all those classes because she insisted. I know I wasn't as good as the other dancers because I just didn't care enough about it, but she kept making me go anyway. Then about six or seven months ago, I found out that they were looking for volunteers to help with the animals at the shelter. You know, feeding them, walking the dogs, that kind of stuff. I started to go there and now I absolutely love it. They've given me more responsibility and sometimes even let me help with the grooming. I'm so happy working with the animals. But she doesn't care. All she worries about is the ballet. I'm starting to really dislike ballet altogether because I'm being forced to take the lessons."

This simple process of speaking and listening had painted a picture of what was happening. I worked with mother and daughter, both together and individually. After some intense sessions, I was able to convince Annabelle that she could not pass her passions on to her daughter. In fact, we came to realize that if she backed off of her insistence on lessons, the two of them could spend many happy hours enjoying ballet performances together. If, however, she did not change and give Rochelle a chance to pursue her own dreams, she would turn Rochelle away from the art altogether and from any pleasure they might be able to share together.

UNDERSTANDING YOUR CHILDREN'S LIMITS AND SUPPORTING THEIR STRENGTHS

In the previous section, you learned how to get to know your children by recognizing the hopes, dreams and passions that motivate them. Now you can take another step that will allow you to better understand your children. You will do this by learning to understand your children's limitations and by supporting their strengths.

We are each endowed with different strengths, but we also have limitations. As an example, look at the examination of three children from the same family. Child number one may have excellent reading skills, but is too shy to speak in front of her class. Child number two may be a whiz at math, but angers easily and becomes argumentative when her ideas are challenged. Child number three may have a wonderful personality, but does poorly in school.

You should never judge your children by their personal limitations or their strengths. You should help them work within their abilities and build on natural talents. While children should be urged to expand their horizons and improve in the areas in which they have limitations, they should also be applauded and encouraged to continue to grow in their areas of strength.

Trying to make your children into something they are not may cause disappointment for both you and your children. Recognizing what your children can and cannot do will allow you to work with them to secure their skills. Taking this path will bring happiness; you will be proud of your children's accomplishments, which will help boost their self-esteem.

All parents want their children to succeed, but there is no such thing as being perfect. As a parent, you must discover the strengths your children possess and work to promote their happiness and success, both now and in the future.

Your View of Your Child's Strengths and Areas for Improvement

To discover how well you think you know your children, you will now create a list of their strengths as well as areas for improvement. On the following pages, you will find two worksheets to fill out. On the first worksheet, list at least five strengths your child exhibits. Below the strengths, describe ways that you, as a parent, will help build on these strengths. For example, does your child have the capability to speak in front of an audience? If this is the case, you can encourage him to join the debate team at school. You can also help your child by encouraging him to practice speaking in front of your family. If your child is a computer whiz, there are many clubs where these talents can be applied, safely allowing growth and enhancing his knowledge.

On the second worksheet, list at least five areas for improvement. Below the areas of improvement, I want you to describe how you, as a parent, will use your knowledge to help your child work within his abilities to improve in these areas. This may include one-on-one tutoring or extra classes for a subject in which he struggles. It may be providing him with safe opportunities to overcome shyness, or working with a specialist to gain a healthy self-esteem. It may require that you encourage your child to participate in a sports program, cheering along as he performs at a personal best. Be sure, however, that your child is involved in the plan for developing his abilities—do not force activities upon him.

My View of My Child's Strengths
(to be completed by the parent)

My Child's Greatest Strengths:

Example: Enjoys and is great at gymnastics.

_____

_____

_____

_____

_____

_____

_____

_____

Ways I Can Encourage These Strengths:

Offer to enroll him in a gymnastics class.

_____

_____

_____

_____

_____

_____

_____

_____

_____

Discovering the Wonderful Complexities of Your Child   187

My View of My Child's Areas for Improvement
(to be completed by the parent)

My Child's Areas for Improvement:

Example: My son has trouble in math class.

_____

_____

_____

_____

_____

_____

_____

_____

Ways I Can Help My Child Achieve These Improvements:

Help him with his math problems; offer to hire a tutor; ask the teacher to help.

_____

_____

_____

_____

_____

_____

_____

_____

_____

YOUR CHILD'S VIEW OF HER STRENGTHS AND AREAS FOR IMPROVEMENTS

Now that you have written down the strengths and areas for improvement that you feel your child possesses, it is time to have your child complete an exercise. On the following pages, you will find two worksheets for your child to fill out. If you feel your child can do it, have her complete this exercise on her own. If your child is younger, sit with her, read each item and write down her responses.

These worksheets are designed to have children think about their strengths and areas for improvement. It will give them an opportunity to describe ways they think that you, as a parent, can help them to achieve these goals. An example will be provided on each worksheet; feel free to provide additional examples.

For the first worksheet, ask your child to list at least five strengths that she possesses. Below her strengths, have her come up with ways that she can develop those strengths. In the last section of the worksheet, have your child describe ways that you can help her develop her strengths.

On the second worksheet, ask your child to list at least five areas where she could improve. Below her areas of improvement, have your child come up with ways that she can achieve those improvements. In the last section of the worksheet, have your child describe ways that you can help her make the improvements.

It is important to encourage your child to be open and honest when filling out these worksheets. Make her feel secure; tell her that your feelings will not be hurt no matter what she writes down. Explain to her that this exercise is important and will bring about positive changes in her life. Explain that you want to help her succeed, and this is the first step in doing so.

My Strengths
(to be completed by the child)

My Greatest Strengths:

<u>*Example:*</u> *Playing hockey*

_____

_____

_____

_____

_____

_____

_____

_____

Ways I Can Develop These Strengths:

Practice; join a league; read books about hockey; attend hockey camp

_____

_____

_____

_____

_____

_____

_____

_____

_____

Ways My Parents Can Help Me Develop These Strengths:

Give me a ride to practice; send me to hockey camp; talk to me about my game

_____

_____

_____

_____

_____

_____

_____

_____

My Areas for Improvement
(to be completed by the child)

Things I Would Like to Improve About Myself:

Example: My math skills

_____

_____

_____

_____

_____

_____

_____

_____

Ways I Can Make These Improvements:

Get extra help from teachers; study more

_____

_____

_____

_____

_____

_____

_____

_____

_____

Ways My Parents Can Help Me Make These Improvements:

Help me practice math problems; hire a tutor for me

_____

_____

_____

_____

_____

_____

_____

_____

Bringing It All Together

After your child has completed both worksheets, sit down with him and discuss what has been written. Discuss what he wrote down as his strengths and areas for improvement. In a non-judgmental manner, ask him why he feels certain ways. Encourage him to talk, and then really listen to what he is saying. Cheer your child on when he discusses methods of how he can make changes. Perhaps you can come up with some other suggestions for how he can make those changes. Finally, review the ways that your child stated that you can help him achieve the goal. Talk it through and tell your child that you will help him out in any reasonable manner. Perhaps you can even come up with some additional suggestions on how you can help.

By reviewing the exercise with your child, you are showing him that you care and that you are making an effort to help him achieve his goals. Follow up on these goals to review the progress that both you and your child have made and the positive changes in his life.

Next, on your own, I want you to compare the responses that you gave with those given by your child. Do they differ a great deal, or are you on the same page as your child? If your responses differ tremendously, then this is a good opportunity to begin to understand your child and the way he thinks. Be open, within reason, to helping your child. Once you have completed this exercise, your knowledge of your child will have expanded significantly, and you will have a clearer understanding of how you can help him build a successful life.

SUMMARY OF CHAPTER FIVE

In this chapter, you began to really look at your children and put goals into action. You learned some important things about your children, several ways of discovering the individuality that each child holds, and how to use that individuality to help them succeed.

You have found that each child is special in her own way. These special aspects of personality make each child different from everyone else. You saw how these differences determine how children react to life and how life reacts to them.

In reviewing the differences that exist between individuals, we recognized that it is unfair to judge or criticize a child according to the abilities of another. Remember, each child has differences, and it is important that we temper our judgments and reactions to these differences. You must keep in mind that you might need to adapt your parenting style according to the differing personalities of your children. While one parenting style may work for one child, it may not work for the other. You must also be flexible with your children. Two children can react differently to the exact same situation. For example, a classmate is joking around at school and makes fun of your daughter. You talk to your son, who attends the same school, and he tells you that it was all in fun and that no one got hurt. Yet, when you talk to your daughter, she tells you that she is being bullied at school and that she is deeply hurt. Each child views situations differently; therefore, you must approach your children with sensitivity and understand the way that they, as individuals, feel and react.

In reviewing different methods of extreme parenting, such as authoritative, permissive and vigilant, you learned the pitfalls of each. You discovered how to develop a healthy parenting style. You also learned to be an objective observer of your child. By completing your child's personality profile, you have come to understand him in a way that will enable you to know his needs. It will also allow you to assist him along the way, feeling the love and security required to grow and be happy.

Each of us holds personal dreams, hopes and passions. In this chapter you have discovered the danger of imposing your dreams on your children. You have learned why it is important to allow them to develop their own interests and give them a chance to pursue these interests without fear of disappointing you. Recognizing your children's passions and acknowledging their right to dream is an important aspect of parenting. Watch closely as your children grow, and you will discover where their interests lie and how you can help to strengthen and improve them.

Finally, you learned that none of us, neither child nor adult, is perfect. In completing the balance sheets, you gained better insight into your child and had a chance to reflect on your own observations of her. As a result, you have discovered how to work within your child's limits to provide a well-balanced, happier life as she matures.

☆ Each child is special; do not compare one child to another.

☆ Do not judge or criticize my children.

☆ Do not impose my own dreams on my children.

☆ Nobody is perfect.

Chapter Six

ATTITUDE AND MOTIVATION

Learn How to Say "We'll Meet Our Goals," Instead of "We'll Never Make It"

CHAPTER OBJECTIVES

- Discover the top two assets on the road to success and how to achieve them.
- Do an assessment of your child's outlook on life.
- Learn how to set realistic goals and how to achieve them.
- Learn the difference between short-term, long-term and lifetime goals.
- Plan monthly family meetings to set new goals and check the progress of current goals.

"Ability is what you're capable of doing. Motivation determines what you do. Attitude determines how well you do it."
— *Anonymous*

In this chapter, you will continue climbing the Pyramid of Success by working with your children to put goals into action. You will learn about the top two assets on the road to success: attitude and motivation. You will set realistic goals and learn how to achieve them. You will then do an assessment of your child's outlook on life. You will learn the difference between short term, long term and lifetime goals. Finally, you will work with your children to plan monthly family meetings in order to set new goals and check the progress of current goals.

TOP ASSET 1: ATTITUDE

When two people of almost equal knowledge and experience are in line for a promotion, the employee who gets the promotion is most often the one with the great attitude. Even if the other candidate is more qualified, the person with the positive and upbeat attitude usually gets further. Think of your own experiences; if you had a choice of doing business with a cheerful and positive company representative or with a negative one, which person would you choose?

Attitude is not how you see yourself, but it is how others perceive you. One aspect of your attitude is that it affects everyone around you. The good thing about this is that each day you have the option to reveal a new attitude. You can set the tone for your day before you even step out of bed in the morning. Your first thought when waking up can be, "I have a desk full of work waiting for me and a meeting with a difficult client today. I just want to pull the covers over my head and stay in bed," or "I have a desk full of work waiting for me and a meeting with a difficult client today. Let's go get 'em!" Which thought do you think will give you a better outlook on your day and lead you to success?

Most children are naturally happy. They awaken cheerfully and ready to delve into every new experience. Their bouncing energy propels them into a full day of adventure. Somewhere along the way to adulthood, a child realizes that life can hold some unpleasant surprises. If their misfortunes are extreme, or if they are permitted to dwell on small setbacks, they may develop negative attitudes toward life. If left unchecked, this negativity may become ingrained in their character. Once a negative attitude is established, it is difficult—but not impossible—to change.

If you notice that your child has a negative attitude, there are several ways you can help. The first thing you should do is check your own attitude. Too often, we do not realize just how negative we are until we actually listen to ourselves and track our attitude. To do this, you need to set aside a period of time, say twenty-four hours, during which you will record each time you gripe, complain or make negative comments. You may be surprised to discover just how often you exhibit the same traits you are trying to eradicate in your children. Before you can help your children, you have to redesign your own thinking.

Martha Washington is quoted as saying, "I am still determined to be cheerful and happy in whatever situation I may be, for I have also learned from experience that the greater part of our happiness or misery depends on our dispositions and not on our circumstances." This comment by our First Lady is as true today as it was so many years ago. A good attitude and cheerful demeanor are easy to present when all is going well, but there are times when things might not go so well and you cannot control the situation. It is at times like these that your determination is put to the test. Whether you are happy or miserable depends entirely on you and the effort you put into your attitude.

If you find, after monitoring your reactions, that you are a sad person and that this unhappiness is reflected in how you relate to others, then you need to do what you can to remedy the situation. First, you need to decide exactly what is causing your distress. If it is your job, then it may be time to look elsewhere for employment. Is it your personal appearance that is causing you grief? Whether you are a man or woman, there are ways to improve your appearance that are not necessarily costly. Are you concerned about some aspect of your health? If so, bolster your courage and consult a medical expert as soon as possible.

From time to time, anyone can find herself in a negative mood. For some people, however, negativity is the norm and this is when it is time for an attitude adjustment. If you have made this discovery, do not delay; take the steps necessary to make your future a reality. Doing something about your situation will give you a better outlook and begin to empower you. There are several techniques that are used to combat negative attitudes. Some of these techniques are listed below.

Techniques for Combating a Negative Attitude

Combating a negative attitude may not be easy to do, but you will find the effort worthwhile. The following are nine techniques to help you along the way:

1) Use humor.
2) Keep it clutter-free.
3) Maintain a balance between home and career.
4) Take care of small tasks.
5) Avoid toxic people.
6) Keep busy with positive activities.
7) Exercise your mind and body.
8) Concentrate on positive thoughts.
9) Help others.

Technique 1: Use humor.

A sense of humor will put you way ahead in the attitude game, especially if you learn to laugh at yourself. People often take themselves so seriously that they cannot tolerate anything that might interfere with their own exceptional opinion of themselves.

To practice engaging in this technique, visualize an embarrassing situation that might have happened to you in the past. For example, did you accidentally spill coffee on an important client you were trying to impress? Now try to imagine how you could put a humorous twist on the story when telling it to your friends. It could go something like, "There I was, trying my best to be graceful and give a good impression, when I was tripped up by a wrinkle in the carpet." Now, the next time an embarrassing situation happens, project ahead and try to see it in that light, as if you were telling your friends a humorous story. This will allow you to push the incident aside and smile.

Bring humor into the workplace, and then address the problems with positive, professional steps. Learn from your mistakes and from others. It will make the working atmosphere lighter, result in a pleasant place to work and deliver an exceptional payoff of greater productivity. Humor is a fantastic ally; use it often and use it effectively.

Teaching Your Children the Importance of Using Humor: Teach your children the vital importance of having a sense of humor. Show them, by word and example, that they should not take life so seriously. If an embarrassing situation should occur, use humor; your children will learn from your example.

Sit down with your children and talk about possible embarrassing situations that could happen to them. Have your children brainstorm ways they could use humor to avoid taking the situation so seriously. By having your children come up with humorous examples, they will be more prepared to deal with these situations when they arise.

Technique 2: Keep it clutter-free.

Relaxation supports the development and maintenance of a positive attitude; clutter does the exact opposite. No one can stay relaxed in an atmosphere that is cluttered with stacks of paperwork, piles of books and lists of telephone messages. Clutter produces anxiety, and anxiety places a negative spin on attitude. You will find that once you establish a routine—and stick to it—you will become a happier and less anxious person.

Focus on the things that need to be done, and then take the time to do them. Clear your desk of all paperwork and catch up on your telephone messages. Become organized by putting your papers in file folders and having a place for everything, then make a concentrated effort to keep things in order. Your work area should serve as a model for yourself and your co-workers. At the end of the day, clear your desk so that when you arrive in the morning, you are not faced with a mess that you dread.

The same principles should apply at home. Eliminate clutter so that you have a place for everything. Keep your kitchen clutter-free. At the end of the day, clean the dishes and put them away so that you are not faced with a messy sink in the morning.

Teaching Your Children the Importance of Being Clutter-free: Encourage your children to pick up their toys at night and put them away. Make it easy for them to follow this rule by providing them with containers and special places that are appropriate for their toys. When your children are of school age, provide them with a desk where they can do their homework. Provide drawers and organizers where they can put their paperwork. Give them a bin where they can keep their pens, pencils and highlighters. Show your children, by example, the virtues of living in a clutter-free house. If they grow up in a household that is clutter-free, they will naturally fall into the same pattern as adults.

Technique 3: Maintain a balance between home and career.

There is no such thing as being perfect; we are not superheroes. It is very difficult to maintain a home, care for children, move up the corporate ladder and try to squeeze in some time for yourself. Usually that time for yourself gets lost in your other tasks. If you are always rushing and have no time to relax, it is no wonder that you feel exhausted and irritable. The key to maintaining balance and finding time in your busy life is routine.

If you stay at the office late, night after night, no time is left to devote to your family or yourself. The establishment of a routine allows you to divide your time effectively; this will positively impact your health and welfare. Make sure you factor in such things as quiet time alone, going to the movies, taking a relaxing bath or enjoying dinner out. What you will find is that, as your life becomes less hectic, your attitude and disposition improve dramatically.

You may love your job, but if you do not provide a balance, both your business life and your personal life will suffer. When on the job, your concentration should be focused on business. When you arrive home, however, the needs of your family should be your top priority. If your children know that once you are at home they have your full attention, they will absorb the idea of balance between work and home, and will use this valuable example in their own lives.

Teaching Your Children the Importance of Maintaining a Balance: Just as you are trying to maintain a balance between your career and home life, it is equally as important to teach your children how to maintain a balance in their own lives. Explain to them that while it is important to do their schoolwork and remain focused on their goals, it is also important to find time to relax and have fun with friends. Teach your children how to prioritize their time so that they can get their homework done and still have time to play outside with a friend or read a fun book. If your children learn how to maintain a balance early in their lives, they will carry this trait with them in the future.

Technique 4: Take care of small tasks.

Have you ever let small tasks slide until you suddenly realize that you have created a mountain of work that is threatening to overwhelm you? This happens so quietly and insidiously that you may not be aware of it until it is out of hand. Our days are filled with thousands of small interruptions and unplanned situations. Allowing tasks to accumulate (building up over days and weeks) will only cause stress and create negative attitudes. Get into the habit of taking care of chores as they occur. If you have already made your office clutter-free, managing each small detail will not be a major issue. When handling paper, for instance, make use of the "TRAF" method: Trash it, Refer it to the proper person, Act on it or File it. At the end of your workday, you can breathe a sigh of relief that you have taken care of everything for that day.

You should run your home in the same manner. Your daily routine may be filled with interruptions, especially when there are children around. It is very easy to tell yourself that you will take care of things later. Unfortunately, by the time "later" arrives, the heap of work has grown into an unmanageable and overwhelming mess, and you are exhausted. By keeping on top of things as they happen, you will be in a better position to manage your home and children. They will learn from your example that it is best not to put things off until later.

There is an old saying, "If you take care of the small things, the large ones will take care of themselves." This is very true. Make sure you attend to both small and large tasks. Do not let messages and memos pile up. Do not let a few pieces of laundry pile up until they become an overwhelming mountain of apparel. Doing small tasks, one at a time, will make them easier to accomplish and eliminate a lot of stress for you.

Teaching Your Children the Importance of Taking Care of Small Tasks: It is important to teach your children how to take care of the smaller tasks, so that they do not let them pile up. For example, explain to your children that it is just as important to finish their ten math problems, as it is to do their twenty-page book report. Explain to them that if they do not do their math homework now, then they will not understand the following set of math problems, and this could affect their math grade for the entire semester. So, just because the book report seems longer and more complex, it does not make it any more important than the seemingly smaller tasks.

Even though your children may be busy with homework or may get home late from a Boy Scouts meeting, it is still important for them to take care of the little things such as cleaning up their desk at night or putting away their clothes. Show them how important it is to take care of both small and large tasks.

Technique 5: Avoid toxic people.

Have you ever noticed how you can be in a good mood, but then talk to a negative person and suddenly feel down? A positive attitude is contagious, but a negative attitude is even more contagious—so beware. If you find that there is a person who holds the ability to pull you down, then the time has come to sever that relationship. It need not be done in a hostile or cruel way, but it does need to be done. Start to wean yourself from regular contact with this individual, and continue until you get to the point where you seldom spend time together.

This may be a friend who you have known for years, and the break may be difficult, but it must be done for your own well-being. This situation becomes even more difficult if the person is a relative.

In this case, you can distance yourself so that your contact only occurs when you feel positive enough to counteract the negativity. To succeed in either case, you will need to remain upbeat and positive, no matter how hard that person tries to bring you down. You owe it to yourself and your family to be surrounded with positive people who will influence your mood in the best possible way. Once you have surrounded yourself with positive people, you will have the ability to infect other people with your contagious positive attitude.

Teaching Your Children the Importance of Avoiding Toxic People: Teach your children the importance of surrounding themselves with positive people and avoiding toxic people. Teach them how to recognize negative people. Have them tell you about their friends and acquaintances at school. Ask them to describe how these people make them feel about themselves, and see if your children recognize any of these people as toxic. Tell your children just how important it is to be surrounded with positive people in order to keep a positive outlook on life.

Technique 6: Keep busy with positive activities.

Busy people do not have time to sit and brood about everything that they perceive to be wrong with their lives. Instead, they keep their minds and bodies occupied with positive activities. By staying busy, we remain active and productive as we execute enjoyable activities in our lives. If you find yourself with a negative attitude and a lot of free time on your hands, it is time to get busy. Find some healthy, fun activities that you can enjoy. Join a gym, volunteer at a local charity, read a good book or take a class. Whatever it is that you do, make sure it is a positive activity that will make you feel good about yourself.

In most workplaces, you can find and observe workers who spend their work hours looking at the clock and trying to appear busy. By day's end, they are worn out from looking busy when they could have been feeling good about themselves and getting the work accomplished. Have you ever noticed how time flies when you are immersed in your work? Not only does the day go faster, but you have put in such a productive day that you are able to feel good about yourself. By occupying your time with productive activities, you will find your attitude changing for the better.

Teaching Your Children the Importance of Keeping Busy with Positive Activities: In my practice, I have heard children as young as five say, "I'm bored." What a shame, and what an opening for negative thoughts to creep in. As parents, we need to keep our children busy and involved in activities that do not revolve around the television. Instead, we must present new horizons and opportunities to them. As a result, your children will develop interests and talents they may never have discovered on their own.

It is equally as important for you to be a part of your children's activities. Keeping busy with your children will benefit both of you by anchoring your relationship and allowing you to bond in a wonderful way. This improved relationship will allow you to spend many happy hours enjoying these activities and each other.

Technique 7: Exercise your mind and body.

Exercise is an excellent way to chase away a case of the blues. Exercise refreshes you and does your mind and body a favor by keeping them fit. Exercise, both physical and mental, clears your mind and prepares you to look ahead with a positive view. Negative thoughts will fly out the window, and solutions to problems will begin to pop into your mind. As you enjoy regular exercise, you will see a positive change in your attitude.

Teaching Your Children the Importance of Exercise: Bringing the many benefits of physical and mental exercise into your home is an exceptional gift to your children. Turn the television off and encourage your children to exercise with you. There are many activities you can enjoy together, such as rollerblading, hiking, trips to the library and arts and crafts. Instead of sitting around on the weekends, plan a family outing to a museum, take a refreshing walk outside, visit a planetarium or stroll through the botanical gardens. Get your children into the habit of regular exercise of the mind and body—they will thank you for it.

Technique 8: Concentrate on positive thoughts.

It is not always easy to focus on the positive, especially when you have problems weighing on your mind. It is, however, of vital importance to focus on the positive if you are going to create balance in your life. In order to do so, you must recondition your mind to promote positive messages. When you hear a message that says, "You can't learn that," counter it with a statement that says, "I have the ability to learn anything I want to." Practice doing this often. Eventually, you will be able to positively reprogram your mind.

For example, say you have an interview coming up for a job you really want and find yourself having negative thoughts such as, "They'll never hire me." This is when you need to employ positive self-talk. Start by changing your thoughts to, "My experience has prepared me for this job." Set your sights on success by telling yourself, "I have every reason to believe that I will be a top contender for the position." If you go to the interview with negative thoughts and a defeatist attitude, it will come through to your prospective employer. If, on the other hand, you go into the interview with a positive and upbeat attitude, your energy and confidence will shine through. You will present a professional and polished image to the interviewer, putting you at the top of the list of candidates.

Teaching Your Children the Importance of Remaining Positive: Doubts and fears are part of each child's life. This is especially true in the years when children are comparing themselves to others. This is a major contributor to a child's low self-esteem. You can help nip it in the bud by providing personal assurances to your children and reminding them that they are able, intelligent and wonderful. Never allow self-doubt to overtake a positive attitude— for you or your children. It takes practice and patience, but exchanging negative for positive thoughts will become easier with time.

A good exercise to practice every day is to think of at least five positive things in your life for which you are grateful. Make this a bedtime ritual for you and your family. Before your children go to sleep at night, have them think of the good things in their life and the positive things that happened to them that day. Some days, it will be easier to come up with a list than other days. The list can include things such as, "I'm grateful for my parents," or "I'm grateful to have a roof over my head," or "I'm grateful for my favorite teddy bear," or "I'm grateful for the compliment that my teacher gave me today," or "I'm grateful for the 'A' I got on my test today." This exercise makes you focus on the positive aspects of your life rather than the negative.

Technique 9: Help others.

When you help other people, it boosts your thoughts about yourself and puts you in a positive mood. When you spend time helping others, you have no time to dwell on your own issues. Also, helping others who are less fortunate than yourself will make you focus on what you have, rather than on what you do not have.

Remember the equation for success that we discussed earlier:

Emotional health + Social health + Spiritual health = SUCCESS

By donating your time and efforts to others selflessly, you are adding to your spiritual health. Through this giving experience, you are sure to feel needed and appreciated. At the same time, you will make a difference in other people's lives.

There are so many worthy causes that need your help; choose one that appeals to your special interests. In making your selection of how to help others, take time to consider what you like to do and where you feel you fit the best. You can volunteer at a local hospital, work with handicapped children at a horse ranch or volunteer at a nursing home.

Teaching Your Children the Importance of Helping Others: Instill in your children the drive to improve the quality of life for those around them. If your children happen to excel in a specific subject at school, suggest that they tutor a classmate who is falling behind. Plan a family volunteer day and have your children help choose the activity. Your children will begin to understand that helping others has a positive result on their attitude and spiritual health.

A Summary of Attitude

One or more of these attitude adjustments may be just the thing to help you improve your outlook on life. Whatever works for you is the method you should use. Different situations may call for different solutions. For one situation, keeping busy may help you. In another situation, it may benefit you to use humor.

Studies have shown that people who approach serious medical problems with a positive attitude have a greater likelihood of beating the illness. We have no scientific explanation for why this is so, but it has proven to be true time after time. Call it "mind-over-matter" if you like, but the simple fact is that a positive attitude works.

At home, you should use the techniques above in order to be a positive role model to your children. Stress to them that perfection is not the goal, but what counts is trying their best. Instead of complaining when your plans do not work as you expected, come up with constructive solutions to problems. Take the high ground and demonstrate to your children that very few things are so serious that they cannot be viewed with a sense of humor. Teach them, by word and by example, the importance of having a positive attitude. While a positive attitude may not solve all of your problems or make difficult decisions for you, it will put you in a better frame of mind to face these problems.

TOP ASSET 2: MOTIVATION

Motivation is a key element to achieving success. There are several ways you can motivate your children, and different motivators work for different people. For some, it is money and fame; for others, it is simply doing a good job. Whatever the reason, motivation gives you that extra push to keep reaching for the top.

Motivating Your Children

Parents, in an effort to do what they consider to be best for their children, may make the mistake of handing them everything on a silver platter. This is an extension of permissive parenting, which you learned about earlier, and it is a common parenting problem. There are, however, many valuable lessons learned from working for what we want. Working for what we want teaches us that there is no such thing as a free ride. Also, when we work for something, we place a higher value on it.

☆ *A Real-Life Example of Motivating Your Children: The Smith Family*

I looked up from my desk as my secretary ushered my new clients into the office. The Smith family was well known in our town. Martin Smith was the owner of a major business in the area. He and his wife, Mildred, were a prominent social couple. Their twelve-year-old son, Sean, was an only child. From the reports I received prior to accepting them as clients, I understood that Sean was turning into quite a problem at school.

Sean was clearly intelligent, but he was failing most of his classes and did not even pretend to try. His attitude was cocky and defiant, almost daring his teachers to challenge him. Now, a new twist had been added: Sean had been caught stealing from other students. Martin and Mildred had been given an ultimatum to either get counseling for Sean or transfer him to a different school.

As they entered my office, I noticed that Sean was a good-looking boy, tall with the bearing and features of his father, combined with the dark eyes and hair of his mother. Martin and Mildred sat on the ends of the sofa, while Sean slouched between them. His parents showed obvious concern for him, but Sean's answers were short, clipped and often bordered on insolence and disrespect. It was decided that our meetings would take the form of a three-week cycle. This first week, I would counsel them as a family, the second session would be for Sean alone and the third would be for Martin and Mildred. Then the cycle would repeat.

The nature of an initial meeting is mostly to get acquainted and put new clients at ease. It also gives me an opportunity to form some preliminary thoughts and evaluate the family as a unit before seeing them separately.

As our sessions progressed, a pattern emerged that was quite simple and not uncommon. Martin and Mildred were both brought up in families from a lower socio-economic status. Through hard work and persistence, Martin was able to become successful; the couple could now afford all of the luxuries they dreamed of when they were younger, and they wanted Sean to feel secure and loved. Because they grew up in families where the lack of money often caused friction and heartbreak, they felt that material things would show Sean how much he was loved. They were determined that their son would not "want for things" as they had.

Their care and concern, however, had backfired. Sean was spoiled to the point where he felt that he was entitled to anything and everything he wanted without having to work for it. When Sean got into trouble at school, his parents bailed him out and made excuses for him. He had no ambition and no motivation to change his ways; he held the mindset that his parents would fix everything.

It took a great deal of work to convince Martin and Mildred that they were not helping Sean by catering to his every desire and excusing his behavior. Eventually, they made some changes and eased off of their giving. It was difficult for them, but eventually they learned to say no to Sean's demands. When he got into trouble, Sean was made accountable and accepted his punishment. Of course, Sean was furious at first—he was being forced to take responsibility for the first time in his life. He threw tantrums, sulked and pouted, but his parents supported each other and remained strong in their resolve.

The payoff came when Sean wanted to go on a school-sponsored trip to the Grand Canyon. The trip was six months away and the cost for each pupil was $1,000. Even though we had been meeting for months and there was real progress being made, Martin was not ready to hand Sean the money. After thoroughly discussing the situation in our sessions, Martin offered a compromise to Sean. If Sean would raise half of the money, Martin would give him the other half. Once Sean realized that his father meant what he said, he got busy. He saved gift money, did odd jobs for neighbors, washed cars and delivered newspapers. In short, he showed creativity, ingenuity and persistence. In fact, he did such a good job that he earned extra spending money for his trip. This marked a real departure for Sean, as it was the first time he had really wanted something and did not have it handed to him. Sean felt proud of himself, and Martin and Mildred were finally convinced of the power of motivation.

Motivation On the Job and at Home

In the workplace, productivity is improved when employees are motivated to excel. This motivation can take many forms. It can be a reward incentive, such as increased pay, bonuses or internal competitions for vacations and other prizes, or, it may be the path to a personal achievement, goal or recognition.

Individual enthusiasm in the workplace is greater when positive outcomes are delivered as a result of good work. Imagine a sporting competition. If winning was not a factor, how well would the team play? Even the Olympics have the reward of a medal for the winner. The motivator for competition is driven not only by national representation, but also by the desire to achieve your personal goals.

Without motivation we tend to stagnate and develop a "why bother" attitude. As you saw with the Smith family, it clearly is not the best practice to deprive our children of the motivation to achieve on their own. Instead of giving your children anything they desire, substitute encouragement, love and parental interest; this will give your children the ambition to succeed on their own. Ultimately, this will instill in them the fire and drive of self-dependence. It will also teach them how to get where they want to go.

AN ASSESSMENT OF YOUR CHILD'S ATTITUDE AND MOTIVATION

It is important to determine what type of attitude your children exhibit. Do they have a positive outlook or are they very negative? It is also important to assess their level of motivation. Are your children go-getters or do you have to ask them to do everything multiple times? In order to identify areas for your children's improvement, you are now going to do an assessment of their outlook on life. Please respond with true or false to the following statements about your child.

Please circle true or false for the following statements:		
1. Goals are an important part of my child's life.	true	false
2. My child knows it is important to work for what she wants.	true	false
3. My child would have more friends if she had a better attitude.	true	false
4. My child would watch television all day if I let her.	true	false
5. My child encourages others to do well.	true	false
6. My child is a team player.	true	false
7. My child has a tendency to bully other children.	true	false
8. My child knows that if she pouts, I will give in.	true	false
9. People often comment on my child's sunny disposition.	true	false
10. My child's school has called about behavioral problems.	true	false

Now let's examine each of the statements from the assessment. Analyze your answers to identify any areas in need of improvement.

Statement 1: Goals are an important part of my child's life.

Goals are vital to a child's success. They provide motivation for achievement and give a reason to continue to strive for fulfillment. From an early age, children should be taught how to set goals and shown the steps needed to reach those goals. Children's goals do not need to be complex; they can be something as simple as mastering a spelling lesson or learning to bake cookies. In early development, the end result is not as important as the knowledge of what path to take in order to get there. As children mature, their goals become more advanced. If children have a strong foundation to build upon, they will learn how to reach their objectives successfully.

Statement 2: My child knows it is important to work for what she wants.

Children who always get their way and get everything they want will be in for a rude awakening when they become adults. By teaching your children to earn their own way to success, you can save them a lot of disappointment and pain as adults. While it is important to encourage your children and help them achieve success, you should not hand success to them. Teach them the importance of working for what they want. When they work for something, they are more likely to appreciate and value it. Think of life as a game. If you get a hole in one all the time, then it would not be worth playing. Part of the sense of success comes from the progress you achieve through even minimal improvements you make as you play. You can appreciate how hard you worked to improve.

Statement 3: My child would have more friends if she had a better attitude.

Is your child often passed over when party invitations are extended, or is she the last to be chosen for teams? Is she always the one who telephones friends, but never the other way around? Take a long, objective look at your child and try to determine if she is pleasant to be around. Does she laugh a lot or is she a habitual complainer? Are her remarks biting and hurtful?

As a parent, you should work with your children to help them achieve a more positive attitude. Their outlook on life may need a few adjustments, and you will be acting in their best interests if you help them make those adjustments now before they become anchored in their personality.

Statement 4: My child would watch television all day if I let her.

Sitting in front of the television all day makes for boring and intellectually-deprived children. To correct this, you need to set expectations and establish rules about TV exposure. Spend time with your children; talk to them and discover key interests (other than watching television of course), then find ways to pursue these interests. Involve yourself and share in the excitement. Set the standard by limiting daily television viewing and replacing it with participation in activities like helping around the house, reading for school or pleasure, playing with friends, learning to garden, doing puzzles or taking long walks. Television is not necessarily a bad thing, but (as with anything else) moderation is the best policy.

Statement 5: My child encourages others to do well.

This is a sign of a confident person, unselfish enough to want others to succeed. People are attracted to this selflessness because it shows confidence. If your child becomes jealous over others' success, she needs to learn that success is for everyone and should be shared.

Children should be happy for the success of others. You can provide the best model for your children by demonstrating support for others. Show them your positive attitude and concern for others, and they will follow your example.

Statement 6: My child is a team player.

A team player is concerned about the team as a whole. To be a team player, you must be willing to give up the spotlight and credit the entire group for the success achieved. Similar to sharing success, people will rally around a team player who recognizes that each person's contribution is important to the end result and that no one person is more valuable than another.

Begin working on this at home by recognizing your family unit as a team and giving each member a responsible part in every project. The entire family will benefit from successful projects.

Statement 7: My child has a tendency to bully other children.

In observing your child playing with other children, do you notice that she usually ends up with all of the toys? When playing one-on-one, does the other child often end up crying? You must make sure that you, as a parent, are not enabling this behavior.

Teach your children the importance of sharing. To do this, you must understand that saying "no" is part of being a parent. Sharing, helping others, controlling tempers and working together are all qualities that add up to happy, successful children. You have the ability to see that your children get started in the right direction early by teaching them to master each of these characteristics.

Statement 8: My child knows that if she pouts, I will give in.

Children are very aware of the power they hold with their parents. While this manipulation may work with you, trying it with others may destroy important relationships with peers, teachers and other adults. While this pouting may melt your heart, it will not work with anyone else and will only cause problems in the future.

Be the parent. Teach your children, in a loving way, that pouting is not acceptable. Show them that disappointments must be taken in stride and, whenever possible, should be used as a learning tool.

Statement 9: People often comment on my child's sunny disposition.

To give your children the gift of a positive attitude and a real regard for others is to give them one of the greatest gifts of their life. Some people are naturally more positive than others, but it is your encouragement and loving guidance that bring this natural inclination to the surface and make it a permanent part of your children's personality. By providing love, happiness and a guiding hand along the way, you help promote a life-long positive attitude.

Statement 10: My child's school has called about behavioral problems.

What type of behavioral problems is the school calling you about? Is your child abusive to others? Does she shirk her work? Is she insolent or disobedient to teachers? Does she exhibit criminal or delinquent behavior, such as stealing or skipping school?

After determining the specific behavioral problem, you need to work with your child to eliminate it. To be successful you need to be firm, while still infusing love into your strategy. Your child may be reaching out for attention. You may want to work with a school counselor to discover the best way to help your child. If the counselor suggests seeing a professional psychologist, then follow that advice.

Your children should be your top priority. Keep in mind that now, while they are still children, is the time to correct unacceptable behaviors. This will help your children reach their full potential on the road to adulthood.

GOAL-SETTING: A WAY OF LIFE

Setting goals is the first step toward bringing about the realization of your dreams. Many people, however, do not understand the process of setting and achieving goals.

A goal is defined as an objective, the purpose toward which an endeavor is directed. When you put your mind to something and set out to achieve an end result, you are setting a goal.

Why is it so important to develop a habit of setting goals? If you do not have a final destination in mind, you may spend your life wandering. To be successful, you need to know what you want. Ask two children what they want for their birthday and one child might answer "toys," while the other child might answer, "A remote controlled robot that walks and talks." Since the second child knows exactly what kind of a toy he wants, his chances of getting the perfect gift rise tremendously.

A goal gives us something to aim for and a sense of satisfaction when we achieve it. As we grow, we have different goals to match different points in our life. The goal for a five-year-old child may be to own the coolest toy on the market, but when he is eighteen years old the goal may be to be accepted into the college of his choice.

GUIDELINES FOR INCORPORATING GOALS INTO YOUR CHILD'S LIFE

First and foremost, teach your children the meaning of a goal, and make sure they understand it. Next, teach them the importance of setting goals. Finally, show them how to set goals by providing examples. Below are guidelines you and your children can use to help set goals. While goals may be very different, the strategies for achieving those goals are usually the same. The guidelines are as follows:

1) Be specific.
2) Make a list.
3) Follow through.
4) Visualize the end result.

5) Be realistic.
6) Get help.
7) Be flexible.

Guideline 1: Be specific.

It is not enough to say, "I want to do well on a test." A much better way of expressing the goal would be, "I want to get a B+ or higher on my math test on Tuesday." By setting specific goals, you have a more definite focus on the objective.

Guideline 2: Make a list.

What steps do you need to take in order to realize your goal? By making a specific list of action items you can take to reach your goal, you are more likely to achieve it. Your list could be something like this:

- I have four days to study before the test. I will study two hours each night.
- I will have one extra session with my math tutor before the exam.
- I will ask my mother to quiz me on some math problems Monday night.

Guideline 3: Follow through.

Now that you have started a plan, you must have the dedication to follow your plan through to the end. Without a plan, it is easy to get sidetracked and lose sight of your goal.

Stay focused. Everything you do should be done with your goal in mind. Whether you take educational courses, join clubs or do a lot of reading, think of how it relates to your goal. When your children set goals, check with them on the progress of their goals. Show an interest and make sure they are following through.

As a parent, you also must follow through on your goals. If your children see you follow through on your goals, they will follow your example and do the same in their own lives.

Guideline 4: Visualize the end result.

Make use of visualization when working toward your dream. It will remind you of your goal and keep you inspired. For example, I have a friend who wanted to own a Victorian-style house. For several years, she saved every penny she earned. During this time of saving and yearning, she came across a Christmas ornament in the form of a house, just like the kind she was hoping to buy some day. She purchased the ornament and kept it on her desk where she could see it every day to help her stay focused. One day a real estate agent showed her a house that was the exact replica of the ornament; it had the spires, the wraparound porch and was even the same slate blue color with white trim. She purchased the house and still keeps the ornament in sight as a celebration of what she had to endure to reach her goal.

Help your children visualize their end result. If they want to become an astronaut when they are older, find a model spaceship they can look at to visualize their goal. If they want to become President of the United States, hang a poster in their room of former presidents in order to keep them inspired.

Guideline 5: Be realistic.

Do not set yourself or your children up for failure. While goals should be challenging enough so that we have to work for them, we should also be realistic when setting goals. All too often we set goals that are impossible to achieve. If we set ones that are unreachable, disappointment, self-doubt and defeat may set in. Sit down with your children and review their goals. Make sure they are realistic and achievable. Then, celebrate your family's successes, enjoying the feeling of satisfaction and pride for meeting challenges.

Setting goals can help you and your children reach further and develop your potential to go beyond the ordinary. Once you have satisfied one goal, set another. Never become complacent and accept things as they are; always strive toward bigger and better results.

Guideline 6: Get help.

You do not have to do this alone. Tell those close to you about your goals and ask for their help from time to time. They will be more than happy to assist you, and they will get a sense of pleasure for themselves when you reach your goal.

Make sure your children know that they can come to you for help setting and maintaining their goals. Let them know that you are interested in their goals and that you want to help achieve them.

Guideline 7: Be flexible.

Keep in mind that goals can change—they are not set in stone. As your ideas and needs transform, your goals may do the same. Suppose your child always wanted to pursue a career in medicine and made that a goal. After beginning her training, she finds that it is not what she thought it would be and, in fact, she dislikes it very much. Teach your children that they should not stick to a goal if they find that it does not make them happy. As things change, explore options and change goals accordingly.

TYPES OF GOALS

There are three major types of goals: short-term, long-term and lifetime goals, all of which are described below. Go through these goals with your children and make sure they understand the meaning of each one. Then, have them set one of each of these goals and discuss it together. See how you can help them achieve their goals.

If you provide your family with the incentive and guidance they need to set goals, they will continue to follow this practice throughout their lives. This practice will help them discover where they want to go, what is important to them and the proper process to get them there.

Short-term Goals

A short-term goal is one that can be reached within six months to one year. Examples of short-term goals might be to go on a vacation, to lose weight or to get an A in a class for the semester. Short-term goals are good because we can see results in a reasonable period of time. Once we have reached our objective, we can set another goal. The excitement of reaching our goal will give us the enthusiasm to continue setting short-term goals as a way of life.

Long-term Goals

A long-term goal is one that is reached over time, about five to ten years. Examples of long-term goals are purchasing a home, earning a college degree or opening your own business. These are things that take time to accomplish. Each of these goals needs planning, dedication and focus.

Long-term goals should be really important to you; you need to think very carefully before deciding to include them on your list. Do not try for too many of these goals at one time. For some people, one long-term goal is all they are capable of handling, while others can handle two or three at a time. Do not set more than three goals at a time, as it is easy to get overwhelmed when you have too many goals.

Lifetime Goals

A lifetime goal should be one major objective that you continue to work toward while achieving your short-term goals. Do not rush into setting this goal. Again, be flexible, as this goal may change as time goes by. Examples of lifetime goals are becoming governor of your state, having enough money to travel extensively or being a recognized and powerful force in your chosen career. Your lifetime goal is tied closely to your life's work.

AN ASSIGNMENT FOR YOU AND YOUR CHILDREN: FAMILY MEETINGS

Goals are important and should become a part of your family structure. In order to put what you have learned about goal-setting into action, sit down with your children and plan monthly family meetings. During these meetings, you and your family should discuss your current goals and the progress you have all made toward achieving those goals. You should also discuss future goals and how you might go about achieving those goals.

The Plan of Action

Call a meeting and have everyone in your family attend. Make it serious enough so that everyone realizes that it is important. At your first meeting, set a charter, establishing what your intent is and how you will proceed with the goal-setting process. Then develop a list of family projects and goals so that everyone will have an understanding of what your focus is and how you plan to get there.

Your process should include a list of short-term, long-term and lifetime goals for each family member. Very young children should be encouraged to work only with short-term goals (about one or two months). As children progress into their late teens, they can add long-term goals to the list. Before ending the meeting, make sure you set up dates for follow-up meetings.

At the follow-up meetings, review and modify your lists and take note of how far each family member has gotten in achieving their goals. Share your goals and give encouragement and aid to all family members. Check for and celebrate successes. Examine the progress of current goals and help your family set new ones if necessary. Stress the value of using a goal-setting system. Be certain to add your own goals to the discussion, providing a good model for the rest of the family to follow. This should be a fun time for the family, but the family should also be aware of the importance of these discussions.

The following chart contains a guide for your family discussion. Use the space as an outline for you and your family to write down your family charter, your family goals and how you are going to achieve them. The chart after that contains space that each family member should fill out with his different goals. Review these individual goals as a family and brainstorm ways each family member can help one another achieve their goals.

Our Monthly Family Meetings: Family Goals

Family Charter/Objective:

Example: *We will meet on the third Friday of every month for dinner and a family meeting. At the meeting, we will discuss our current goals and the progress we have all made toward those goals. We will also set new goals and brainstorm ways to achieve them.*

_____

_____

_____

_____

_____

_____

_____

_____

_____

_____

_____

_____

Family Goals/ Projects:

Keep the house clean and organized.

_____

_____

_____

_____

_____

_____

_____

How We Will Achieve These Goals as a Family:

Mom take out trash, Dad do dishes, Suzie clear table, Mike dust coffee table.

Our Monthly Family Meetings: Individual Goals

Name   *Example:* Mike

Short-term Goal   *Get a B in math*

Steps to Goal   *Study; get help from teachers*

Long-term Goal   *Go to college in the Northeast*

Steps to Goal   *Study; set up a savings account*

Lifetime Goal   *Become an accountant*

Steps to Goal   *Intern at a big company*

Name _____

Short-term Goal _____

Steps to Goal _____

Long-term Goal _____

Steps to Goal _____

Lifetime Goal _____

Steps to Goal _____

Name _____

Short-term Goal _____

Steps to Goal _____

Long-term Goal _____

Steps to Goal _____

Lifetime Goal _____

Steps to Goal _____

Name _____

Short-term Goal _____

Steps to Goal _____

Long-term Goal _____

Steps to Goal _____

Lifetime Goal _____

Steps to Goal _____

Name _____

Short-term Goal _____

Steps to Goal _____

Long-term Goal _____

Steps to Goal _____

Lifetime Goal _____

Steps to Goal _____

Name _____

Short-term Goal _____

Steps to Goal _____

Long-term Goal _____

Steps to Goal _____

Lifetime Goal	_____
Steps to Goal	_____
Name	_____
Short-term Goal	_____
Steps to Goal	_____
Long-term Goal	_____
Steps to Goal	_____
Lifetime Goal	_____
Steps to Goal	_____

SUMMARY OF CHAPTER SIX

In this chapter, you learned that the top two assets on the road to success are attitude and motivation. You were given attitude adjustment techniques and methods of motivation. You also learned how to use these attributes both on the job and at home. You learned how to work with your children to improve their attitude and increase their motivation.

You completed an assessment of your child that gives insight into her attitude, motivation and goal-setting abilities. This helped you identify areas of your child's life that may need special attention.

Since goal-setting is such an essential step on the road to success, you learned the proper way to set goals and the steps needed to achieve them. You also learned the three major types of goals. You were shown the importance of making goal-setting an important part of your life. These are all valuable skills that you will share with your children to help them set their goals.

You had a task of setting up a monthly family meeting in which you and your family reviewed the progress of current goals, made new family and individual goals and discussed how to achieve those goals. By doing this assignment as a family, you emphasized the importance of setting goals and demonstrated the proper way to set and achieve those goals.

> ☆ Practice one attitude adjustment technique.
>
> ☆ Use motivation to help my children explore a new interest.
>
> ☆ Set realistic goals for my family and myself.
>
> ☆ Teach my children successful methods of goal-setting.

Chapter Seven

GETTING TO THE HEART OF IT ALL

An Analysis of Your Child's Capacity to Empathize

CHAPTER OBJECTIVES

- Discover the definition of empathy and where it comes from.

- Do an assessment of your children's capacity to empathize.

- Learn how to teach your children the importance of empathy.

- Learn how to enhance you and your children's ability to empathize.

- Discover how to use your empathic skills both at work and at home.

- Study your children's capacity to empathize over one month's time.

*"To understand any living thing, you must, so to say, creep within
and feel the beating of its heart."*
— *W. MacNeile Dixon*

In this chapter, you will continue your family's climb up the Pyramid of Success by working with your children to put goals into action. You will learn the definition of empathy and see where empathy comes from. You will then do an assessment of your children's capacity to show empathy. After discovering your children's strengths and areas of improvement regarding empathy, you will learn how to teach your children the importance of having empathy and compassion. You will then be provided with life-coaching tips and tips for working with your children to enhance their ability to empathize. Finally, you will discover how you can use your empathic skills both at work and at home. Throughout the chapter, you will read examples of people using empathic skills to solve problems, manage their employees and work with their children. Finally, you will plan to study your children's capacity to empathize over a one-month period of time so that you can work with them on any areas that may need improvement.

WHAT IS EMPATHY AND WHERE DOES IT COME FROM?

Webster's Dictionary defines empathy as, "identification with and understanding of the thoughts or feelings of another." The word empathy is derived from the Greek work "empatheia," which means "feeling into." To understand the feelings of others, you must first understand yourself. In any relationship, the base for caring and empathy comes from emotional harmony and inner peace. In other words, you must have the capacity within yourself for empathy.

Empathy is not confined to any one area of life but encompasses every aspect of our existence. It comes into play in business, parenting, romance, politics and almost every other area of life.

Theoreticians have conducted studies and tests to determine the ability of a person to perceive the subjective experiences of others. Their studies have shown that empathy can be traced all the way back to infancy. At only a few months of age, a baby will react to the distress of another baby. In a room with two infants, if one infant starts to cry, usually the other will begin to cry or fuss as well. As children mature, they begin to understand that the distress of others belongs to others rather than themselves. Children this young are uncertain as to what they can do about others' distress, but will try to bring whatever comfort they can. Studies have shown that toddlers will bring their own toys, or even their own parents, to help comfort another child who is upset.

By examining various levels of empathy in the development of children, it is easy to understand just how important parents' roles are in instilling the capacity for empathy in their children. Wise parents who are interested in their children's happiness and success will work to see that empathy and compassion are integral parts of their children's character development.

AN ASSESSMENT OF YOUR CHILD'S CAPACITY TO EMPATHIZE

Before going any further, you will now evaluate your child's level of sensitivity toward others. The following assessment will help you determine how empathic your child is. It will also assist you in finding areas that need improvement.

For the following scenarios, respond with how you think your child would react. Once you are done with your assessment, pose the scenarios to your children to see how they respond.

☆ *Scenario 1*

One of the more popular students at school is having a birthday party and your child is invited. Everyone is talking about this party and how great it is going to be. After the invitations have been distributed, your child notices that all but two students in his grade have been invited. The host of the party keeps making fun of those two students and is saying how he would never invite them to his party. What would your child do?

    a) Go and have a good time.
    b) Feel a little guilty about the situation, but go to the party anyway.
    c) Confront the host about why he did not invite the other two people and, if that does not work, decline the invitation.

☆ *Scenario 2*

Christmas is coming and your child has a long list of gifts that she hopes to get. She hears about a toy drive at school to help get toys for children of poor families who cannot afford any. Your child's reaction would be:

    a) "Gee, I'm glad I'm not one of those unfortunate people without toys this year."
    b) "I feel sorry for those people. I hope someone helps them out."
    c) "I want to help those people. I'm going to donate one of my toys."

☆ *Scenario 3*

The school bully is picking on a new student. The bully tells people that anyone who is friends with the new kid is a total loser. Your child would:

    a) Avoid the new kid and not even think about it.
    b) Feel bad about the situation, but not do anything about it.
    c) Invite the new student to eat lunch with him and introduce her to his friends.

☆ *Scenario 4*

Your sister and her husband just got divorced, so she and her child are staying with you temporarily until they get back on their feet. When they move in, your child would:

    a) Complain about the inconvenience of having to share a room.
    b) Ignore the cousin as much as possible and tolerate her only when necessary.
    c) Make the cousin feel welcome and introduce her to friends.

☆ *Scenario 5*

A club has formed at your child's school in order to help the needy by shopping for them, cutting their grass, and shoveling their snow. Your child:

    a) Does not join in because it would interfere with the activities that she enjoys.
    b) Thinks it is a good idea, but feels that she has enough to do.
    c) Becomes an active member, giving up some of her own activities to make time to help.

Rating Your Child's Ability to Show Empathy

Add up all of the a's, b's and c's from the five scenarios above. If your child mostly answered "a," she either may not be aware of the needs of others or may be too self-centered to care. You need to gently and lovingly work with your child to increase compassion and empathy. Give her a good example to follow. Explain how she can make a difference in the lives of others, and tell her why empathy is so important. The following sections in this chapter give more tips on how to raise your child's empathy level.

   If most of the answers fall into the "b" category, your child probably has feelings for others and some good intentions, but has not yet figured out what she can or should do about them. You can help her by suggesting a behavior that will be more in line with showing concern for the plight of other people, and actively working to alleviate the problem.

If "c" is the answer to the majority of the scenarios, then you have a child who has a healthy amount of empathy. If fact, if she has all "c's," you may have to keep an eye on her to make sure she takes time for herself and does not spend all of her energy helping others and ignoring her own needs.

TEACHING YOUR CHILDREN THE IMPORTANCE OF EMPATHY

Teaching your children about empathy begins at a very early age through your actions as both a parent and a human being in general. If children's emotions, such as happiness, tears or the need to cuddle are consistently ignored, those children might avoid expressing their emotions later in life.

Children learn by example. They imitate the actions of their parents, whether good or bad. Some children are not even aware that, in the eyes of society, some behavior patterns are unacceptable. For most children, their parents are the ultimate role models. **The philosophy of a child is simple: if my parents do it, it must be right.** Therefore, your duty as a parent is to show, through words and actions, how to exhibit compassion and do the right thing.

There are many times when it is not easy to show compassion, even when your child is an innocent little baby. For example, on nights when the baby is teething or has a cold and is inconsolable, it is difficult to be compassionate when you are so exhausted from lack of sleep. You are only human and it is natural to feel the way you do. This is, however, one of the most important times to show love and compassion to your suffering child.

The effect of parents' actions and reactions to their babies is truly amazing. For instance, think about the very necessary, but often unpleasant, task of changing a dirty diaper. If parents show anger or resentment toward their babies when changing their diapers, the babies will eventually think they have done something wrong. Holding them, talking softly and showing concern and love in times of distress will provide a good base for developing your children's sense of empathy.

Empathy should be present in everyday interactions between you and your children. Each small, repeated action with your children, such as eye contact and reassuring sounds, adds to the building blocks of empathy. If you reassure your children, they will realize that their emotions are being tended to and that they are loved. As a result, your children will learn to be sensitive to the feelings of others. If children are treated with respect and cared for, they will, over time, begin to feel empathy toward others who are less fortunate, such as the homeless, the elderly or the sick. Encourage them to help others faced with difficult situations, and this will in turn also increase their ability to empathize.

As your children enter their toddler and pre-school years, encourage them to participate in projects that help others. Keep in mind that children of that age can be messy and uncoordinated; therefore, do not expect everything to be done perfectly. Instead, make it a happy time that you both will remember; worry about cleaning up later. For example, if you are making cookies to give to the new neighbors, allow your children to mix the dough. Use the cookie cutters to make fun shapes and allow your children to sprinkle some sugar on top for decoration. In addition to making other people feel good, you will be making memories that you will both treasure for years to come. If you help an elderly or disabled friend by shopping for him, take your children along and give them a small bag with unbreakable items to carry into the house. Let them feel like they are contributing too.

Consider planning a family outing to your local charity. This will provide a great bonding opportunity for your family, will teach your children about the importance of helping others and will be a great contribution to those less fortunate. After the activity, praise your children and let them know what a good service they just did. Encourage them so that they will want to help out again in the future.

Once your children enter school, many opportunities will be present for lending a helping hand. Many schools sponsor clubs whose sole purpose is to help the needy. Many organizations such as the Girl Scouts and Boy Scouts are known for their volunteer efforts. Whatever the activity, encourage your children to become active participants in these charitable causes.

Once your children enter junior high and high school, volunteer opportunities are expanded even further. Organizations such as the Salvation Army, local hospitals, animal shelters and homeless shelters are in constant need of volunteers. Encourage your children to volunteer; it is one of the best gifts you can give them.

A Discussion with Your Children: A Family Scenario

It is especially important to teach your children that their actions and decisions not only impact their own lives, but also impact the lives of others. Explain to your children how their actions affect many people, including their family, their friends, their teachers, etc. Give them examples of situations where their actions and decisions affect others. The following is a scenario that you should share with your children on the importance of thinking of others. Have your children come up with examples of how the following behavior may affect others.

☆ *John*

John was in junior high school. He had a lot of friends and did well in school. One day, after school, John's friends were smoking cigarettes in the schoolyard. His friends asked him to join in and, without thinking, he agreed. Discuss this scenario with your children.

Ask your children whom John's behavior might affect. Jot down their responses and review them together. Go through the people this behavior may affect (from your children's list and from your own). Explain to your children how their behavior and lack of empathy may affect others. For example:

- Unbeknownst to John, his little sister, Sarah, was watching him smoking and now thinks it is okay to smoke.
- John could get suspended and have to be out from school, but both of his parents work full time. One would have to stay home with him, resulting in financial hardship.

Go through some other examples with your children, so that they fully understand the importance of relating to the feelings and well-being of those around them.

METHODS OF ENHANCING THE ABILITY TO EMPATHIZE

There are many ways to heighten you and your children's ability to empathize. Below are a few methods that empathic people use to understand others. While you are reading, note which traits you and your children possess and which you might need to develop more. Below each method is a life-coaching tip that you and your children can use to help develop that particular characteristic. The methods are:

1) Step into someone else's shoes.
2) Trust your intuition.
3) Maintain good communication skills.
4) Create energy and motivate others.
5) Read non-verbal cues.

Method 1: Step into someone else's shoes.

One way to heighten empathy is to try to "step into someone else's shoes." Try to understand where people are coming from and how your actions and behaviors may affect their lives. As a general practice, you should avoid categorization. When you place people into certain "boxes," it is easy to automatically lump them in with everyone else in that box. By seeing people as individuals, you will be more readily able to relate to how each person views different situations. You will see what pleases them, what angers them and what motivates them.

Working with your children: Discuss different scenarios with your children about how they can step into someone else's shoes. Tell them to imagine what it would feel like to be homeless or what it would feel like to be bullied by someone. You will be amazed how this will open your children's eyes to the feelings of others.

Life-coaching tip: By thinking about the way your actions might make someone else feel, it allows you to empathize and be compassionate to others. Before speaking or acting, think about your words and actions and how it would make you feel if you were in that person's shoes.

Method 2: Trust your intuition.

If your intuition is fine-tuned, you can trust the feelings or impressions you get about other people. Sometimes a lot of facts or data are not available to us. In these cases, trusting your intuition will prove to be a valuable resource.

Working with your children: Discuss with your children moments when intuition might come in handy. For example, if they are walking home from school and a stranger approaches them, they will probably have a gut feeling or intuition that tells them they should not interact with this person. In this case, it is good to trust their intuition. You should, however, explain the vital difference between trusting their instincts and jumping to conclusions. For example, when it comes to classmates at school, they should get to know people before judging them, instead of simply judging people by their appearance.

Life-coaching tip: Learn to trust your instincts. Use positive affirmations to reinforce your reliance on intuition.

Method 3: Maintain good communication skills.

Communication is a two-way street. It is not enough to be clear, distinct and convincing when delivering information. It is just as important to actively listen to other people and really understand what they are saying. By really listening to and understanding others, it shows that you respect them enough to want to understand their points of view.

Working with your children: Practice effective listening with your children. Talk to them about something important. Have them write down the vital points about what you were saying. When you are through, review the points your children wrote down. Did they get the gist of what you were trying to say? Have a discussion about the importance of listening and having good communication skills.

> **Life-coaching tip:** Practice effective listening by writing down the important messages others are trying to relay when they are speaking to you. After you are done, read through the notes you have made and reflect on how much more of the conversation you were able to absorb because you really listened.

Method 4: Create energy and motivate others.

In order to excite others about your ideas and plans, you have to understand what motivates them and what will make them enthusiastic about working with you. In order to do this, get to know the people with whom you interact. Learn about what excites and motivates people and try your hardest to work with that knowledge.

Working with your children: Talk it over with your children and brainstorm on a project that they can do within your family or at school. For example, perhaps your son would like to organize a trip for your family to do a park cleanup. Perhaps your daughter would like to get her soccer team to raise money for new uniforms. Whatever their ideas, encourage them and have them write down ways they can get others on their team motivated. Review their ideas with them and brainstorm additional solutions. Emphasize the importance of creating energy and motivating others.

> **Life-coaching tip:** Think about one idea you have for a project, whether it is at work with your colleagues or at home with your family. For example, do you want to start an intramural softball league at your company? Do you want to institute a monthly family game night? Take one idea at a time, and write down ways in which you can create positive energy and motivate the people on your team. Implement your ideas and record the results. Have your child do the same when he is old enough.

Method 5: Read non-verbal cues.

A key element in developing empathy is the ability to read non-verbal signs such as tone of voice, gestures and facial expressions. Studies have shown that people who are able to read feelings relayed through non-verbal cues have proven to be more emotionally adjusted, more outgoing and more sensitive to the feelings of others.

Working with your children: Coach your children and encourage them to develop the skill of reading non-verbal cues. Emphasize the importance of possessing this skill and teach them how to develop it. One thing you can do is record a television show. Play the tape but mute the sound, so that they can only see the characters' actions, rather than hear their words. After your children watch the show, ask them to analyze what they think the characters are feeling based on watching their actions. Watch the show with the sound and review your children's responses. This is a good exercise to get both you and your children accustomed to reading non-verbal cues. You can also do this exercise with younger children substituting magazine pictures. Ask your children to tell you what feelings the people are showing by their facial expressions. Your children will start to associate feelings with non-verbal cues.

Life-coaching tip: Work every day on reading non-verbal cues. As you are talking with friends or family, look at their facial expressions, their hand gestures and other clues into what they are feeling and trying to express.

☆ *A Real-Life Example of Enhancing Empathy: Tricia*

Several years ago, I opened my office door to a new patient. Tricia and her mother, Mona, came to my office one day by recommendation of Tricia's school. Tricia had become a major problem in her school. She was extremely uncooperative, doing only what pleased her and ignoring everyone else's feelings. In addition, she had become a bully. Tricia had become the leader of a small group of students in her classroom that would tease and torment other students. Under Tricia's leadership, the activities of the group escalated to include petty theft and vandalism. The situation had reached the point where school authorities insisted that Tricia either see me or be expelled from school.

Tricia was an attractive twelve-year-old girl, but dressed in a way that made her appear five or six years older. It was clear from the moment Tricia and Mona entered my office that Tricia was the one who was in charge. She walked ahead and immediately sat in the chair opposite me, while Mona trailed behind in a hesitant manner.

Tricia's look as she faced me was one of defiance. Mona began immediately to fuss. She insisted that the principal—in fact, all of the teachers—picked on her daughter. "They're jealous of her because she's so pretty and because she has friends," she said. I asked her about the bullying behavior and the vandalism. She said, "Tricia said that she and her friends didn't do any of that and I believe her. She wouldn't lie to me." Tricia sat listening, looking smug and unconcerned. Her attitude gave the impression that she was secretly laughing at the entire situation, and was already thinking about how she would joke about this with her group of followers.

"Tricia," I said, "You look very nice today." This brought a smile to Tricia's face, indicating that the compliment was deserved and that I had done well to pay it to her. I continued, "But do most twelve-year-old girls dress like you do? You seem to dress a lot older than other girls your age. Why is that?" "I don't like those little kid clothes," Tricia answered. At this point Mona chimed in, saying that her daughter had excellent taste in clothes, which was why she let Tricia wear whatever clothes she wanted.

The rest of our session continued in this same way. When the time was up, I advised that I would need to see both of them on a regular basis. Tricia pouted and acted annoyed, which triggered the same response in Mona. I explained that to satisfy the requirements set forth by the school, I would have to meet with them until I was satisfied that Tricia had received proper counseling. They reluctantly agreed and we arranged to meet every Tuesday.

As our weekly sessions progressed, it became evident that Mona had devoted her life to her daughter; she did everything in her power to see that Tricia got whatever she wanted. Tricia became accustomed to having things handed to her, and soon learned that a few tears or sulking would have Mona eating out of her hand. She became a perfectionist at manipulation.

I determined that one of the major issues I had to confront with Mona was her total devotion to Tricia to the extent that she had no real life of her own. I had to convince Mona that she was not helping Tricia by giving in to her every whim. The first hurdle was for Mona to say "no" to Tricia when she thought Tricia's demands were inappropriate. After twelve years of giving in to every whim, that first "no" was very difficult. She finally did it and, despite her daughter's rage, she stuck to her decision.

Our next project was to wean Mona away from being constantly at her daughter's beck and call. Over the last twelve years, her devotion to Tricia had caused Mona to drift away from friends and activities that she had previously enjoyed. I urged her to reconnect with some of her friends and to set aside one day a week as "Mona's Day." Initially, Tricia was upset to find her mother's interest diverted to other activities and people, but over time she accepted the new routine and learned to live with it.

Once Mona had become accustomed to her new role and was comfortable with herself, I recommended that she give back to the community. I gave her a list of charities that needed volunteer help and suggested that she choose one and devote some time to it. She chose a nursing home and volunteered every Wednesday helping the elderly. Mona became a changed woman and discovered that she was missing so much by allowing herself to be dominated and manipulated by her daughter.

In the meantime, I worked with Tricia to help her understand the changes in her mother and how she, herself, must also change in order to become a happy and productive member of society. Tricia was an intelligent girl and a born leader. It was up to me to help her turn her good qualities into useful tools.

Although Mona did not give in to Tricia's every whim, she was still available to her when Tricia actually needed her. She still showed her an abundance of love; in fact she found this to be even more pleasurable now that she was not bound so tightly to her daughter. It took many sessions before Tricia could accept this new situation, but eventually she had to admit that Mona was happier than she had been for a long time. She also noticed that when Mona did anything for her, it was with more interest and love. At some point, after many sessions, Tricia started to look up to and admire Mona. She began to see her as an individual who took charge of her life and was enjoying the results.

Eventually, I was able to guide Tricia away from the negative activities toward some positive actions. She became involved in a daycare center located within the school and spent her days after school, when Mona was busy, helping to care for other children. She worked with them on craft projects, read to them and did whatever she could to help. Her friends followed her in this project, and the daycare employees were thankful for the help. After a while, Tricia realized that she felt really good after she helped others.

This particular problem took time but worked out well. There were multiple problems to solve with both the mother and daughter in order to help Tricia. I had to help Mona understand that, although she thought she was being a good parent, she was actually contributing to Tricia's problems. She had to relearn how to be an effective parent, while allowing time for herself. By doing volunteer work, she was satisfying her need to help others, while also being a positive role model for Tricia.

With Tricia, I had to help her realize that she could not spend her life as a manipulator. I worked with her intelligence and her leadership skills to guide her into paths that would encourage her to help others. Using life-coaching techniques, I helped to develop her compassion and empathy. Although it took a lot of time and effort, Tricia reached a point in her counseling where her natural intelligence took over; she understood why positive changes in her life were necessary. As her admiration for Mona slowly grew, Tricia saw her as a role model. Mona's volunteerism and genuine concern for the people she helped spurred Tricia into her own volunteer activities.

This was a typical situation in which a devoted parent, wanting the best for her child, ended up with a spoiled youngster who felt nothing for anyone but herself. As Mona resumed some independent pursuits, Tricia found that she was expected to shoulder more responsibility. Tricia was surprised to find that she actually enjoyed being responsible and helping others.

As a result of weeks of counseling, a mother's love and openness to change, this situation had a happy ending. Although it was not an easy process, both Tricia and Mona feel better about themselves and are helping others on a regular basis.

USING YOUR EMPATHIC SKILLS AT WORK AND AT HOME

The life of an office manager would be greatly simplified if each of her employees had the same personality, likes and dislikes. If this were the case, the manager would be able to develop one pattern of behavior that would be effective for everyone. This, however, is not a reality in the workplace. In the same vain, it is also not realistic to expect all children to be alike. Just as every employee is different, so is every child. Each child has his own talents, abilities, insecurities and needs. Effective managers and effective parents alike realize that every employee and every child must be treated differently.

The following is an example of a departmental manager who learned that each of his employees had their own talents and shortcomings. He learned to adjust his management style to suit each employee. Similarly, he was able to use the skills he learned on the job with his own family.

An Example of Empathy in the Workplace and Home

☆ *Workplace Example: Dennis and Mike*
When Dennis took the job of departmental manager at his company, his predecessor briefed him about the temperaments of the various employees he would be managing. "Watch out for Mike," he was told. "He's a great salesman, but he's loud, tends to dominate a meeting and his crude remarks turn many people off." Just as Dennis had been told, Mike did like to dominate any group he was part of. His loud voice tended to override comments from others. After keeping an eye on Mike for a month or so, Dennis came to the conclusion that, although Mike was loud and crude at times, he

knew the product inside and out and was very well informed on company policy and procedure. His price quotes to customers were right on target every time. Dennis looked over Mike's personnel file and discovered that Mike had come to the company straight from high school and had worked his way up from the factory to the sales office.

One day, Dennis called Mike into his office to have a discussion with him. It turned out that Mike felt he was at a disadvantage because he lacked the amount of formal education most of the other salespeople had. To make up for this, he tried to show that he was good at the job by dominating other employees. Dennis explained to Mike that he was one of the best salespeople in the company and that he did not need to prove himself. Furthermore, with a little polish to smooth out the rough edges, he could climb up the corporate ladder rather quickly. Dennis arranged for the company to pay for courses for Mike at the local community college. Through these courses, he learned how to dress, speak and behave in appropriate ways that would help him present himself in a positive light. Mike was a good student and was grateful to Dennis for working with him. As a result, Dennis' sales figures rose to a new height, as did his position with the company.

☆ *Family Example: Dennis and Kandy*

Dennis found that this same formula worked with his family. Kandy, his middle child, situated between her older sister and her younger brother, often felt overlooked. To compensate for these feelings, she would get into trouble often, which would get her the attention she craved.

As a result of his management experience, Dennis was able to see Kandy's behavior for what it was. He had a meeting with Kandy and listened very intently to what she had to say. He learned that she felt inadequate because she was always compared to Misty, who got much better grades in school, and to Junior who, being the baby, could do no wrong.

Dennis began to spend more time with Kandy. They agreed to spend private father/daughter time with each other every Tuesday evening. This would be their special time together when Kandy could have his full attention. After spending time together, Dennis discovered that Kandy had a beautiful singing voice and that her greatest wish was to learn how to play the piano. He made a deal with Kandy: he would arrange for her to take piano lessons, and, in return, she would work to bring up her grades, modify her behavior to be more tolerant of her siblings and be more helpful around the house.

Dennis was able to recognize the similarities between Mike, his employee, and Kandy, his daughter. He understood that both felt inadequate, both had talents that needed to be uncovered and both believed that inappropriate behavior was the key to receiving the attention they craved. He demonstrated that he understood their feelings and was able to use that to identify the difficulty each one was experiencing. He was then able to turn a potential problem into a satisfying resolution.

☆ *Workplace Example: Dennis and Sammy*

Mike was not the only challenge that Dennis inherited when he assumed his new position. Mike's predecessor told him that he was on the verge of letting Sammy go. Sammy was quite the opposite of Mike; he seemed to be introverted, shy and hesitant when contacting potential customers. The only reason he was not yet let go was because the manager knew he had a family to support and hoped his performance would improve enough to justify his employment.

In watching Sammy, Dennis noted that he never spoke up at meetings. He also noted that when speaking to potential clients or when asked questions about the product, his response showed his obvious lack of confidence. Despite these drawbacks, Dennis felt that, with the right guidance, Sammy could become a good salesman.

In his review with Sammy, Dennis made sure that Sammy received a thorough tour of the plant and studied manuals that explained the product. During the review, it became clear that Sammy knew his material, though he lacked the confidence and skills necessary to communicate this to others. Dennis also arranged for Sammy to have a one-on-one meeting with Mike. This gave Mike the opportunity to share his knowledge and gave Sammy someone he was comfortable with to ask questions when he needed product answers. As a final step, he saw to it that Sammy received a course in assertiveness training to show him the proper way to approach customers. Sammy also met regularly with a life-coach who was able to allay some of his fears and build his self-confidence.

Dennis and Sammy agreed on another review in six months. By that time, it was apparent to everyone that Sammy had gained a great deal of confidence, and his sales were steadily increasing. Sammy discovered that his sense of humor gave him a knack for talking to people that often resulted in a sale. With each new sale, his self-esteem rose even more.

☆ *Family Example: Dennis and Misty*

Dennis was able to use similar tactics with his older daughter, Misty. Like Sammy, Misty was shy. Even though she got excellent grades in school, she was intimidated by the easy way her sister Kandy could make friends. She spent most evenings and weekends by herself, reading or doing some other solo activity. She longed to have more friends and venture out to do more exciting things. Dennis was able to use his experience with Sammy to help Misty. By listening, Dennis ascertained that Misty had a great interest in photography. He made several inquiries and found a local photography club that welcomed beginners. Once she began to associate with people who held the same interest as she did, her shyness started to evaporate and she emerged from her shell to become more self-confident. For her birthday, Dennis gave her a camera that she had been eyeing; this brought her out of her shell even more. She was able to summon some assertiveness when taking photographs. After receiving positive comments from the other members of the club, her confidence grew to the point where she entered a few contests and won some prizes.

A Summary of Dennis' Experiences with Empathy:

Dennis made it a priority to bring out interests and talents that were previously undiscovered, simply because no one took the initiative to find them. The management training Dennis received served him well both at work and at home. The most important lesson he learned was that no two people are exactly alike.

Whether it is at work or at home, we must see that each person's individual needs, talents and feelings are addressed. Once Dennis learned to do this in a work environment and was able to help employees achieve success and satisfaction, it became clear to him that the same methods could be applied to his family, with equally positive results.

The important difference between these workplace examples and family examples was the ingredient of love. Mike and Sammy knew and appreciated the sensitivity and compassion Dennis showed by taking the time to speak to them and help them reconcile their difficulties. Kandy and Misty had the additional ingredient of love. The words may not have been spoken, but the actions said, "My father is doing his best to help me because he loves me." Although it was his management training that showed Dennis the right path to take to bring out the best in his employees, it was the love he showed his family that made the biggest difference.

AN ASSESSMENT OF YOUR CHILD'S CAPACITY TO EMPATHIZE

Over the next month, use the chart on the following pages. Write down instances in which you would expect your children to show empathy or compassion. Beneath each instance, note whether or not your child showed a suitable amount of empathy in each situation. When reviewing these instances at the end of the month, note areas in which you feel your children need improvement. You can then work with your children to fill in any gaps. Review some of these instances with your children, and note whether they think they showed empathy in these situations. Discuss additional ways they could have shown empathy, and praise them for the empathy they did exhibit.

Studying My Child's Capacity to Empathize

Situation: *Example:* Neighbor's son has chicken pox

Was Empathy Shown?:   *No.*

Ways to Show Compassion: *Offer to get child's homework; lend child games*

Situation: _____

Was Empathy Shown?: _____

Ways to Show Compassion: _____

Situation: _____

Was Empathy Shown?: _____

Ways to Show Compassion: _____

Situation: _____

Was Empathy Shown?: _____

Ways to Show Compassion: _____

Situation: _____

Was Empathy Shown?: _____

Ways to Show Compassion:	_____
Situation:	_____
Was Empathy Shown?:	_____
Ways to Show Compassion:	_____
Situation:	_____
Was Empathy Shown?:	_____
Ways to Show Compassion:	_____

SUMMARY OF CHAPTER SEVEN

In this chapter, you learned all about the importance of having empathy and compassion. By assessing your children's strengths regarding their feelings for others, you were able to teach them the importance of empathy. Your concentration in this chapter was to help your children realize that they must care for and associate with the feelings of others. You were given some life-coaching tips to enhance your own capacity for empathy, as well as some tips for working with your children to enhance their ability to exhibit empathy. You were then shown examples of how you can use your empathic skills both at work and at home. Finally, you were asked to prepare a list, making note of events that call for compassion and your child's reaction to them.

Each day brings new opportunities to show compassion. These situations provide you, as a parent, opportunities to instill values in your children. When you help others and take the time to explain to your children why helping others is so important, you are confirming the idea that it is the right thing to do. A compassionate child is one who is emotionally healthy. It is never too early or too late to instill empathy and walk the path to emotional health and maturity.

☆ Volunteer my time to those less fortunate.

☆ Plan a family volunteer day at a local charity.

☆ Listen to my children and realize that they each have special qualities.

☆ Show my children, by word and example, the importance of stepping into someone else's shoes.

Chapter Eight

THE FOUNDATION OF YOUR CHILD'S SUCCESS: BUILDING YOUR CHILD'S SELF-ESTEEM
Nurture a Fragile Self-Esteem

CHAPTER OBJECTIVES

- Learn about the consequences of poor self-esteem.
- Do an assessment of your children's level of self-esteem.
- Discover how you can help boost your children's self-esteem.
- Learn the four steps to a healthy self-esteem.
- Develop a plan of action to help your children increase their self-esteem in at least 3 ways.

"What a man thinks of himself, that it is which determines,
or rather indicates his fate."
— *Henry David Thoreau*

Self-esteem enables people to accept and embrace the role of leader. This chapter will help you identify the negative consequences of having poor self-esteem. It will also help you assess your children's level of self-esteem and discover ways to help boost their self-esteem. You will learn four steps to a healthy self-esteem and develop a personalized plan of action to help boost your child's self-esteem.

ARE YOU ENERGIZING YOUR FAMILY TO SUCCEED?

Any worthwhile manager will take the time to assess the individual talents of his employees. Too often, an employee is given a job to do that he is not ready for, does not have the aptitude for, or lacks interest in. Placing an individual in a position where he cannot perform at an optimum level can result in poor self-esteem. This person might have become a leader in another position, but will never try because he has developed such a poor sense of self.

Effective managers foster their employees' self-confidence in a number of ways. The skills needed to instill this in others can be easily transferred to use within the family. For example, good managers know and understand the backgrounds of their employees by studying their applications and interview reports, in order to understand their employees' capabilities and strengths. In a family situation, parents know their children well. Do you, as a parent, take the time to think about your children's likes, dislikes, strengths and weaknesses? If your son is a computer whiz, do you assume that your other son is also? Do you compare your children to each other?

If you do, this can be detrimental to their self-esteem, since every child has his own individual likes, dislikes, strengths and weaknesses. You do not want your children growing up thinking that they can never measure up to their siblings, or that they cannot make their parents happy. The longer this continues, the more their self-esteem suffers. By the time they reach high school, they could be labeled as underachievers, not because they do not have the ability to do better, but because they are convinced they cannot do as well as their siblings.

What you should do is use your children's differences to the best advantage. **Celebrate their differences, as these are what make them unique and special.** How many parents fail to recognize the individualism of their children? How many talents and skills are buried because they were never permitted to develop? How many adults are unhappy in their life work because, as children, they were put into a mold and were never able to break out of it? How many grown people suffer from poor self-esteem because their interests were never taken seriously?

It is your responsibility as a parent to seek out the differences in your children and to give them the chance to develop their interests, even if these interests do not appeal to you. Your children are not you and will never be you. Do not make them feel that they are not good enough. Do not stifle their creativity. Give them a chance to grow and watch the beautiful blossoms that will appear.

Perhaps you were never given the chance to pursue your dreams as a child. Now is the time; if there is something you always wanted to do, go for it. Perhaps you have always wanted to learn how to be a gourmet cook, play the piano or paint. Even if you do not bring home a masterpiece or make a tremendous amount of money pursuing your dream, you will be setting a fantastic example for your children. They will see the importance of going after their dreams. In addition, this will allow you to understand the importance of giving this opportunity to your children.

Be lavish with your praise for a job well done. Too often, parents do not give credit where credit is due. While they may not be intentionally insensitive, by not acknowledging hard work and efforts, children's sense of accomplishment is taken away. If you take away pride, you subsequently destroy self-satisfaction. This is displayed in the workplace all the time. If you encourage good work, your employees will feel a great sense of pride and try hard to do a good job the next time. If you do not acknowledge their efforts, they may wonder why they should even bother in the first place.

Children are constantly learning new skills. They need the positive reinforcement of parents to make them feel good about their accomplishments. It does not matter if your son's picture of a cat looks more like an abstract painting of a house, or if your daughter's science project resembles a hodge-podge of sticks and cans. They did their best and need to be commended for that. It does not matter if anyone else likes their work; the approval children are constantly seeking is that of their parents. If they do not receive this attention and praise, they will feel their efforts are worthless. I know of cases in which parents actually laughed at the attempts of their children, thinking that the children would not care or even understand. Unless you are a comedian, being laughed at is no laughing matter. It belittles them, and instead of feeling good about themselves, they assume they are an object of humor and will never be taken seriously.

Remember your first day on a new job? How did you feel as you walked into a room full of strangers? Timid? Nervous? Frightened? Your supervisor probably took you to your workstation and told you what to do. Then you were on your own, feeling very left out as co-workers talked to each other and joked about things you were not a part of. A good supervisor would have been conscious of your first-day jitters and would have introduced you to several nearby workers. Maybe she could have told you which co-worker could be most helpful if you had any questions. A good supervisor would have understood your distress and helped smooth the waters for you.

Good supervisors and good parents are very much alike. Parents must recognize and acknowledge their children and see to it that each child feels special and accepted. A child's ego is extremely fragile. There may be times when he feels on top of the world, but that can all change in an instant.

Who has such power and control over another person's feelings? It is you, the parent, who helps determine the self-esteem of your children. Take a minute, right now, to transport yourself back in time to when you were the age your child is now. What was a typical day like? How many times did you hear the word "no," or the phrase, "don't do that," or worse, "you never do anything right." Contrast those words with the number of times you were praised, even if what you did was mediocre. How often were you encouraged when you took the initiative and tried something you were hesitant to do? When you were in a school play, a dance program or a music recital, did you receive the support and encouragement you needed?

Now come back to the present and think about how you interact with your children. Are you repeating your own childhood with them? Children are bombarded daily with a large amount of "do's" and "don'ts." There has to be a balance in order to give their sensitive egos a boost. I'm not advocating permissiveness; children do need boundaries and they need to be taught what they can or cannot do so they can function as successful adults. However, there are times when parents concentrate so hard on teaching perfection that they neglect the care and attention that is absolutely necessary to a child's self-esteem.

If your child has a day filled with roadblocks, he will come to you for support. Be careful not to undermine your children's feelings. Listen to them—don't minimize their feelings, but help them express what they feel. Be sure to validate their feelings and, when necessary, give constructive feedback. However, if, time after time, that support is withheld, your child will be convinced that he is unworthy of your time. This is not something he will outgrow; it will be with him for life. This could potentially keep your child from reaching for the stars and becoming successful because, in his mind, he does not feel worthy of success.

Know the Danger Signals of Poor Self-Esteem

Is your child shy, or does he suffer from low self-esteem? Do you know the difference? The following is an example of two students. See if you can tell which student has a positive self-esteem.

☆ *A Real-Life Example of Signals of Poor Self-Esteem: Lenny and Michael*
Lenny did not make friends easily. He often stood on the outskirts of conversation groups, and it was difficult for teachers to get him to

participate in class discussions. His grades were a little above average, but it was torture for him to speak before the class. When he had to give an oral report, his discomfort was apparent by the quiver in his voice, his shaking, sweating hands and his downcast eyes.

Michael had many friends, often laughed at himself and was considered something of a clown. He often called attention to his faults and laughed about them. Michael seemed genuinely surprised when he did something well. If he received a compliment on anything at all, he was likely to mumble something like, "Yeah, I guess I lucked out," or, "I accidentally got it right." He usually went along with the crowd, did not put forth too many ideas of his own and did not make waves.

Which child has the low self-esteem? Did you know it was Michael? He had the classic symptoms. He was quick to call attention to his faults and laugh about them. He would have been crushed if these faults (usually blown out of proportion in his own mind anyway) were brought up by others and laughed at, so he beat them to the punch and pretended it did not matter. If he did well and received a compliment, he put himself down because he actually believed that he did not deserve praise. He went along with the crowd and did not voice his own opinions because he felt his ideas had no value and they would only be ridiculed. Michael used a disguise and he used it well. He appeared to be easy-going and comfortable with himself, but in reality he was filled with doubt about his own worth.

When paying attention to the behavior of your children, the following are some guidelines you can use to determine your child's self-confidence. Be sure to keep in mind that low self-esteem can be indicative of other problems.

A child exhibits high self-esteem when he:

- Takes pride in his accomplishments
- Acts independently

- Takes on responsibility
- Handles frustration well
- Is enthusiastic about challenges
- Feels capable
- Demonstrates a good sense of humor
- Feels a sense of purpose

A child exhibits low self-esteem when he:

- Avoids risk
- Feels powerless
- Is easily frustrated or overly sensitive
- Requires continuous reassurance
- Feels isolated or appears withdrawn
- Is influenced easily by others
- Complains often and/or has a negative attitude
- Blames others for his shortcomings
- Is angry or refuses to cooperate
- Is dependent

ASSESS YOUR CHILD'S LEVEL OF SELF-ESTEEM

Using the self-esteem guidelines above, I want you to observe your child over a period of several days and in various circumstances. For example, how does your child handle conflict, disappointment, rejection or failure? Think about your child's coping strategies and openness to new activities and relationships, then complete the chart on the following pages. Your observations will provide insight into how your child feels about himself. Remember, these are just guidelines and may be indications of other problems.

For each feeling or behavior below, rate the number that best reflects your child's level of self-esteem, on a scale of 1 to 10. A score of 1 indicates that your child always exhibits this behavior, while a score of 10 indicates that this behavior is never exhibited.

	Always									Never
1. My child takes pride in accomplishments.	1	2	3	4	5	6	7	8	9	10
2. My child acts independently.	1	2	3	4	5	6	7	8	9	10
3. My child takes on responsibility.	1	2	3	4	5	6	7	8	9	10
4. My child can handle frustration.	1	2	3	4	5	6	7	8	9	10
5. My child is enthusiastic about challenges.	1	2	3	4	5	6	7	8	9	10
6. My child feels capable.	1	2	3	4	5	6	7	8	9	10
7. My child demonstrates a sense of humor.	1	2	3	4	5	6	7	8	9	10
8. My child feels a sense of purpose.	1	2	3	4	5	6	7	8	9	10
9. My child avoids risk.	1	2	3	4	5	6	7	8	9	10
10. My child feels powerless.	1	2	3	4	5	6	7	8	9	10
11. My child is easily frustrated /overly sensitive.	1	2	3	4	5	6	7	8	9	10

12. My child requires continuous reassurance.	1 2 3 4 5 6 7 8 9 10
13. My child feels isolated or withdrawn.	1 2 3 4 5 6 7 8 9 10
14. My child is easily influenced by others.	1 2 3 4 5 6 7 8 9 10
15. My child complains often or has a negative attitude.	1 2 3 4 5 6 7 8 9 10
16. My child blames others for his shortcomings.	1 2 3 4 5 6 7 8 9 10
17. My child is angry or refuses to cooperate.	1 2 3 4 5 6 7 8 9 10
18. My child is dependent.	1 2 3 4 5 6 7 8 9 10

If you were able to answer questions 1 through 8 with a score between one and five, and questions 9 through 18 with a score of six to ten, then your child exhibits a healthy level of self-esteem. Scores of four to seven show that there is room for improvement in these areas, and this is where you need to concentrate your efforts when helping your child.

The Importance of Increasing Self-Esteem

Low self-esteem in children can lead to a lifetime of misery and missed opportunities. They may not even attempt more difficult college courses or seek advancement in the workplace because they feel they cannot do it. Their brain tells them they just are not good enough. Use every available opportunity to praise your children. Never dwell on a failed attempt. Instead, praise them for doing their best. Always encourage your children to try their best for the highest position they want to achieve. Never use negative descriptions, such as stupid or clumsy. These will stick in their brain and they may never overcome the effects.

Very often, children do not fit into their parents' preconceived mold. Instead of recognizing the talent that is there, parents may stifle it in favor of their own plans. Recognize that your children are unique and that they have their own ideas about what they want to do in life. Encourage them and give them every opportunity to excel in the areas that are special to them. Never put them down for not falling into the pattern you expect of them.

☆ *A Real-Life Example of the Effects of Poor Self-Esteem: Edward*

Several years ago, a baseball player, Edward, came to my office. Edward was the younger son in a family of sport fans. During football season, the family could be found gathered around the television watching games. Edward's mom always made sure there were plenty of snacks available and planned the dinners so they would not interfere with watching the game. When they were not involved with football, hockey was the big interest, and in summer baseball took the spotlight.

Edward's older brother, Sam, was an all-around athlete and played on every team he could join. He was known as a jock and loved the attention it brought him. Edward's parents were positive that Edward would follow his brother's lead. Edward liked sports all right, but he was not too interested in playing. He joined the different teams only because his parents expected him to.

What Edward really liked to do was read, especially if the book pertained to any aspect of business. He read biographies of every business magnate he could get his hands on—from Andrew Carnegie to Nelson Rockefeller. He found the business world intriguing and wanted to be part of it some day.

At first, he tried reading while a game was going on, but it was too distracting and he was teased too much about always having his nose in a book; so he tried to slip away to his room while the rest were gathered around the television. This did not work either; he was always discovered and dragged back into the family fold. His parents began to refer to him as "our scholarly son," making it sound as negative as possible.

Edward gave in.—He gave up his dream and concentrated instead on his parents' interests. He focused on sports and became a good player. He was picked up by a major league baseball team and sent to their farm club to be groomed for the big time. It was the same team that had picked up his brother, and the managers began to call him "Little Sam."

His parents were happy and proud to have two sons playing for a major league team. Sam was proud of his little brother and happy to be doing what he always dreamed of doing. Edward, however, was not happy. He knew he was in an enviable position, and that millions of young men throughout the country would love to be in his shoes; but deep in his heart, he still harbored a yearning for the world of business. Of course, he would never be good enough to do well in it; at least that was the message he had received for many years from his family.

At the time Edward came to my office, his game was suffering; he was not doing as well as expected and he worried he might be let go. When I asked if this would bother him a lot, he answered, "Not really, except that my family would be disappointed, and I'm not prepared for anything other than baseball."

We talked for quite awhile, and I asked Edward what he would like to do if he could not play ball. This was when his dream of a business career came to light. "But," he said, "I could never do it. Dad always told me I wasn't smart enough to really make it big in business. Even though I never thought about making it 'really big,' I just wanted to be involved in the process. I don't even know for sure what kind of business I'd like to be in. But, it doesn't matter because I'd never be able to hold my own there anyway."

Edward had more than one hurdle to jump. First, he had to learn to recognize his interest and understand that he could make a go of it. To begin with, I had him sign up at a local college for a few business courses. The important thing now was to start; he could decide what area to focus on at a later date. Second, Edward needed to realize that he was not required to fill the role written for him by his family. If he chose a different path, they would have to accept that and learn to live with it.

It was a slow process, because we were trying to undo years of negative messages to the psyche and replace them with a positive self-image. As Edward progressed along his path to recovery, he became happier and more self-assured. His game improved to the extent that his worries about being let go vanished. Edward left the game of baseball voluntarily to pursue a career in business, where he now owns a successful company. His family has come to terms with his decision.

Edward's story demonstrates the effects that poor self-esteem can have throughout a person's lifetime; it can affect career and personal choices. As parents, you need to recognize your children's passions, strengths and weaknesses. Identify what makes them special and nourish those qualities. Watch your children carefully. Notice how they react when with friends. If you see that they often put themselves down and constantly acquiesce to the ideas of others, or if they venture an opinion but dismiss it with laughter, then you need to step in and help them. Be your child's biggest fan. Support his dreams and help him become the best person he can be.

BOOSTING YOUR CHILD'S SELF-ESTEEM

Parents can have a negative or positive impact on self-esteem. Your words and actions can help or hinder your child. Even a little remark meant as a joke can sting deeply. In order to be an effective life-coach for your child, you must learn to help her feel good about herself. The questions on the following pages will help you determine the effect you may be having on your child's self-esteem

Are You Boosting Your Child's Self-Esteem?

Please circle yes or no for the following questions.

1. Is your child comfortable about expressing opinions?

Yes   No

2. Do you try to change your child into what you consider to be "acceptable?"

Yes   No

3. Do you regularly attend events that your child participates in, such as sports, theatrical productions or award presentations?

Yes   No

4. Do you cause feelings of low self-appreciation by using phrases such as, "You're so stupid," "You never do anything right" or "Why can't you be more like your brother?"

Yes   No

5. Do you make derogatory comments about your child in front of others?

Yes   No

6. Do you make an effort to accept your child's friends?

Yes   No

7. Do you encourage talents that are different from other family members?

Yes   No

8. Do you praise efforts, no matter how minor?

Yes   No

9. Do you take time to listen to your child with your full attention?

Yes   No

10. Do you tell your child often that you love her?

               Yes   No

Questions 2, 4 and 5 should be answered "no." All others should have received a "yes" response. If your answers differ, then these are the areas in which you need extra work. Make a conscious effort to change your methods of dealing with these types of situations. Work on yourself and watch how the changes in you will be reflected in your child. If you feel good about who you are, you are more likely to foster positive feelings in others around you.

The Magic of Encouragement

There is no greater incentive to your child and no greater way to boost a lagging self-image than through the magic of encouragement. The following five life-coaching tips have been used extensively by successful managers and by effective parents. Pay close attention to each of the tips and practice them often. Whether in the workplace, in the home or in personal relationships, these are natural self-image boosters that are necessary for everyone.

Life-coaching Tips:
- Comment on what others are doing right. Focus on what is right instead of what is wrong, in order to bring out the good qualities already there.
- Demonstrate appreciation. Cooperative and helpful behavior needs to be appreciated in order to be repeated.
- Support others while they are learning a new skill or changing a behavior. Avoid the temptation to interfere when others are working on a new task.
- Demonstrate your confidence in people. Provide opportunities for learning and an environment for forgiving mistakes.
- Build on success. Children and adults need to experience success in relationships and in work. Encouragement will help them develop a "Yes, I can" attitude.

THE ESSENTIAL ELEMENTS FOR HEALTHY SELF-ESTEEM

There are four essential elements needed to lay a foundation for good self-esteem. If just one of them is weak or absent, it will make meeting life's challenges difficult. Compare this to a company with an inept CEO. Adjustments are always necessary on the part of the employees to cover for her. Even though the workers know who is at fault, they still will blame themselves for failures.

When children have the four basic needs for self-esteem met, they can climb the Pyramid of Success with confidence. The following are essential elements your children need in order to develop positive self-esteem:

1) Sense of connection with others
2) Uniqueness
3) Empowerment
4) Satisfaction of emotional needs

Essential Element 1: Sense of connection with others

Children, particularly as they approach their teen years, tend to travel in packs or groups. There is a good reason for this—children need to feel connected to peers. This need to belong is met through relationships that make them feel loved and special. They develop this feeling through responses and interactions with others in the group. The behavior of a child who shuns group contact is considered to be an anomaly and, if this behavior is excessive, could be cause for concern.

Consider people who commit crimes. They will often be described by those who know them as, "a nice guy, but a loner." People who are loners have never developed a sense of belonging. There are times when children will become part of a group that is not healthy or wholesome. They join this "gang" because, as a member, they receive the sense of belonging that is absent from their life. When these teens, many of whom have gotten into serious trouble, are interviewed and asked why they feel such loyalty to a group that is known for trouble, they answer, "because they're my family, they're there for me when I need them." They are receiving from the gang what is lacking at home.

It is not easy for children who are not part of a group to break into one. If they are the "new kid on the block," friendships and affiliations may have already been formed; therefore, they may be considered an outsider. Your child's peer group may also affect her sense of self, either positively or negatively. Be open and encourage your child to discuss her feelings about her interactions with peers. Help her come up with ways to counter negative comments from others.

Essential Element 2: Uniqueness

Children need to know that they are individuals, special and different from anyone else. As tempting as it is for parents to pay attention to and have their children develop characteristics that are similar to their own, it is not in the best interest of the children to do so. Parents need to recognize and accept the differences in their children. Children should be free to develop likes and dislikes, find their own individuality and know that they are accepted and loved. This knowledge will increase self-esteem and help them to be proud of their uniqueness.

As they mature, they may want to be more like their peers and conform, such as in their style of clothing, in order to feel accepted. This is normal, but always encourage them to be who they are. When your children feel confident in their ability to be who they are with their own thoughts and feelings, they will be better able to combat peer pressure.

Essential Element 3: Empowerment

Empowering your children gives them the confidence to trust their own judgment in decision-making situations. If their opinions are constantly dismissed, they will feel they are not worthy of consideration. This is a huge blow to self-esteem and will take a lot of work to rectify.

Start empowering your children as soon as they are old enough to express an opinion. Begin early and give them choices. Do they want an orange or an apple for a snack? Do they want their stuffed animal or their doll to take in the car? This is not to say they should always have things their way, but giving them a chance to choose some things that affect them gives them a voice and lets them know their opinions matter. As they grow older, include them in family decisions, such as what movie to see or where to go on vacation. Just because their ideas are included, they should not always prevail. They also need to learn that the thoughts of others must be respected. If what they propose is not acceptable, they should still be encouraged to continue to contribute. You can encourage your children by using statements such as, "That's a good idea. We can't use it right now, but we'll remember it for next time." Or, "I can tell that you really put a lot of thought into that. Thank you. We can't use your idea right now, but we'll keep it for a later time. Please keep the ideas coming; you're doing a terrific job and they're such a big help to the family." Take ideas and contributions seriously and let your children know that what they think matters. Never just gloss over them, or worse yet, laugh at them. If you laugh at their ideas, you laugh at them. If you consistently reject their input, you are rejecting them. Let your children know that they count—their self-esteem depends on it.

Essential Element 4: Satisfaction of emotional needs

Children are rarely unemotional; rather, they tend to feel in extremes. Either they are ecstatically happy or their world is falling apart, they feel loved or everyone on the planet hates them. They can experience extreme joy or profound sadness. Through all of these complex emotions, parents are responsible for creating a positive self-image in their children, because how a person feels about himself determines how his life will unfold. Self-esteem is critical because it may influence:

- Who they choose as friends
- How they cooperate with others
- How productive they are
- Who they will marry

Self-esteem is closely related to a child's personality. The more positive children feel about themselves, the more easily they will interact with others. If they feel loved, they will give love in return. Self-esteem touches every aspect of life and may determine:

- Level of creativity
- Future leadership qualities and skills
- Integrity
- Stability

PLAN OF ACTION FOR DEVELOPING A POSITIVE SELF-IMAGE

Listed next are three life-coaching activities that your family can engage in to help bolster self-esteem. By involving the whole family and making the project fun, you can accomplish a great deal in your quest to help improve your children's self-esteem. Perhaps your family can think of more activities, but these will give you a good start. Be sure that all family members are aware that there are no right or wrong answers and that no one should criticize anyone else's responses.

Life-Coaching Activity 1: Discussion

At the end of the day, discuss your children's accomplishments and successes of that day. Help them by pointing out successes and new skills learned. Share some of your own accomplishments of the day as well.

Life-Coaching Activity 2: Family poster

Make a family self-esteem poster. Each family member who witnesses another member doing something good should write about it on the poster. Older family members can write for the younger members. Read the comments aloud when the family is together. Examples: "I saw Johnny putting away his toys," or "I saw Katie help her younger brother."

Life-Coaching Activity 3: Sentence-Completion Game

Play a sentence-completion game. Share with your children the feelings behind their answers to the following statements:

- "I am happy when..."

- "I feel hurt when..."

- "One of the things I do well is..."

- "One of the things I'm getting better at is..."

SUMMARY OF CHAPTER EIGHT

In this chapter, you learned about the effects of low self-esteem in the workplace and in the family. You were able, through assessing your children, to determine their level of self-esteem and discover methods to boost their self-image.

You learned several ways to help increase your children's self-esteem and the four essential elements necessary to develop a positive self-image.

Finally, a three-step plan of action was detailed to assist you in helping your children accept and like themselves. It is only through self-acceptance and self-love that others will have the same regard for them.

☆ Watch my children carefully for signs of low self-esteem.

☆ Praise my children at least once each day.

☆ Find ways I can help my children improve their self-esteem.

☆ Plan a family meeting in which accomplishments can be praised.

Part Three

REACHING YOUR FAMILY'S FULL SUCCESS POTENTIAL

Monitoring and Modifying Behavior to Achieve Goals and Improve Interactions With Others

Chapter Nine

SOCIAL SKILLS: ONE OF THE MOST ESSENTIAL KEYS TO SUCCESS

Communicate Your Way to Success

CHAPTER OBJECTIVES

- Learn the difference between good and bad communication.
- Assess both you and your child's communication skills.
- Discover different forms of communication.
- Develop an action plan to improve your communication skills.

> *"He understands badly who listens badly."*
> — *Welsh Proverb*

Social interaction is one of the most important skills in life. This chapter will explain the difference between good and bad communication. It will help you and your children assess your communication skills, discover different forms of communication and learn how to use them. You will also be asked to give five examples of poor communication and learn how to improve these interactions. This chapter will, ultimately, improve your family's social skills and enable you and your children to develop excellent communication skills.

EFFECTIVE COMMUNICATION SKILLS

Communication can be your best friend or your worst enemy—you get to choose its role. If you take the time and trouble to develop effective communications skills, this will unlock many doors for your future success. This will allow you to excel in innumerable situations, both business and personal. This will also hold true for your children and will also greatly enhance their social skills.

Communication is not "I talk—you talk." **Communication is "You talk, I listen. I talk, you listen."** Without listening, there is no understanding; and without understanding, communication is pointless. The following are just a few skills associated with being a good communicator. As you read through them, see how you can use these qualities in your family life. Think about ways you and your children can use these communication skills:

1) Motivate people to take action.
2) Build cooperation and trust.

3) Maintain focus on the issues.
4) Provide accurate information.
5) Prevent communication breakdowns.

Communication Skill 1: Motivate people to take action.

A good communicator has the ability to guide people in the proper direction and motivate them to take action on an issue that is relevant to them.

Life-coaching tip: Realize that you can be an inspiration to others. Foster this talent by leading others to discover their own hidden strengths.

Communication Skill 2: Build cooperation and trust.

When you listen to a convincing point of view, you can be swayed in that direction. If you feel that you and your ideas are being listened to and taken seriously, you will begin to trust that person and will be more willing to cooperate with them.

Life-coaching tip: Give serious consideration to other people's ideas, but do not change your mind unless you are convinced that their plan is better. Having an open mind does not necessarily mean giving in.

Communication Skill 3: Maintain focus on the issues.

Avoid getting sidetracked when participating in group discussions. Stay focused on the issues. This is where your communication skills will come into play. Through good communication, you can keep the focus where it belongs and eliminate any extraneous discussions

Life-coaching tip: Learn to focus your attention on one thing at a time. This will help you retain the information received on one particular subject.

Communication Skill 4: Provide accurate information.

By being a good communicator, you are able to gather information that contains accurate facts. You can then transmit this knowledge to others so that rumors and false data are not spread.

Life-coaching tip: Become a fact checker and eliminate many problems by knowing—through your own research—what the truth really is.

Communication Skill 5: Prevent communication breakdowns.

A breakdown in communication occurs when one person does all the talking and the other is expected to do all the listening—there is no equal give and take. Your skills can keep the lines of communication open so that all parties can come to a satisfactory resolution.

Life-coaching tip: Be firm, but polite, when informing other parties that, although they have some worthwhile ideas, you would like to give your thoughts now—then do it.

☆ *A Real-Life Example of Using Communication Skills: Diane and Kim*

The most common source of friction between parents and children is a lack of communication. Communication is a difficult skill to learn within a family, but in order to work as a unit, it is necessary that all family members listen to each other.

When Diane and her daughter, Kim, entered my office, it was obvious they were not on the best of terms. As they took their seats, they left a lot of space between them. Diane looked frustrated and Kim was sullen. Kim slouched in her chair, folded her arms and stared at the floor.

I began with Diane and asked her to describe the problem she was having with Kim. She shrugged and said, "Nothing I say ever gets through to her. I tell her things over and over, and she just ignores me and does what she wants to do. I just can't get her to listen to me." As her mother spoke, Kim raised her head and rolled her eyes in an exaggerated motion. "Do you disagree with that, Kim?" I asked. "Boy, do I ever!" Kim said. "She says I don't listen to her, but she doesn't listen to me. I try to talk to her and explain stuff to her, but she doesn't pay any attention to me."

The complaints from Diane and Kim were exactly the same. Neither party was willing to listen to the other. Diane, as the parent, felt that she knew best and Kim, as the child, felt that her thoughts and opinions were ignored. Both individuals wanted to change the other, so neither listened.

We began by having communication sessions in my office. The first of those sessions focused on the issue of Kim staying home alone. She felt that, at twelve years old, she was old enough to stay home alone when her parents were out. Diane thought Kim was much too young and would not consider allowing it. At first, they sat and stared at each other, neither willing to talk. When they did begin to talk, Diane spoke non-stop at Kim. When she paused for breath, Kim would jump in and shout her opinion at her mother. It was then that I stepped in and helped them see that this pattern was the same one they always followed—it was unproductive. I then set some ground rules. The first rule was that one person spoke at a time while the other person listened. The second was that there would be no shouting at, talking over or interrupting the other person. Finally, the last rule was that each person must consider what the other was saying and not immediately dismiss it.

We began the session again, this time following the rules. At the end of the session, both mother and daughter had agreed that Kim would be permitted to stay alone for no longer than three hours at a time during the day, but not at night. They would try this for six months. After six months, they would review the situation and, if all had gone well, they would renegotiate another agreement.

We continued to practice communicating for the following six weeks. During that time, Diane and Kim were to practice the rules at home. Eventually, our sessions were changed to a monthly basis. After six months, they were able to discontinue counseling. Through this process, they learned the proper way to communicate.

By listening to each other with open minds, they grew closer and their entire relationship moved to a higher level of understanding.

The Three V's of Effective Communication

The responsibility for effective communication lies with both the speaker and the listener. The following guidelines will help you and your children ensure productive communication in all of your interactions.

Effective Communication "V" 1: Visual

Use appropriate eye contact.

- *Speaker:* Speak directly to the other person. Do not allow your eyes to wander around the room or settle on an object beyond the other party. Show, by looking at the listener, that he is the focus of your attention.
- *Listener:* Eye contact will confirm your attention to what the speaker has to say. It lets him know that you are interested and believe the statements have value.

Maintain the proper distance.

- *Speaker:* Keep a respectful distance from the party to whom you are speaking. Do not crowd or lean in too close. He might become uncomfortable and possibly feel threatened. Either of these situations can result in distraction, and the effectiveness of your speaking can be lost.
- *Listener:* Stay with the speaker. Just as your eyes should not wander around the room, neither should your body.

Words and facial expressions should match.

- *Speaker:* You would not say, "I'm sorry to hear about your problems" with a laugh in your voice, or, "I'm so happy for your success" in a flat, expressionless monotone. For maximum effect, let what you are saying reflect in your face.
- *Listener:* If the speaker is relating a serious concern, you should not be smiling or laughing; instead, you should be showing your respect for the words by the expression on your face.

Avoid distracting gestures.

- *Speaker:* Relax. Fidgeting, drumming your fingers on the table or any other mannerisms can be annoying to the listener and take attention away from the message you are attempting to convey. If you find that you have habits that are distracting, make it a point to rid yourself of them.
- *Listener:* The same bothersome gestures on your part can break the concentration of the speaker, in addition to giving the impression that you are bored and not paying attention.

Use proper posture.

- *Speaker:* Your posture reflects your attitude. To give the most weight to your words, you should assume an alert, tension-free stance, one that will hold the attention of your listener while giving you an air of confidence.
- *Listener:* Remain relaxed but focused on the words of the speaker. Nod from time to time, or give verbal clues such as "yes," or "I understand," to let the speaker know that you are listening.

The next two sets of guidelines refer particularly to the speaker and give rules for holding the attention of the listener and making your statements effective.

Effective Communication "V" 2: Vocal Qualities

Tone of voice

- How loud you speak must suit the circumstances of the conversation. Do not whisper so that the other person has a difficult time hearing, but do not use a loud and overbearing voice. A controlled, convincing tone will be most effective and reinforce your message.

Rate of speech

- Speak neither too quickly (causing the listener to miss much of what you say) nor too slowly (causing the listener to be bored). A smooth, even rate of speech is most relaxing, engaging and easy to understand.

Fluency

- The flow of your speech should be even, without any distracting filler words such as "um," "uh" or "like."

Inflection

- If the message you are delivering is exciting, let the inflection in your voice show it. If the news you are imparting is of a serious nature, show that in your voice.

Effective Communication "V" 3: Verbal

Use complete sentences

- Be articulate when expressing yourself. Always use complete sentences and avoid leaving your listener with a half-finished thought. Avoid using filler words.

Express ideas clearly

- Your main message should be expressed clearly, leaving no doubts about the intent of your words.

Avoid qualifiers

- Qualifiers weaken your statement. Phrases such as, "This probably isn't a good idea, but…" or "I'm not very good at this, but…" only serve to weaken the confidence you want to express.

AN ASSESSMENT OF YOUR COMMUNICATION SKILLS

Effective communicators must be able to utilize their skills in all areas of life. Communication in the workplace is essential for a well-run organization. In the home, effective communication sets the tone for fewer misunderstandings and more cooperation. In the classroom, utilizing effective communication ensures that your child will have a voice.

How well do you currently communicate? By answering the questions on the following pages, you should have an accurate idea of areas you and your child need to improve upon.

An Assessment for You as the Parent

The following assessment should be filled out by you, the parent, keeping your communication skills in mind.

Please circle always, sometimes or never for the following statements:

1. Raising my voice helps get my point across.	Always	Sometimes	Never
2. Instead of listening, I am busy composing my comments.	Always	Sometimes	Never
3. I do not say much, but I am known as a good listener.	Always	Sometimes	Never
4. I can usually sway people to my way of thinking.	Always	Sometimes	Never
5. I find my mind wandering when someone else speaks.	Always	Sometimes	Never
6. I often must repeat myself to be understood.	Always	Sometimes	Never
7. People pay attention if I monopolize the conversation.	Always	Sometimes	Never
8. It is better to interrupt than to lose my train of thought.	Always	Sometimes	Never

An Assessment for Your Child

The following assessment should be filled out by your child.

Please circle always, sometimes or never for the following statements:

1. Raising my voice helps get my point across.
   Always   Sometimes   Never

2. Instead of listening, I am busy composing my comments.
   Always   Sometimes   Never

3. I do not say much, but I am known as a good listener.
   Always   Sometimes   Never

4. I can usually sway people to my way of thinking.
   Always   Sometimes   Never

5. I find my mind wandering when someone else speaks.
   Always   Sometimes   Never

6. I often must repeat myself to be understood.
   Always   Sometimes   Never

7. People pay attention if I monopolize the conversation.
   Always   Sometimes   Never

8. It is better to interrupt than to lose my train of thought.
   Always   Sometimes   Never

Points of Discussion for You and Your Children

Statement 1: Raising my voice helps get my point across.

In this statement, you see the overbearing person who thinks that by talking over everyone else, she will be more effective. In fact, the exact opposite is true. No one likes to be preached to. There is no communication involved, because this person tends to overpower anyone who has a different opinion or who would just like to participate in the conversation. Instead of getting ideas across, this person's point will be lost because she will also lose the other people's interest and respect.

Statement 2: Instead of listening, I am busy composing my comments.

This statement shows disrespect for the speaker that will not go unnoticed. Focusing only on what you want to say and disregarding other people's opinions demonstrates that 1) you are a self-centered person who thinks your thoughts are the only ones of importance, and 2) you miss many good points because you are not paying attention.

Statement 3: I do not say much, but I am known as a good listener.

Although good listening skills are an important ingredient in communication, you are short-changing yourself and others when you keep your ideas to yourself. You need to learn to share your ideas and feelings in order to fully participate in the communication process.

Statement 4: I can usually sway people to my way of thinking.

Number four shows a good quality to possess if it is accomplished correctly. Do you sway people to your way of thinking by persuasive arguments, by talking over their attempts or by ignoring their ideas? If you can convince others to adopt your way of thinking through positive statements that prove your point of view, then you have a rare skill that should be expanded upon.

Statement 5: I find my mind wandering when someone else speaks.

If your answer to number five is "always," or even "sometimes," then you might have a problem with your ability to listen. Practice focusing when you find your mind beginning to wander. Bring it back immediately to the subject at hand. Exercise control over your thoughts by keeping them directed to a focus point, not allowing them to jump from topic to topic.

Statement 6: I often must repeat myself to be understood.

The goal of number six is to be able to answer "never." A good communicator projects her thoughts clearly, and in a manner that the listener can easily understand. If you need to repeat often, then you must learn how to be distinct and concise when conveying your message, so the listener understands immediately what point you are trying to make.

Statement 7: People pay attention if I monopolize the conversation.

When you monopolize a conversation, people will desert you in favor of someone who will include them in the discussion. The only people who will stay and listen are those who are too timid to risk hurting your feelings if they leave. Rather than holding their attention, you will be considered a bore to be avoided.

Statement 8: It is better to interrupt than to lose my train of thought.

Number eight will stop a conversation cold. It is extremely frustrating for people to talk when they are constantly interrupted. It also gives the impression that your thoughts are the only important ones. People who interrupt use the excuse that if they do not voice their opinions immediately, they will lose their train of thought. What they do not consider is that, by interrupting, they are causing the speaker to lose a train of thought, again giving the impression of seeing themselves and what they have to say as most important.

Some children tend to interrupt often, as a result of their excitement for learning about a subject. If this is the case with your child, teach him the virtue of writing down his thoughts about a topic. When the other person is finished speaking, your child can then refer to his notes.

Identifying Non-verbal Communication: An Essential Social Skill

Up to this point, the focus has been on the most obvious form of communication—verbal. It is now time to learn about non-verbal communication. We are surrounded by non-verbal communication each time we are with other people. A shrug of the shoulder, a crossed leg or playing with a strand of hair are all types of communication with which we need to become familiar. By reading these signs, you will have insight into the actual feelings of the people with whom you speak. If you can interpret the non-verbal cues, you can adjust the method of delivering your message and obtain the desired response from other people.

Non-verbal communication can be the key to helping you when you need to interact with others. If you can zero in on the attitude of the person you are speaking to, you can prevent a lot of misunderstandings and hard feelings. Reading non-verbal clues can turn any opportunity into a win-win situation.

The following are some non-verbal gestures that convey certain unspoken judgments, behaviors or perceptions that others may be thinking or feeling. Recognizing these in yourself and others will make you a more effective communicator:

1) Openness
2) Defensiveness
3) Evaluation
4) Suspicion
5) Insecurity
6) Willingness to cooperate
7) Confidence
8) Nervousness
9) Frustration

Non-verbal Gesture 1: Openness

If you are aware that the people you are speaking to are willing to listen to you, then half the battle is already won. It takes much of the pressure off of you, and you can concentrate on your message, rather than getting and keeping their attention. Signs of openness include open hands or an unbuttoned coat. These show that people are willing to listen with an open mind.

Non-verbal Gesture 2: Defensiveness

When people come into a room feeling as though they or their ideas are going to be attacked, they will exhibit signs of defensiveness as a protection against your possible blow. If you notice defensive behaviors in others, you will have to work hard to assure them of your sincerity and openness to their opinions. A defensive person might cross his arms on his chest, sit with crossed legs, make fist-like gestures or use pointing motions.

Non-verbal Gesture 3: Evaluation

Most people have experienced a time when they wondered if the person talking to them knew what they were talking about. Unfortunately, this is not a one-way street, and you can be assured that people will evaluate your speech and knowledge as well. If your listeners place their hand to their face, tilt their head or stroke their chin, they are evaluating you. If they peer over their glasses, take them off and clean them or place the earpiece in their mouth, they are evaluating you. If they put their hand to the bridge of their nose, you are being evaluated. Have your facts straight and know your subject well enough to come out on the high end of the evaluation.

Non-verbal Gesture 4: Suspicion

Occasionally, when you present an idea contrary to popular beliefs, you are viewed with suspicion and must earn respect and trust. Crossed arms, sideways glances, touching or rubbing the nose, rubbing eyes and buttoning the coat (an indication of drawing away) are all clues that you are being viewed with suspicion. Gain trust by allaying fears and speaking in a confident manner. Be able to answer questions truthfully and with authority.

Non-verbal Gesture 5: Insecurity

It is difficult for people who are insecure to become full participants in any discussion. They need to be handled in a particular way and drawn into the conversation through encouragement to ask questions and voice their opinions. At times, these are the people who have the best ideas, but are too insecure to state them. You need to assure these people that their thoughts have value and will be considered. To spot an insecure person, look for those who pinch their flesh, chew on a pen or pencil or rub thumb over thumb. They may also bite their fingernails or keep their hands in their pockets.

Non-verbal Gesture 6: Willingness to cooperate

There is nothing more heartening to a speaker than to sense that the audience, whether it is one person or a group of people, is ready to cooperate and be receptive to what he has to say. Knowing you have a cooperative audience allows you the freedom to relax, and this relaxation gives you a more sincere and confident appearance. Cooperative listeners will lean forward, similar to a sprinter's position. Their hands will be open, and they may be sitting on the edge of the chair. They will use hand-to-face gestures, tilt their head or unbutton their coat.

Non-verbal Gesture 7: Confidence

Whether you are the speaker or the listener, there are signs to watch for that can help you determine the confidence of others. Confident people may sit with their hands together, fingers forming a steeple. They may stand with their hands behind their back or with their back stiffened. Watch for the position of the hands in a coat pocket; if the thumbs are out, you are in the presence of a confident person.

Non-verbal Gesture 8: Nervousness

Knowing whether or not you are relating to a nervous person can be a big advantage to you. Nervousness manifests itself in a number of ways. Nervous people may clear their throat, whistle or pick or pinch their flesh. They may tug at their slacks while seated, jingle money in their pockets, tug at an ear or wring their hands. If you observe any of these clues, you can advance your cause by putting them at ease and assuring them that there is no need for nervousness.

Non-verbal Gesture 9: Frustration

Frustration makes a worthwhile conversation impossible. If you notice other people becoming frustrated, you need to slow down, take a deep breath and listen with an open mind to what they have to say. You can tell if they are frustrated if they take short breaths, have tightly clenched hands, wring their hands or make fist-like gestures. They may also point the index finger, rub their hand through their hair or rub the back of their neck.

Ask, Listen and Learn

There are times when the best way to gain insight into the thoughts of another person is to ask a relevant question, then wait for the answer before going on to the next question.

Life-coaching tip: Never feel that your question will be considered silly or that you will be perceived as unintelligent. The opposite is true; it is the intelligent person who asks questions that will further his knowledge.

☆ *Asking, Listening and Learning in the Family*

The following is an example of dialogue between a father and his son.

> *Father:* I know you're upset because I won't allow you to go to Stanley's party on Saturday night. Do you know why I'm refusing permission?
> *Son:* Yeah, you think I'll get into trouble.
> *Father:* Why would I think that?
> *Son:* Oh, I guess it's because there was some problem at the last party he threw.
> *Father:* What was the problem?
> *Son:* Oh, you know, because a couple of guys drank. But I'm not gonna do that.
> *Father:* Why do you think you won't drink at the party?
> *Son:* 'Cause I know better. I won't let them push me into it again.
> *Father:* You said, "again." Have they pushed you into things before?
> *Son:* Well, maybe once or twice.

Father: Why would this time be different? Didn't you believe last time that you could resist their pressure?

Son: Yes, and I almost did.

Father: If you couldn't resist the peer pressure before, why do you believe you can now?

Son: I think I can try.

Father: But what if you fail?

Son: Then I'd get into a lot of trouble, especially since I'd have the car.

Father: Do you believe it's worth taking the chance?

Son: No, I guess I'll hang out with Jim and the gang instead.

Note that the father's questions allowed his son to think the problem through and reason for himself. **By asking the proper questions, you can open the door to understanding.** Another instance in which this type of questioning can be utilized is if your daughter makes a statement like, "My teacher always sides with the other person if I'm in an argument." Some of the questions you might ask her are:

- "What's an example of that?"
- "Why did you feel that your teacher took the other side?"
- "Do you feel that your teacher doesn't like you?"
- "When was the last time this occurred?"
- "Why do you think this has happened?"

By urging your children to think about and verbalize their beliefs, you can help them better understand and change those beliefs that might be false. There are many forms of communication, and not all methods work in all situations. The above examples are a form of communication that helps the person examine his own belief system and discover the flaws that lead to unhappiness and misunderstanding.

Improving Social Skills Using the Seven Rules of Communication

The following rules will help improve your communication skills, opening the door to better social skills:

1) Have patience.
2) Keep your answers simple.
3) Avoid technical terms when possible.
4) Define any technical terms you must use.
5) Never be too busy to explain something.
6) Never make anyone feel stupid for asking questions.
7) Answer only questions that are asked of you.

Communication Rule 1: Have patience.

When you are asked a question, you must realize that although the answer may be obvious to you, it is not obvious to everyone. If it were, they would not have asked you in the first place. Whether it is an employee asking about the company policy or a child asking about the proper way to set the table, take your time and answer in such a way that they are satisfied and understand your answer.

Communication Rule 2: Keep your answers simple.

Answers that become involved not only confuse the issue, but also overload the listener with more information than he can process at one time. Follow the old saying that tells you, "When someone asks you what time it is, don't tell him how the watch was made." Too much information can discourage the person from asking a question the next time he does not understand something.

Communication Rule 3: Avoid technical terms when possible.

Your answers cannot be understood if the language you use is over the heads of your listeners. Remember the age and/or experience level of those you are trying to reach. Use terms that may seem oversimplified, but will make perfect sense to them. It does not solve anything if your answer is not understood.

Communication Rule 4: Define any technical terms you must use.

Never assume that your listener knows all the proper names for items or situations. Long explanations with unfamiliar names will cause your listener to give up before they even begin to grasp the meaning of your answer. If you stop often and ask, "Do you have any questions? Do you understand what that term means?" you will have the opportunity to educate as well as provide information.

Communication Rule 5: Never be too busy to explain something.

Time is one of the most valuable commodities we have, and to give of your time to help another by providing an explanation will be appreciated by them. If someone has a question but it is not a convenient time for you, tell him to come back later when you are less busy. Give him the impression that he is important and you want to help him.

Communication Rule 6: Never make anyone feel stupid for asking questions.

If you make others feel bad for asking questions, you will immediately close the door to further communication. A better way to handle the questions is be to use comments such as, "That's a good question and I'm glad you asked it," or, "I used to wonder about that myself." Comments such as these will encourage others to continue to question and grow, and the line of communication between you both will be a good one.

Communication Rule 7: Answer only questions that are asked of you.

Giving the whole picture will only cause confusion. If your child asks, "Mommy, where did I come from?" he may only want to know what part of the world he was born in. Imagine his confusion if you go into a detailed explanation of the entire reproductive process from start to finish. If a new employee asks, "What happens when you press this button?" An answer of, "It summons the guard" is better than a detailed description of the company's security system. If a friend asks where you went on vacation this summer, don't recount every summer vacation you've ever taken.

CONSTRUCTIVE CRITICISM AS A COMMUNICATION TOOL

Criticism that is meant to be constructive can often end up being destructive. You might be too quick to jump in and "help," and not take the time to fully understand the situation or take into account the effect your words can have on the recipient. Before offering critical advice, ask yourself the following questions:

- Do I always look for what others do wrong rather than what they do right?
- Do I use my own preconceived ideas as criteria for what is right and wrong?
- Do my comments provide helpful guidelines for future actions?
- Will my comments improve the situation in any way?
- What will my comments do to our working relationship?
- Is the other party seeking improvement or will my comments anger him?
- Has he heard similar criticism before and not made any changes?
- Why would my advice have more weight than what he heard previously?
- Would praise be more effective in this case?
- Would a problem-solving technique be of more use in this situation than criticism?

If, after weighing the answers to the above questions, you still feel that criticism is an appropriate way to take care of a situation, be extremely careful of how you go about it. Using criticism as a form of communication can be dangerous and must be used with extreme care.

THE WRITTEN WORD

We have discussed verbal communication, as well as non-verbal communicative signs and gestures. You will now learn about the third type of communication—the written word.

Each piece of mail that we receive or send is an interchange with another person. Every interoffice memo or note to a friend tells something about us and about the way we relate to others. Correspondence has the same qualities as a verbal exchange; it can be approving or disapproving, praise or criticize, show warmth or coldness and can be constructive or destructive.

It has often been said that you should never put anything in writing that you would not want the world to see. Keep this in mind when you are composing a written message. Choose your words carefully. Remember that the person reading your letter cannot see your face, and it is difficult to judge if you are serious or making a joke. Many misunderstandings have occurred because a writer thought he was being funny and the reader took it as a serious matter. Before putting words to paper (or computer) imagine the reaction of the person who receives your message. Remember, too, that written correspondence is often shared with others, so never write anything to anyone that you would not want someone else to see.

AN EXERCISE FOR IMPROVING COMMUNICATION SKILLS

Since communication is such an important part of our lives, it is time to work on a plan to improve your communication skills in any way possible. This plan will be two-fold and will involve you and your children.

The first part of the following assignment will be a life-coaching tool for you, the parent, to complete by yourself. In the first row of the first worksheet below, list a situation in which you feel you could have communicated better. Then, list ways that your communication affected others around you. Finally, in the last row, list ways you could have communicated better in those situations. Repeat this for a few situations. Once you have completed your worksheet, take a look at it and see if there are any common trends throughout. By doing this, you prepare yourself to recognize a similar situation in the future and thus be able to communicate more effectively, utilizing your newly acquired communication skills.

For the second part of the assignment, have your child fill out the next worksheet in a similar way. Before he does so, make sure he understands what to do. There are examples in the worksheets that will help you and your child brainstorm some of your own ideas. When your child is done completing his worksheet, talk to him about what he wrote. See if he can notice any common trends in the way he reacts to situations and the way he communicates with others. Review the ways that lack of communication affected others around him, and ask him to tell you how he thinks that might have made others feel. Finally, review the improvements he listed. Again, by doing this, you are coaching your child and preparing him to recognize similar situations in the future and to ensure better communication skills for those situations.

Improving My Communication Skills
(to be completed by the parent)

Situation in Which I Could Have Communicated Better:

Example: Raised my voice when telling my wife to pick up the kids from school.

How My Communication Affected Others:

Wife got defensive and started yelling at me.

Ways I Can Improve My Communication in Future Situations:

Don't yell; speak calmly.

Situation in Which I Could Have Communicated Better:

_____

_____

How My Communication Affected Others:

_____

_____

Ways I Can Improve My Communication in Future Situations:

_____

Situation in Which I Could Have Communicated Better:

How My Communication Affected Others:

Ways I Can Improve My Communication in Future Situations:

Situation in Which I Could Have Communicated Better:

How My Communication Affected Others:

Ways I Can Improve My Communication in Future Situations:

Improving My Communication Skills
(to be completed by the child)

Situation in Which I could Have Communicated Better:

Example: Yelled at my little sister and demanded that she get out of my room.

How My Communication Affected Others:

Little sister cried and ran to her room.

Ways I Can Improve My Communication in Future Situations:

Ask her to leave my room calmly. If that doesn't work, ask for mom or dad's help.

Situation in Which I could Have Communicated Better:

_____

_____

How My Communication Affected Others:

_____

_____

Ways I Can Improve My Communication in Future Situations:

_____

_____

Situation in Which I could Have Communicated Better:

_____

How My Communication Affected Others:

_____

_____

Ways I Can Improve My Communication in Future Situations:

_____

_____

Situation in Which I could Have Communicated Better:

_____

_____

How My Communication Affected Others:

_____

_____

Ways I Can Improve My Communication in Future Situations:

_____

_____

SUMMARY OF CHAPTER NINE

Many conversations are sabotaged either by one who monopolizes the talk or by one who is so involved with thinking about her next comment that she fails to listen to the speaker. In this chapter, you learned that communication is not a one-way street where one person does all of the talking. Rather, it is an effort by both parties to talk and listen. This reciprocal process has been a major component of becoming a life-coach to your child. It has not been a one-way conversation in which you do all the talking or lecturing and your child does all the listening. Instead, it is now an exchange of thoughts, feelings and ideas between you and your child.

You and your children have had an opportunity to assess your communication skills in order to discover any areas that you need to improve upon. You learned that verbal communication is not the only way we interact with one another. You have learned how to read non-verbal signs and signals and, in that way, better your own social skills. The written word is another form of communication that is sometimes overlooked. Your exact verbal message may be forgotten over time, but what you write lasts for many years and can be seen by many who were not the intended recipient of your message. A wise person will put much thought into what they place on paper or computer.

Finally, you were asked to ponder instances in which communication failed and discover what could have been done or said differently to achieve a better outcome and avoid misunderstandings.

☆ Think of five instances this week in which I could have communicated better.

☆ Be aware of my listening skills and work toward improvement.

☆ Have a conversation in which I use good communication skills.

Chapter Ten

CONFLICT AND PROBLEM-SOLVING

Monitoring and Modifying You and Your Children's Coping Methods

CHAPTER OBJECTIVES:

- Learn how proper conflict resolution can equal success.

- Do an assessment of you and your child's reactions to conflict.

- Through personal life-coaching, learn alternative methods of handling conflict.

- Discover what your children learn from your behavior during conflict situations.

- Develop a family conflict-resolution plan.

"The best way to escape from a problem is to solve it."
— *Brendan Francis*

How your children cope with the fluctuations of life is in large part determined by your reactions to problems. In this chapter, I will show you how proper conflict resolution can equal success. You and your children will do an assessment of your reactions to conflict. By using a life-coaching approach, you and your children will discover the secrets to handling conflict. You will also discover what your child learns from your behavior during conflicts. Finally, you and your family will develop a conflict-resolution plan.

YOUR CHILDREN AND CONFLICT

Children are faced with the issue of solving problems from the moment they are born. It takes an extremely short time for infants to realize that if they cry, they will be fed or cuddled. As children get older and journey into adulthood, their problems become larger. How will they cope with the challenges they face on a daily basis? Will they storm off to their room, slam the door or pout? Will throwing a tantrum get the sought-after results? Or, will your children become bullies and take what they want without regard for anyone else? How your children react to adversity throughout life depends on the methods you employ to solve problems.

Before you can teach your children to face the difficulties they may encounter, you must be able to face these same difficulties. Every relationship, whether business or personal (employer/employee, husband/wife or parent/child), will encounter times when ideas differ, personalities clash or miscommunication results in conflict. When we speak of parents and children, it is a sure thing that there will be disagreements and conflicts. Not all conflicts, however, have a negative effect. If a resolution is achieved utilizing proper methods of problem-solving, the encounter will become a positive learning experience for all concerned.

Children's lives involve daily conflicts with siblings, parents and friends. They are confronted constantly with new situations. In addition to the struggles of family life, they have school to contend with and the challenge of getting along with classmates. This stage of life is not easy, but if they have training in conflict resolution, as well as love and understanding at home, they will make it through.

The following assessments will help you recognize both you and your children's current styles of conflict resolution.

AN ASSESSMENT FOR YOU AS THE PARENT

The following assessment should be filled out by you, the parent.

Circle the answers that best reflect your responses to the statements below:

1. When someone is hostile toward me, I tend to:
   a) Respond angrily
   c) Take the abuse
   b) Use persuasion
   d) Walk away

2. When addressing others during a serious conflict, I tend to:
   a) Shout
   c) Listen actively
   b) Listen a little
   d) Apologize

3. When I'm involved in an unpleasant confrontation, I:
   a) Use sarcasm
   c) Use humor related to myself
   b) Occasionally joke
   d) Use no humor

4. Following a serious conflict, I:
   a) Settle things my way
   c) Worry, but hide it
   b) Negotiate an outcome
   d) Let it go

---

5. Others tell me that when I'm faced with conflict, I:

    a) Fight for my way   b) Show cooperation

    c) Am easygoing   d)Avoid confrontation

6. When I'm involved in a dispute, I generally:

    a) Sway others   b) Use logic

    c) Compromise   d) Back down

AN ASSESSMENT FOR YOUR CHILD

The following assessment should be filled out by your child.

Circle the answers that best reflect your responses to the statements below:

1. When someone is hostile toward me, I tend to:

    a) Respond angrily

    b) Use persuasion

    c) Take the abuse

    d) Walk away

2. When addressing others during a serious conflict, I tend to:

    a) Shout

    b) Listen a little

    c) Listen actively

    d) Apologize

3. When I'm involved in an unpleasant confrontation, I:

    a) Use sarcasm

    b) Occasionally joke

    c) Use humor related to myself

    d) Use no humor

4. Following a serious conflict, I:

    a) Settle things my way

    b) Negotiate an outcome

    c) Worry, but hide it

    d) Let it go

5. Others tell me that when I'm faced with conflict, I:

    a) Fight for my way

    b) Show cooperation

    c) Am easygoing

    d) Avoid confrontation

6. When I'm involved in a dispute, I generally:

    a) Sway others

    b) Use logic

    c) Compromise

    d) Back down

Analyzing You and Your Children's Responses

Once you and your children have completed the assessments, take a look at your sets of responses. Which responses are more predominant in your style of reacting to conflict? For example, do you often back down and avoid confrontation at all costs? Do you give in while compromising your own needs? Or, do you usually settle things your own way, regardless of the other person's feelings or desires? If you have a tendency to react to conflict using these types of unproductive methods, then you may consider altering your conflict-resolution style.

More productive methods of conflict resolution include using logic and compromise, while actively listening and cooperating so that both parties can be satisfied with the outcome.

You may notice a difference in how you and your children responded to the above assessments. As a life-coach to your children, you can begin to help them by recognizing how they respond to conflict. You can also help them find ways to alter their unproductive resolution styles. Later in this chapter, you will discover the secrets of productive conflict resolution.

HELPING YOUR CHILD WITH CONFLICT RESOLUTION USING A LIFE-COACHING APPROACH

How do you and your children resolve disagreements? Being able to resolve conflicts is a necessary skill in life. However, there are some unproductive behavior patterns that inhibit people's abilities to successfully resolve conflict. Those unproductive behavior patterns are:

1) Dominance
2) Avoidance
3) Self-pity
4) "Mr. Nice Guy"
5) Temper Tantrum

Below are descriptions and examples of these behavior types. Do any of these behaviors remind you of the way you or your children resolve conflict? Remember your answers to the previous assessments and see if you or your children fall into any of these behavior types. Discuss these behaviors with your children and make sure they understand them, using the examples to help illustrate the points. After reading through each behavior, have a discussion with your children about how that behavior is unproductive. Have your children come up with their own examples of that behavior, as well as alternatives to that behavior that would better resolve the conflict. This will help optimize your ability to turn a conflict into a win-win situation.

Behavior 1: Dominance

Communication is a two-way street; it consists of listening as well as speaking. A dominant person must have his way and will demand it, disregarding other people's feelings and desires. Dominant behavior will only push people away from you. No one wants to be around a bully or someone who always has to have it his way. You may get what you want initially by being dominant, but how far will that get you?

Bringing it home:
If your impressionable six-year-old sees that daddy gets his way by being stern and bullying mommy, his mind will unite the two, and that will become his method of getting what he wants. Imagine this same child is aware that there is a difference of opinion and sees mommy and daddy discussing fair compromises. Rather than observing a dominant approach, instead he hears a calm tone of voice and sees his parents resolve the conflict amicably. What does this do for his conflict-resolution model? He begins to associate reasoning with resolution, and, without even realizing it, he has learned a valuable lesson in successful negotiation.

Behavior 2: Avoidance

Being around conflict can be very upsetting to many people, and, therefore, they will go to any lengths to avoid it. However, running away from conflict is only a temporary patch. By discussing ways you can help resolve conflict, rather than avoiding it, you will achieve a more permanent solution.

Bringing it home:

Let's say that thirteen-year-old Susie comes home from school one day and informs you that she's going on a date. Not just a date, but a party with a boy four years older than she is, and she intends to stay out past midnight. Before you can say anything, your husband, Bob, begins to yell and scream that she certainly is not going on this date. You can feel your stomach begin to tighten up into a familiar knot while the shouting match continues between Bob and Susie.

Your first instinct is to leave the house until it is over, as you have done every other time Bob and Susie argue, giving Susie the impression that if you walk away from a disturbing situation, it will go away. Instead, you force yourself to remain calm and start to discuss the matter with Bob and Susie. This, in turn, has a favorable effect on them and they cease shouting. You ask Bob to give his reasons for refusing to allow Susie's date. He cites good, sound reasons and the more he talks, the more Susie slumps in her chair. You then ask Bob to listen while Susie gives her reasons for her actions. Susie is pleased that she can speak and be heard. It turns out that she had asked permission a week before to attend another party with a boy in her class where she would be home by 11 p.m., but consent was refused. She adopted this attitude in retaliation. After thinking it over, Bob admits that Susie is growing up and needs a little more freedom, and Susie admits that her father has valid reasons for being upset about her date with an older boy.

With your help, they compromise; Bob agrees to listen more often to Susie's reasoning, and Susie agrees to follow the rules laid down for her. Susie learns that running away solves nothing. By sitting down and talking things over in a placid manner, they got to the heart of the issue, and everyone was happy with the result; a real resolution was reached, and Susie's relationship with her father improved tremendously.

Behavior 3: Self-pity

There is a time in our lives when we must stop resorting to tears. Don't feel sorry for yourself or try to have others feel sorry for you. Self-pity will get you nowhere. No one wants to be around someone who has a defeatist attitude. As an adult, you must take full responsibility for your actions. If that means you need to apologize for what you have or have not done, do it and let the issue be finished.

Bringing it home:
Gloria, your eight-year-old, has never gotten over using tears and self-pity when confronted with a wrongdoing or while trying to get out of chores. You see what is happening and it bothers you; however, when you think about it, you realize that she is modeling her behavior after you. You make a concentrated effort to change for Gloria's sake.

One day, your sister, Paula, is visiting and she tells you that she took your mother shopping—again. Paula goes on to say that this was to be a shared duty, each alternating weeks, but you have not taken your turn for a month. Paula begins to get agitated; it is obvious that this is a sore spot with her. You can feel the tears stinging your eyes, and your brain is developing the story of how you've had so much work lately that you just could not do it. You think to remind her that you have taken mom for her last few visits to the doctor, so you feel you have done your duty. You notice, however, that Gloria is watching you. You manage to keep the tears from falling and your voice from trembling as you say, "I'm sorry, Paula. I have been very busy and you've had to handle everything. Thank you for doing that and I promise to take my turn in the future. Just to make sure I don't mess up again, will you call me the day before to remind me?"

Gloria has seen you apologize. She noted that you did not resort to tears and, instead, admitted being wrong. Talking with Gloria after Paula leaves, explaining to her why your response was better than tears, will be more effective because she actually witnessed these actions for herself.

Behavior 4: "Mr. Nice Guy"

Do you always play Mr. Nice Guy? While being a good person is an excellent attribute to possess, there also comes a time when you must stand up for yourself and what you believe in. **You can't please everyone all of the time.** Sometimes you will have to say no or tell someone something he doesn't want to hear. Although you may not win a popularity contest at that moment, you will win respect in the future because you stood up for what you believed in.

Bringing it home:
When it comes to the home, you cannot always be Mr. Nice Guy. As parents, we have all had to say no to our children at times. Often we are met with the response, "But Jimmy's parents let him do it. You're mean not to let me do it too!" This is always difficult. As parents, we naturally want our children to love us, respect us and be our friend; however, you must remember that you are not your child's buddy. You are his parent, and you have the knowledge which allows you to decide what is good or bad for him.

It is good to talk to your children when you make decisions. Explain that the right choice is not always the popular choice, but because you are the parent, you know what is best in that particular instance. Open communication is vital; do not ever say, "Because I'm the parent, that's why," and end the conversation. Instead say, "Because I'm your mother/father, I know this would not be good for you because..." Never shut your children out; listen to them, let them air their thoughts and feelings and keep an open mind. However, if you are convinced you must say no, do not back down.

Behavior 5: Temper Tantrums

Do you get what you want through tantrums? Temper tantrums only increase your blood pressure and give you the reputation of being a difficult person to be around. If you don't get your way, don't throw a tantrum. Instead, talk things through with the others involved to come up with an amicable solution.

Bringing it home:
Does throwing a temper tantrum get your children what they want? Are you enabling them in this behavior by giving in to avoid an unpleasant scene? If your child runs to his room and slams the door, give him fifteen minutes to cool down before going in to him. If he lies on the floor and kicks his feet, walk away from him. If he has no audience, he will stop. Later, go back to him and talk. If he begins to act up again, walk away again. He will learn that if he wants your attention, he has to stop carrying on. Always talk with him and find out what is behind the behavior. Let him know that you love him and will listen to him, and do it. If he wants to talk to you, do not put him off with, "I'm busy now." **Make time for your children, because the best gift you can give your children is time.**

A Practical Scenario

The following is a practical scenario to share with your children. The example shows a possible conflict between friends. At the end of the scenario are some extreme examples of negative responses from each of the unproductive behaviors we just reviewed. Discuss with your children why they think these behaviors are unproductive. Brainstorm positive resolutions with them.

You and two friends are planning an afternoon at the movies. One friend wants to see the latest romantic comedy, and the other wants to see the new action film. You really want to see the new horror flick. The discussion soon becomes heated and you find the tension rising. What happens next?

Dominance: You tell your friends that you want to see the horror flick and that you're going to go see it whether they like it or not.

Avoidance: You make an excuse to leave the room and read a magazine while your friends argue. You completely avoid the conflict.

Self-Pity: With a pout on your face, you tell your friends, "Poor me. I never get my own way. I always have to give in to you. I suppose I have to do it your way."

Mr. Nice Guy: Although you really want to see the new horror flick, you don't voice your opinion because you don't want to be the bad guy. You want your friends to like and accept you, so you compromise your own feelings and desires.

Temper Tantrum: You begin to kick your feet, jumping up and down saying, "You guys are jerks. You're so stupid to want to see movies like that. You're always making me go places I don't want to go." You throw the movie schedule on the floor and start yelling at your friends some more.

Does any of this ring a bell? Do you recognize you or your child's reaction patterns in any of the above scenarios? If you do, it is time to work on your own method of dealing with conflict so you can help your child know how to act in situations in which he will encounter disagreements. **You can help no one until you help**

yourself. If you examine your response to conflict and see a pattern of dysfunctional reactions, the sooner you change, the sooner you will help yourself and, in turn, your children. By encouraging your children to recognize and examine some of their own dysfunctional reactions, you will be giving them a gift they can use throughout life.

Change is not easy, but if children are going to become successful adults, they must know how to properly handle conflicts. They may not realize it at the time, but they are depending on you to show them the way. It will be impossible to help your children in this area if you are lacking appropriate conflict-resolution behavior.

Sit down with your children and make up possible conflict scenarios of your own. Come up with productive and positive resolutions to those conflicts. The more practice they get, the more prepared they will be to handle conflicts when they arise. The problem-solving skills they will develop will prove invaluable within any work, social or academic setting.

INCORPORATING PROBLEM-SOLVING SKILLS INTO YOU AND YOUR CHILDREN'S LIVES

In both work life and personal life, there are skills we need to incorporate into our lives in order to prevent conflicts and solve problems. The essential skills to possess are to:

1) Use effective communication.
2) Avoid overreacting.
3) Eliminate confusion.
4) Identify and avoid disruptive behavior.
5) Use creativity and keep an open mind.

The following are explanations of the above problem-solving skills that will help you present yourself in the most favorable manner. These skills should also be reviewed with your children. An understanding of problem-solving skills will prepare your children for resolving conflicts throughout their lifetime. After reading through each of these skills, have a discussion with your children about how these skills can be incorporated into their lives.

Problem-Solving Skill 1: Use effective communication.

Any time there is a confrontation in the workplace, the fault can almost always be placed on miscommunication. Usually one person assumes the other knew exactly what a statement meant. Many managers give more responsibility to a promising new worker, only to have their hopes dashed if the worker fails to succeed at the task because he is unfamiliar with it. The manager needs to give clear, precise instructions, stopping after every few statements to ask, "Do you understand? Do you have any questions?" The worker needs to listen very carefully and ask about anything that is unclear. If both parties fully understand what is involved, the chance for success skyrockets.

Bringing it home:

These same rules apply in the home. When you tell your ten-year-old son to mow the lawn for the first time, don't assume he knows what is expected of him. You must make clear what you want and how you want it done. Manager or employee, parent or child, everyone needs to learn a few basic rules of communication and practice using them until they become natural.

Give your children the same attention and courtesy you would give to a co-worker or an employee when communicating. Listen and pay attention to what your children have to say; do not dismiss their ideas without testing them for merit. Discuss any issues that could evolve into a conflict.

Some of the advantages your children will receive from using effective communication are:

- Gaining understanding that conflicts can be resolved through open, two-way communication
- Increased self-esteem because others are giving credence to their ideas
- Sharpened negotiation skills, leading the way to more effective communication and, in turn, more profitable interactions with others

- Rising leadership potential because they are not afraid to voice their opinions and will be known as good communicators and listeners

Problem-Solving Skill 2: Avoid overreacting.

It is important not to overreact when in conflict. Instead, redirect your energy in a positive light, turning something potentially destructive into something constructive. An unexpressed emotion is similar to a small cut on the finger; if left alone, it will become infected and fester. When you hold emotions inside and do not express what you are feeling, the emotions can take over and overwhelm you. What may have begun as a mild annoyance becomes a major concern; this can result in overreacting. Do not let all of your emotions build up. Discuss your feelings when you are calm. If possible, wait twenty-four hours before you react to a highly emotional issue. In the meantime, write down your thoughts and feelings so that you can discuss them once you've calmed down.

Bringing it home:

Teach your children that they have a voice within the family. They do not need to keep their emotions inside until they feel like exploding. The family unit is the first and primary source for learning how to handle emotions. The methods children learn from their family about reacting to situations will be carried with them through adulthood.

By learning not to overreact, some of the advantages your children will receive are:

- Realizing that hiding their feelings only worsens physical and emotional issues
- Increased ability to understand others and relate to the emotions others express because they know feelings are okay
- Feeling relaxed and confident in themselves because they are free to express their emotions

Problem-Solving Skill 3: Eliminate confusion.

Confusion can leave arguments deadlocked with no chance of resolution. In the heat of any conflict, accusations may be addressed that have no bearing at all on the present situation. Additionally, each time we become engaged in a dispute, we are quick to label the other person as the problem. This immediately shifts the focus of the confrontation to the person and away from the actual problem. When in a conflict, diffuse anger by insisting that everyone concentrate on the initial problem and put aside any extraneous issues. This can sometimes be a difficult task but a worthwhile one in the end.

Bringing it home:

Teach your children by word and example how to stick to the issues at hand in order to avoid confusion. For example, if your children begin to argue with each other about what television program to watch and then quickly change the argument into something like, "He ripped the head off of my Barbie last week" or, "She threw my toy car out the window yesterday," it confuses the situation at hand. Pretty soon, no one knows what the original argument was about. If you see your children get sidetracked, remind them to stay focused on the issues at hand. This skill requires patience and tact; however, through constant practice, children can learn to focus on the immediate problem and keep it from getting out of hand.

Some of the advantages your children will receive from eliminating confusion are:

- Eliminating conflicts that get sidetracked with unrelated information
- Using logic to make important decisions
- Mastering the ability to maintain focus and attention on the task at hand

Problem-Solving Skill 4: Identify and avoid disruptive behavior.

Anyone who engages in behavior that we consider difficult is doing so for a reason. It is up to us to discover what that underlying reason is before we can take steps to resolve an issue. The big question we need to ask is why. Put yourself in the place of the person you consider difficult and ask yourself, *Why is he acting like this? What is he getting out of it?*

Studies have shown that when a person is rewarded for any type of behavior, that reward acts as reinforcement to continue along the same path. So what is the reward this particular individual is receiving from acting in such a manner? Determine if this is a one-time occurrence or if the difficult behavior is habitual. It is possible that the individual enjoys the attention he receives from acting that way, or he may feel it is the only way of getting his point across.

Bringing it home:

Teach your children the skills necessary to recognize if they or someone they know habitually uses explosive behavior to get their way. This will allow them to reflect on their own ways of behaving and recognize others' behavior, whether exhibited by their siblings, friends or classmates. **Remember, you cannot change other people's behavior, but you can change the way you react to their behavior.**

Notice the way your children handle conflict. Do they behave a certain way to get what they want? Do they whine or throw tantrums to get their way? Teach your children to take into account all of the different personalities and styles of dealing with conflict in your family.

If one child in your family utilizes disruptive behavior, try to get to the bottom of things to see why he might be doing so. Talk to him one-on-one, not in front of the entire family. Ask him what he is gaining by behaving that way. Ask him how he would feel if others acted that way. Speak in generalities at first. For example, you can say something like, "When I don't get my way, I sometimes feel like jumping up and down and screaming. Do you ever feel that way?" This will encourage your child to open up and express his innermost feelings. Behind every behavior, there is often a core reason for that behavior.

Some of the advantages your children will receive from knowing how to identify disruptive behavior are:

- Thinking before they react
- Adjusting their response patterns accordingly because they are able to recognize others' predominant ways of reacting
- Showing more empathy because they will understand reasons behind others' disruptive behavior

Problem-Solving Skill 5: Use creativity and keep an open mind.

It is a rare individual who can maintain an open mind when faced with a controversy and welcome ideas and solutions other than his own. A person who assumes and insists that his is the only solution is doomed for failure. The greatest asset an individual can bring to the table is an open mind.

Sometimes it takes the combined efforts of more than one person to get ideas flowing. Not all suggestions will be good, but they can lead to ideas and thoughts that will help determine the best outcome. The ideal situation is one in which, after a problem is recognized, all parties involved meet to brainstorm alternative methods of compromise.

Bringing it home:

Teach your children the importance of keeping an open mind in all situations. Show them how creativity leads to solutions. For example, if your children are arguing about who gets to choose the program on television, instead of having to decide that one child gets to pick the shows for the entire day, have them come up with creative solutions to this problem. A creative solution might be that one son gets to pick the show in the morning, while the other gets to pick the show in the evening. This solution satisfies both parties and makes for a happier family. It also shows them the importance of finding creative solutions to conflicts.

Some of the advantages your children will receive from using creativity and keeping an open mind are:

- Learning how to come up with creative solutions to problems
- Avoiding being stuck in a never-ending argument—instead knowing how to compromise using creative alternatives
- Discovering the importance of brainstorming various compromises before presenting their position to the other parties involved

A Practical Scenario

The following is a practical scenario to share with your children. The example shows a possible family conflict. At the end of the scenario are ways the problem-solving skills you learned above can be utilized to resolve the conflict amicably. You and your children should brainstorm other ways these problem-solving skills can be utilized in everyday life.

Your family is planning a two-week summer vacation. You sit down as a family to discuss the trip. Your ten-year old son wants to go hiking and fishing, but your fifteen-year-old daughter wants to go somewhere with a beach. Pretty soon, the argument gets heated, and the two kids are yelling at each other. They start bringing up old arguments, placing blame on each other, calling the other's ideas stupid, etc. They start throwing things at each other, and before you know it, the situation is out of control. How can your family use the skills they just learned to resolve this conflict and avoid arguments like this in the future?

Use effective communication: With all of the yelling, screaming and name-calling going on, the children didn't have a chance to really hear and understand what the other's ideas were. If each child makes his points clear to the other, without disruptions, an amicable resolution to the problem can be reached.

Avoid overreacting: Obviously, both children have their opinions and desires regarding this vacation. As a result, they are each overreacting by yelling and screaming. They're letting their emotions get the best of them. Without the overreacting, there would have been more clear and open communication, thus leading to a faster solution.

Eliminate confusion: By bringing up former arguments and unrelated things, it is only adding confusion to the situation. It is important to stay focused on the task at hand, which is to find a vacation spot that everyone will be pleased with.

Identify and avoid disruptive behavior: Yelling, blaming each other and throwing things is achieving nothing in this situation. Will that make the siblings agree on a vacation spot? No. It is only delaying the argument and adding fuel to the fire.

Use creativity and keep an open mind: Instead of arguing and insisting that theirs is the only solution, the children need to keep an open mind and get creative. Where can your family go on vacation for some summer fun on the beach, as well as outdoor activities, such as fishing and hiking? Have your children sit down with each other and brainstorm some places they can go to please both of them. How about Hawaii or the Caribbean, for example? Your son can go deep-sea fishing while your daughter tans on the deck of the boat or back at the hotel beach. No matter the outcome, having your children learn how to sit together to come up with a creative compromise is a lesson that they will use throughout their lives.

IMPROVING YOUR FAMILY'S PROBLEM-SOLVING SKILLS

You and your family must be ready to overcome certain hurdles if you are to be effective in your role as problem solvers. Before you all adjourn to your think tank, each person must make sure to invoke the Rule of the Five P's: Proper Preparation Prevents Poor Performance.

Prior to solving a problem, be sure to know what the problem is. Do not assume that all information you receive is accurate and valid. Check your sources and determine that they are reliable and that you have been given honest, unbiased information.

It is also important to determine exactly what outcome you are after. If your sons are fighting about who has to mow the lawn more often, what do you want to end up with? You probably want them to come up with a schedule. Have them brainstorm ways they can resolve this problem by coming up with a schedule that satisfies both parties. Know what you are aiming for, and reach for that goal.

If you teach your children the art of listening to one another's points of view and help them become adept at skillful negotiation and communication, you will have given them invaluable insights into achieving a successful life.

DEVELOPING YOUR FAMILY CONFLICT-RESOLUTION AND PROBLEM-SOLVING PLAN

If you and your family are to put what you have learned about yourselves in this chapter into good practice, you must have a conflict-resolution and problem-solving plan in place. Now I want you to sit down as a family to come up with a plan that you can use if problems or conflicts arise.

First, come up with a set of guidelines that you can use when you meet. Read the examples in the chart below and then have your family come up with your own guidelines for your meetings.

My Family's Guidelines

Examples: *Each family member will share his feelings and needs.*
Each family member's ideas are welcome.

_____

_____

_____

_____

_____

_____

_____

_____

_____

_____

_____

_____

Model Plan for Conflict Resolution and Problem-Solving:

Now that you've come up with some guidelines for your family meeting, I want you to come up with a plan that you can follow should a conflict arise in your family. Below is a model plan. Read through this plan, then modify it on the following pages to fit your family's needs:

- Assign different roles to family members (e.g., one person is moderator, one person records the meeting, one person writes down goals, etc.)
- State the problem/issue/conflict in writing.
- Write down each family member's suggested solutions.
- Come up with resolutions to the problem and write them down.
- Write down ways that the resolutions will be carried out.
- Follow up later on and write down the results of your hard work.

Model Family Plan for Conflict Resolution and Problem-Solving

Problem/Issue/Conflict

Example: *Family members complain they get stuck with the worst chores.*

Family Members' Solutions

Name of Person Proposing Solution:

Maria

Proposed Solution:

Make a rotating chart, so no one does the same chore two weeks in a row.

Ways This Can be Carried Out:

James will make a list of indoor chores. Rudy will list outdoor ones. Beth will design and decorate a chart.

Follow Up

Was this issue resolved?

Yes.

What, if anything, could have been done differently to better solve the problem?

We could have assigned teams of two family members to the unfavorable chores, so no one has to do the worst chores alone.

How did each family member help with this issue?

Maria proposed the solution, James and Rudy listed chores, Beth designed the rotating chart and Connor attached the chart to the refrigerator and filled in family members' names.

My Family's Plan for Conflict Resolution and Problem-Solving

Problem/Issue/Conflict

_____

_____

Family Members' Solutions

Name of Person Proposing Solution:

_____

Proposed Solution:

_____

_____

_____

Ways This Can be Carried Out:

_____

_____

_____

_____

Follow Up

Was this issue resolved?

_____

What, if anything, could have been done differently to better solve the problem?

_____

How did each family member help with this issue?

SUMMARY OF CHAPTER TEN

In this chapter, you learned that how we cope with the fluctuations of life is in large part determined by our reactions to problems or conflicts. You learned how proper conflict resolution can equal success. You and your children did an assessment of your reactions to conflict. You learned how to help your children with conflict resolution using a life-coaching approach and learning about unproductive behaviors. You also discovered methods of handling conflict and resolving problems. Finally, you and your family developed a conflict-resolution plan.

> ☆ Be a role model to my children when it comes to resolving conflicts.
>
> ☆ Effective conflict resolution can lead to success.
>
> ☆ Remember the Rule of the Five P's: Proper Preparation Prevents Poor Performance.
>
> ☆ Brainstorm with my family for new solutions to old problems.

Chapter Eleven

DISCIPLINARY STRATEGIES
Friend or Foe?

CHAPTER OBJECTIVES:

- Understand why children misbehave.
- Learn why discipline is necessary.
- Assess your current disciplinary strategies.
- Learn how to discipline your children properly.

"The secret cruelties that parents visit upon their children are past belief."
— *Dr. Karl A. Menninger*

In this chapter, you will learn why children misbehave and why discipline is necessary. You will assess your current strategies of discipline and discover the effects of improper discipline. You will then help your children develop appropriate self-discipline measures that will be invaluable throughout their lives. You will create a list of behavioral problems that your children currently face. You will then learn appropriate disciplinary methods for specific behavioral problems.

WHY DO CHILDREN MISBEHAVE?

There are many reasons why children misbehave. Below are some common reasons for misbehavior, followed by effective responses you can use to react to those behaviors.

Attention

Very often, misbehavior stems from a child trying to gain his parents' attention. When parents don't spend a lot of time around their children, they might see behavior problems develop. For example, if there is a new baby in the family, or if you travel on business often, you may notice that your child misbehaves; he may be trying to gain your attention, even if it is negative attention. Some effective responses to a child who misbehaves because he is trying to gain attention are:

- Ignore the inappropriate behavior.
- Give attention to the proper behavior.

- Redirect the child's behavior in a cooperative direction.
- Schedule some special one-on-one time with your child on a regular basis.

Revenge

Another reason for misbehavior could be revenge. If a child does not get his way, he might try to retaliate by misbehaving. If you give in to his improper behavior, then you are showing him that it is okay to fight back when he doesn't get his way. Be strong and be consistent; don't give in too easily. Some effective responses to a child who misbehaves because he is trying to get revenge are:

- Remain calm.
- Engage cooperation.
- Encourage kind behavior by redirecting your attention to positive tasks your child engages in.

Feelings of inadequacy

Some children's misbehavior stems from a low self-esteem or feelings of inadequacy. If a child is always compared to his sibling who is "perfect" in his parents' eyes, then he might feel like giving up. His attitude may become, "I can't do anything to please them anyway, so I might as well just do things my way." Some effective responses to a child who misbehaves because of feelings of inadequacy are:

- Stop all criticism immediately.
- Encourage all your children's efforts.
- Don't compare your children to their siblings or peers.
- Never give up on your children. Always look to encourage their strengths.

Power Struggle

Another reason for misbehavior could be a power struggle. If your child does something wrong, you may feel angry or provoked by his defiance, especially when your attempts to correct his behavior are unsuccessful. This could result in a power struggle between you and your child. The anger and frustration that both of you feel as a result just adds fuel to the fire. Some effective responses to a power struggle are:

- Withdraw from the struggle and give yourself time to cool down.
- Redirect your child's behavior in a cooperative direction.
- Act kindly, but firmly.
- Take a moment or two before deciding what action to take.

TOO MUCH OR TOO LITTLE?

So what should you do when your child misbehaves? When it comes to disciplining children, it is difficult for parents to find a happy medium. Some are convinced that their children should have everything they desire and should never be disciplined in order to grow up happy and well-adjusted. There are others who believe in the old "spare the rod and spoil the child" adage. This kind of parenting involves watching for any small infraction of the rules and strict retribution for any defiance. Neither of these styles is ideal.

I am reminded of two separate, real-life cases in which parents swayed to opposite extremes. In the first case, the child was spoiled to the point where no one could do anything with him, which was a result of overindulgence from his parents. In the second instance, the child was quiet and introverted, and was obviously frightened of anyone who might raise his voice at him. He was suffering from parents who were too strict.

If you are not careful, discipline can escalate into a form of child abuse. Parents are often cited for child abuse when, in their minds, they feel they are doing their parental duty by inflicting physical punishment for misbehavior. When punishment becomes cruel or threatens the welfare of the child, it crosses over into the arena of abuse.

A complete lack of discipline can be equally abusive, but in a different way. Outwardly, the child may appear to have the ideal life. What happens when that ideal comes face to face with reality? How does this child handle a situation in which he is treated like any other person his age? It is not an easy thing to adjust to and can cause mental and/or behavioral problems.

If you discipline your children properly, you will not be punishing them; rather, you will be teaching them acceptable behavior. Punishing without explanation leads to feelings of anger. It confuses children and can lead to rebellious conduct. To be successful, people need to have a sense of self-worth and accomplishment. They need to place a high value on themselves. No one will think highly of you if you do not think highly of yourself. Inappropriate methods of punishment can destroy the delicate self-esteem if a child.

I know of one parent who loved his child very much; however, when the child misbehaved, the parent would shout over any explanation the child tried to give. He would listen to no one whose opinion differed from his own and would constantly say to the child, "You must be crazy!" or "Are you crazy?" Imagine what this did to the child as he grew up. Not only was he never permitted to explain his actions, but he was told over and over again that he was mentally deficient. His self-image plummeted, and it took a long time for him to appreciate himself.

Remember that you are a model for your children. If you react to an adverse situation by lashing out at anyone within striking distance, your children will react in the same manner. **You are a hero to your children.** Little boys want to do everything "just like daddy," while little girls are anxious to emulate mommy, and often turn out to be miniatures of the parent. If they imitate your good points, they will copy your negative points as well. This is one reason why a personal life-coaching approach is so important. It prepares you to help your children as well as yourself. Always avoid any type of discipline that involves physical violence. Violence begets violence; children exposed to hitting as a solution will solve their problems the same way.

YOUR PERSONAL ASSESSMENT

Before we talk about the appropriate methods of discipline, we need to assess your current methods of disciplining your children. Fill out the next form with your responses to the following statements.

Please circle agree, possibly or disagree for the following statements:

1. A child should enjoy childhood as long as possible. Agree Possibly Disagree

2. Children should be seen and not heard. Agree Possibly Disagree

3. It is okay for a child to see how much he can get away with. Agree Possibly Disagree

4. There are times when it is permissible to hit a child. Agree Possibly Disagree

5. If I scream at my child, she will know I mean business. Agree Possibly Disagree

6. If I show too much affection, my child will take advantage. Agree Possibly Disagree

7. You can never give a child too many material things. Agree Possibly Disagree

8. I think it is cute when my child talks back to adults. Agree Possibly Disagree

9. If I do not give her what she wants, my child will not like me. Agree Possibly Disagree

10. An occasional smack will prepare my child for the world. Agree Possibly Disagree

Analyzing Your Responses

Now that you have completed the assessment above, let's take a look at your set of responses and how it pertains to your disciplinary style.

Statement 1: A child should enjoy childhood as long as possible.

Years ago, childhood lasted a lot longer than it does today. At an age when a girl was still playing with dolls, she is now imitating a favorite singer. Girls are growing up quickly and leaving childhood behind at an earlier age. It is a pity, because no matter how grown up she looks or sounds, mentally she is still a child. She is not ready for the adult world that is being thrust upon her. She goes through a period where she is caught between childhood and adulthood with confusion and anxiety. Do not add to her problems by pushing her to mature before she is ready.

Often, parents are eager to see their child become one of the "in" crowd, and they push him from one stage of development to the next before the child is mentally capable of handling it. Another problem that may surface is one of sexuality. In trying to emulate those who are older in both looks and actions, your child may get into a sexual situation that will lead to severe problems, such as an unwanted pregnancy or disease. Boys are not exempt from this push into an older world. They are now expected to be a "hunk" or a "stud" before they are even aware of what those titles entail. If they do not measure up to the standards set by other boys, they could be bullied. In the majority of school violence cases, it was boys who were picked on and bullied who finally could not take the pressure any longer and rebelled in a violent manner.

Allow your children to grow up naturally. If you allow them to grow up at a natural pace, they will have many happy childhood memories because they were able to enjoy that time of their lives.

Statement 2: Children should be seen and not heard.

It is important for children to know when it is appropriate or inappropriate for them to speak, but do not shut your children out completely and keep them from expressing their ideas. This would not be fair to the children or to you. Children have valuable insights and can add to a conversation. Children must, however, be taught when it is proper to participate in an adult conversation and how to speak in a respectful and non-intrusive manner.

If you have ever been in the presence of another adult whose child insists on saying what is on her mind by constantly interrupting you and your friend, you will understand. Your friend either thinks his child's behavior is cute, or he ignores her. You, on the other hand, might find it so frustrating that you cut your visit short and leave with the reinforcement of "children should be seen and not heard." This is a shame, because if the parents had only taken the time to teach their child some manners, this would never have happened. You cannot blame the child—she did not know any better. The blame lies with improper coaching.

Most children are naturally boisterous, inquisitive and prone to expect all attention to be on them. It takes love and tender training to teach children how to act. You must also remember that it is unreasonable to expect a child of two or three to sit quietly. They should be exposed, a little at a time, to adult talk-time and reminded gently when they are being presumptuous. In addition to good manners, children's self-esteem increases if they are permitted to voice their opinions. They gain a sense of value that they would not have otherwise.

Statement 3: It is okay for a child to see how much he can get away with.

Every child, no matter what age, will push the limits to see how far he can go before hitting the "no" wall. It is up to you, the parent, to set a limit and stay firm in your decision. The trick is to adjust your limits to coincide with your child's growth and to remain flexible.

For instance, when your child is six years of age, you may have a bedtime set at 8 p.m. By the time he is eight years of age, that bedtime may be increased to 9 p.m. In the summer months, when there is no school, this time may be extended; but as long as school is in session he should have a bedtime of no later than 9 p.m. Children need to get their sleep if they are to do well in school. Many teachers can tell you about children who fall asleep during class and, when they are asked what time they went to bed the night before, they reply, "Eleven or twelve o'clock." This is grossly unfair to the child. Children cannot be expected to concentrate and retain information when they cannot stay awake. Yes, they will try to get you to bend the rules. Expect to hear a whine that begs, "Just this once...Pleeeeeze. Everybody else watches this show."

You need to assert your authority as a parent and do what you know is right for the health and welfare of your children. **The**

push and pull between child and parent is a good thing. It indicates that the child is reaching for independence. He thinks he is ready to grow a little more and is ready to test his wings. This is an excellent sign, but you must learn to let the attachment string out a little at a time so he is not overwhelmed with freedom he is not equipped to handle.

Statement 4: There are times when it is permissible to hit a child.

If you agree with this statement, then you need to consider when those times are and why hitting is your solution. What do you think children learn through spankings and hitting? Remember that violence begets violence. Do you want your children to grow up with the idea that the only way to solve a problem is through violence? Children learn through modeling, and you are the primary model for your children. Do you want that model to be one of violence?

Do you find that you quickly lose your temper, or have a problem keeping it under control? Are you often at a loss when it comes to dealing with your children? Parenting classes offer solutions to most problems you will encounter. These classes also give you the knowledge that you are not alone—others have your same questions and face your same problems. If you want the best for your children, you will steer them away from a life that includes violence, and instead gear them toward one that concentrates on love and understanding.

Statement 5: If I scream at my child, she will know I mean business.

If you scream at your child, what she will know is that you are out of control. Just because this is your child is no reason to feel that you can yell at her at will. Children have the same feelings as adults. Think about how you would feel if you are yelled at by another person, especially one who is bigger than you or holds a position of authority over you. Is this how you want your child to feel? Do you want her to live in fear of you? To grow into a successful adult, she needs to feel love; she does not need to feel threatened by you.

You are probably wondering how you can be calm and loving when your child is giving you a terrible time and not listening to you. It is not easy. One word gives you the answer—control. Consider the bedtime issue. You know it is important for your child's health and welfare that she gets the proper amount of sleep, so you stick with the schedule you have set. Sticking to this schedule takes some effort on your part. Your task of getting your child to bed on time will be made easier if you make it a pleasant experience for her. Include a bath, a story and a few minutes of tender togetherness. Make it a time she will look forward to, instead of just putting her in bed and running back downstairs. We must give up something that is precious to each of us: time. We have so little of it and we are so busy, that we hesitate to give up any we may have set aside for ourselves. Yet, this is all part of parenting. It can bring you closer together or pull you apart. How you deal with each situation will determine the direction your relationship with your children will take.

Statement 6: If I show too much affection, my child will take advantage.

You can never show too much affection to your children. Children will take advantage of you only as far as you allow them to. If they have a clear understanding that you are the parent and you establish rules that you adhere to, they will only gain from your affection. Studies show that children who are deprived of affection may have trouble showing affection to others. Many will need counseling, either as a child or when they reach adulthood. They may have trouble forming lasting relationships; and their marriages often fail, due to their inability to give or receive the necessary affection.

Love and affection are parts of the same package—they go hand-in-hand. They are two of the most important things in your children's lives. **You can live in poverty or you can live in luxury, but as long as love also lives there, your children will have a good growing experience.** Affection and love are free; everyone can afford them. Do not shortchange your children by withholding these crucial elements in their lives.

Statement 7: You can never give a child too many material things.

This is often the attitude of people who grew up having very little themselves. They recall the things they wanted, but did not get, and vow that their children will never know how that feels. If parents were unhappy as youngsters, there may have been other underlying causes, not just because they did not have the latest and best of everything.

When children are showered with gifts that they never have to earn and therefore have no idea of the value, they believe they have everything coming to them and they do not have to work for any of it. You are not helping your children by treating them in this manner. You will be helping them if you occasionally have them earn the money for what they want. Even a very small child can do this. He can earn a part of the needed money by helping with minor chores, such as setting the table or feeding the dog. It is not necessary for him to earn the entire amount; earning even a small portion will teach him responsibility.

Material things do not provide happiness—love and attention do. Show your children how to rely less on material things and more on emotional responses, such as love. Teach your children the importance of sharing. Twice a year, go through his toys and clothing with his help. Allow him to help you decide which items can be donated to those less fortunate.

Statement 8: I think it is cute when my child talks back to adults.

Talking back does not show independence; rather, it shows a lack of discipline and manners. Would you consider these same actions by an adult to be "cute?" As stated earlier, children should not be stifled; however, they need to learn how and when it is appropriate to speak. If they are permitted to butt into every conversation, getting all of the attention for themselves and speaking rudely, they will continue to do this throughout life.

Take time to help your children understand when it is proper to speak and in what manner they should speak. If your child does act or talk inappropriately, you should discuss this when the two of you are alone. If he acts as he should, praise him for his good behavior. Praise will provide positive reinforcement, which gives an incentive to continue with the same conduct.

I do not advocate the "children should be seen and not heard" rule, but I do feel that children should be respectful and well-mannered. Once again, the onus of providing a good model falls on you. You may have met a friend's child and, after listening to her for a few minutes, thought to yourself, "My goodness, she sounds just like her mother." This is not unusual. Children will pick up mannerisms, speech patterns and behavioral attitudes from their parents. This is a prime example of modeling. See that your children have a good example from which to learn.

Statement 9: If I do not give her what she wants, my child will not like me.

While she may not like you at that moment, or even if she says she hates you, this is only the outburst of a child who is being denied what she wants. You should know that: 1) your decision is in her best interest, and 2) this is a natural reaction on her part and will pass quickly. Her intention is to hurt you so you will give in to her. If it works, she will do it again and again until she has gained complete control over you.

We all want our children to like us, and they will love us as we love them. The one thing to remember is that your job is to be a parent, not a buddy. You will sometimes have to make decisions that will not be popular with your children. If you want to do your job in the best way possible, then you will understand that you are sometimes cast into the role of the "bad guy." Your children do not need you to be their best friend; they need you to guide them in making important decisions, keeping them on the right path.

Statement 10: An occasional smack will prepare my child for the world.

No, it will not. Prepare him instead by assuring him of your unconditional love. Help him to get over the bumps and bruises that are a part of living. Show him how to concentrate on the good that is in the world and how to reach out to people who need assistance. You cannot shield your children from the realities of life, but you can give them the assurance and confidence they need to succeed.

GUIDELINES FOR APPLYING PROPER DISCIPLINE TO YOUR CHILDREN

With your discipline assessment from earlier in mind, read the following guidelines. They will help you incorporate healthier and more effective strategies into your discipline style. It is likely that different methods will work at different times, depending on circumstances. The most important thing to remember is to make sure that discipline does not turn into verbal or physical abuse.

- Never punish in anger. Allow time to lapse and tempers to cool before deciding on punishment for an infraction.

- Make sure to hear all sides with an open mind.

- Yelling, screaming and hitting are never appropriate or effective methods of discipline.

- Although there are many ways of enforcing discipline, different ways will work with different children. You must find the most effective method for your children. You may also need to use different methods for children in the same family. Just because they are siblings does not mean they will respond well to the same type of discipline.

- Children will use disruptive behavior if they feel it will get them attention. If you feel this is the case with your children, make sure their behavior is not harmful to themselves, then completely ignore them. For this to be effective you must have the cooperation of all other adults in the room; no one should pay any attention to the child. When the child realizes he is not getting anyone's attention, he will stop. It is then that you need to praise him for stopping the poor behavior. One way of ignoring him is to simply walk away; if you distance yourself from him, you will not be tempted to give in to his tantrums.

- When considering suitable disciplinary methods, think about the option of denial or revocation of privileges. However, if you say you are going to revoke a privilege, then be sure to follow through. It is only through consistency that your actions can be meaningful.

- Bear in mind the temperament of your child. For some, the strong actions described above would be most effective. Others would benefit most if you take the time to talk calmly to them.

- Never embarrass your child in front of others. Wait until you are alone, then calmly talk to him about what he did wrong, why it was wrong, and what you expect of him in the future.

- If your child's behavior is so disruptive that she must be spoken to immediately, take her aside and speak softly, but with authority, explaining the situation to her. If she continues the same actions, remove her from the group and take her home. She will understand that you are in control of the situation and you will not tolerate inappropriate behavior.

- When you remain calm and speak in a calm voice, you will lessen your child's anxiety and help him see his actions in a rational way. He will be more likely to understand the unsuitability of his behavior. He will take his cue from you and follow your lead.

It is not always easy to remain calm, but doing so will prevent violent reactions on your part. There are times when you become very angry at the behavior of your children, which may result in shouting and possibly physical discipline. When your anger begins to take over your good sense, remove yourself from the situation. After you have had time to cool down and can think rationally, you will be in a better position to speak to your children about their behavior.

Score Points with Your Children

One of the most effective ways to work with children is through the use of a behavior chart. On a poster board, I want you and your children to make a weekly chart containing the different days of the week and different duties for each of those days. These duties should be ones that both you and your children think are fair. Responsibilities should be age-appropriate. For example, a seven-year-old child should have no more than seven tasks for the week. A ten-year old should have no more than ten tasks for the week.

For every goal/responsibility that your child fulfills, put a sticker or a star in that box. If your child does not complete a duty, she should not get a star for that task; remain consistent and steady. At the end of the week, add up the number of stickers. For example, your seven-year-old child can have a total of 49 points possible for the week (seven tasks times seven days a week = 49 possible stars). The goal is not to get a perfect score. Instead, add up the number of stars and then give certain privileges/rewards based on that. For example, for your seven-year-old with a total of 49 stars possible, you can do the following:

> Greater than 30 stars = Reward Category 1
> Greater than 40 stars = Reward Category 2
> Greater than 45 stars = Reward Category 3

Both you and your children should come up with these privileges/rewards together. For example, perhaps greater than 30 stars could mean an extra half hour at the pool this weekend.

- Be sure to praise your child if she falls into a reward category. If she does not get enough stars for a reward that week, then talk to your child about why this is so, and what she could have done differently.
- As a child grows and matures, so does her behavior. Keep this chart up to date and modify it as needed. Keep the chart visible so that your child can see her stars multiplying, which will serve as a motivator.

- Be consistent, and, whenever possible in a two-parent household, have both parents decide together whether the child accomplished her goal for each task listed.

The following is an example of what one chart might look like for a seven-year old. As you can see, she has seven tasks. In this example, Sarah received more than 30 stars, so she can choose a reward from Category 1.

Self-Motivated Behavior Chart for Seven-Year-Old Sarah

	Sun	Mon	Tue	Wed	Th	Fri	Sat
Set table		☆		☆			
Wash dishes	☆	☆	☆	☆	☆	☆	
Take out trash	☆	☆		☆			
Do homework	☆	☆	☆	☆	☆	☆	☆
Help mow lawn		☆		☆		☆	
Help younger brother with homework		☆	☆	☆	☆	☆	
Feed the dog		☆	☆	☆	☆	☆	

Negative Effects of Improper Discipline

You have undoubtedly heard about studies that say people who were abused as children may become abusers as adults. You have also heard about instances of abuse leading to criminal behavior. The offices of therapeutic counselors are filled with people who have lasting emotional scars due, in a great part, to the violence they witnessed or experienced as children. Hospital emergency rooms deal on a daily basis with children who have been injured by parents in their efforts to discipline them. When improper discipline enters the picture, children are scarred both emotionally and physically. How does this happen? Where does it start? How can you recognize actions on your part that are harmful to your children? The following are real-life examples that were successfully resolved, but could easily have gotten worse.

☆ *A Real-Life Example of How Improper Discipline Can Affect a Child: Jake*

They entered my office for their first visit looking every bit the happy family. Before meeting with Bob, Ellen and Jake, I read the school report thoroughly. Jake was intelligent and attentive in his classes, but between classes, he was a bully, often hitting children younger than him. The report said in part, "Jake has a difficult time adjusting socially. He seems to be fine until his temper flares up. At that time, he hits other children or destroys property. Although only ten years of age, this is his second school. His parents were asked to remove him from the first school because of his uncontrollable temper." His anger has caused him to be abusive to other children and destroy school property, including a computer that he threw onto the floor.

Watching Jake, relaxed and smiling, it was difficult to imagine him as a boy with an uncontrollable temper. "I see you went to another school before this one, Jake. What happened there? Why did you leave?" Ellen jumped in before Jake could answer. "Some kids were fooling around in the computer room and a computer got knocked to the floor. Jake was blamed for it."

"Jake," I said, "I understand that you were hitting some other children at school. Do you want to tell me about that?" This time, it was Bob who jumped in. "They were always picking on him. He was only defending himself."

"I'd like Jake to tell me what happened," I said. Jake glanced quickly at his parents and the smile was gone from his face. "Jake, what happened at the other school?" I asked again. "I dunno," Jake muttered as he slouched further down into his chair. Not wanting to push him too hard on his first visit, I dropped the matter. The time was almost up, so I ended the session, making sure to plan for next week.

"When you bring Jake next week I would like to start seeing him alone. Please drop him off and pick him up again in an hour. Or, if you prefer, you can wait in the reception area." Bob and Ellen exchanged looks. "I'd really like to be in here with him," Ellen said. "Yes," Bob echoed, "One of us should be with him."

"I appreciate your concern," I said, "and from time to time we will have a family session. But Jake is my client and he and I must work together as a team for the counseling to be effective. I will need to enlist your cooperation and I will keep you updated on any major developments. The majority of my time, however, needs to be one-on-one with Jake. If you do not agree, you will have to find another counselor." They agreed, but reluctantly. It was decided that I would meet with Jake in one week.

When he arrived at my office, Jake bounced in and settled into one of the comfortable chairs facing me. He was happy to talk about his life and chatted on in the way ten-year-olds do. This continued until I brought up the subject of his removal from his first school. He skillfully avoided answering my questions, and when I insisted, he became visibly anxious. He began to clench and unclench his fists and his mouth changed from a cheerful smile to an angry grimace. "I don't want to talk about that," he insisted. I could see that he was trying to fight for self-control, so I tried to reassure him that he need not be afraid to talk to me. After much patient prodding, he finally stated, "Sometimes they just make me mad so I hit them." Our time for that day was over, but I asked Jake to begin thinking about what kinds of things make him angry and what he could do instead of fighting to get rid of the anger.

As time went on, in subsequent sessions with Jake, he became more comfortable with me and I gained his trust. He told me about the family structure and the punishment methods employed in his home. What finally emerged was the picture of a family that was generally happy, but when Jake broke a rule, he was spanked. If one of his parents, usually Bob, became angry, he pushed and smacked Jake. Bob was always sorry after he did this, but that did not stop him from repeating this behavior the next time Jake misbehaved. There were times too, when Jake would witness arguments between his parents that resulted in objects being thrown to the floor and broken. All of this had a negative influence on Jake and his way of managing anger.

In later sessions with Bob and Ellen, they admitted to this behavior and were willing to undergo therapy to change, in order to give Jake positive role models to emulate. In addition to their sessions with me, Bob and Ellen attended an anger management workshop where they learned how to dispel their anger in non-violent ways. I continued to work one-on-one with Jake. Slowly, but surely, Jake's aggressive attitude changed and he was once again accepted by his peers. His trouble at school decreased dramatically and his grades improved.

☆ *A Real-Life Example of How Improper Discipline Can Affect a Child: Anne*

Physical abuse is one matter; verbal abuse can be just as devastating. Anne was a shy child, timid and withdrawn. When people met her, they considered Anne to be a very well-behaved girl, which is exactly what her mother, Denise, wanted.

When they came to my office for their first meeting, my door was slightly ajar and I could hear them, or rather I could hear Denise, as they entered the reception area. She was saying, "Now, don't go saying anything stupid like you usually do. Think before you answer anything; don't just open your mouth and let the words fall out." I opened my office door to greet them and invite them in. Anne looked frightened and entered cautiously, taking a seat and primly folding her hands. I offered her a piece of candy from the jar on my desk and she quickly looked to Denise for approval before carefully choosing the flavor that appealed to her.

It was not easy to talk to Anne. Denise would either answer for her or would contradict Anne's reply, making it appear that Anne did not know what she was talking about. As the session progressed, Anne spoke less, leaving Denise to instead assert her opinions only.

In my first session alone with Anne she was very tentative with her answers. It took much encouragement from me over many weeks to get her to speak openly. In my work with Denise, I was able to monitor her outbursts and allow Anne's answers to stand on their own. She needed to recognize that, although many statements from Anne did not coincide with her own ideas, this did not necessarily make Anne's ideas wrong. It was a hard thing for Denise to do, but slowly and with practice, she was able to control her urge to constantly correct and admonish Anne.

The two factors together, Anne's growing sense of self assurance and Denise's willingness to step back, helped Anne to become a more outgoing person. She readily joined school groups and was even elected class treasurer the following school year.

Denise was unintentionally guilty of verbal abuse. She considered her continuous verbal attacks a form of discipline. She wanted Anne to be perceived as a bright child and felt that her attempts at correction would turn Anne into a confident, knowledgeable speaker. She actually produced the opposite effect. **Verbal abuse is just as debilitating to the receiver as physical abuse.** It leaves no outer scars, but the mental scars go deep.

Summary of the Above Real-Life Examples

The two cases cited above are examples of two forms of discipline harmful to children: physical and verbal abuse. Fortunately, these were discovered before permanent damage was done, and the parents were willing to make necessary changes in their own lives in order to become a positive force in their children's lives.

> **Life-coaching tip:** Parents and parents-to-be should study good, positive methods of discipline before embarking on a negative path for themselves and for their children.

IMPROVING YOUR DISCIPLINARY SKILLS

It is time to think about yourself and your reactions to situations. Are you a good role model for your children? How can you improve? What are your worst situations? We are not always aware of our responses. A good way to see yourself is through the eyes of others. Enlist the help of your spouse or a best friend. Ask questions such as: Do you think I overreact when I discipline? How does it make you feel when I allow anger to control my actions? Am I usually fair in my discipline? Do others consider me to be a controlled or uncontrolled person? Consider their answers carefully. Do not take any criticism as negative—instead think of it as a positive force that will help you improve.

There are mental health clinics nationwide that offer courses on anger management. Even if you feel that you do not have a problem at this time, it would be a wise move to take such a course to help head off future problems.

Take a critical look at your disciplinary methods and how your children react to anger. Can you see the similarities? Consider the past several months. Do any incidents come to mind in which you or your children gave in to anger and behaved irrationally? Do you see a pattern emerging?

Now, I'd like you to look at your own disciplinary methods and how you handle situations. In the chart on the following page, I want you to list some behavioral problems you observed in your children over the last month. For each problem, describe exactly what led up to the unwanted behavior. Then, describe your disciplinary method and its effectiveness. Next, describe how you could have reacted differently. What did occur and what should have occurred? Consider the proper discipline for each.

After you have made this list and are satisfied with your answers, sit down with your children and calmly discuss an approach for instituting change. If your children see that you are working toward a change, they will also have the desire to change.

Work together on this project. Do not keep it one-sided. Ask your children what you do that makes them angry or fearful. If you are known to be a hot-tempered individual, your children may be afraid to speak up at first. Do not intimidate them. Be gentle and assuring, slowly gaining their trust. Show by your actions that you are in control of your emotions.

An Activity to Improve Disciplinary Skills

Behavior problem I observed in my child:

_____

_____

What led up to this behavior in my child?

_____

_____

What was my disciplinary method?

_____

_____

Was my disciplinary method effective?

_____

_____

If not, why?

_____

_____

What was the desired outcome?

_____

_____

What was the actual outcome?

_____

_____

Could I have reacted differently?

_____

_____

What might be a better form of discipline to use?

_____

_____

SUMMARY OF CHAPTER ELEVEN

In this chapter, you examined your methods of discipline. You discovered that discipline is a very necessary part of childhood. To grow into successful and productive adults, children must be taught the proper way to behave in any circumstance, so they will fit into society and be valued citizens.

Discipline means different things to different people. You were given the opportunity to examine your own views on the subject and to assess the value of your responses.

There are various methods used to discipline children. What is appropriate? What is considered abusive? These are difficult questions. Most parents want their children to have the best possible life, and parents often go overboard in trying to keep their children in bounds.

Improper discipline has a negative effect on a person's life. Harsh behavior by parents becomes harsh behavior by their children. Physical or verbal abuse can be devastating and should be dealt with as early as possible to prevent permanent damage.

You were asked to examine your methods of discipline and make every effort to correct any negative actions. You then were asked to look at your children and see where any problems might lie. Talk with them and gain their trust. Show by your own improved behavior that change is possible and that you expect them to exhibit proper behavior patterns in their own lives.

☆ Never punish in anger.

☆ Never embarrass my child in front of others.

☆ Try to analyze the underlying reasons behind my child's misbehavior before taking action.

☆ Keep in mind the temperament of my child when disciplining.

Chapter Twelve

SEEING YOUR INVESTMENT PAY OFF
Family Success Through Teamwork

CHAPTER OBJECTIVES:

- Learn the value of teamwork as it applies to your family.
- Learn coaching tips to instill a team spirit in your family.
- Assess you and your family's ability to work as a team.
- Plan a group family function.

> *"Each of us depends on the rest of mankind for the bare fact*
> *of survival."*
> — *Emmanuel Cardinal Suhard*

This final chapter will help bring everything you've learned thus far together. You will begin by learning how teamwork applies to your family. Then, I will teach you how to instill team spirit. Next, each member of your family will assess her own abilities for being a team player. As your final activity, your family will plan a group function in which each family member is responsible for specific duties. In order to see what it is like to play a different role within your family, each person will have an opportunity to perform duties that another family member usually does.

By the end of this chapter, you will feel educated, enlightened and empowered for the most rewarding job of your life. You will begin to feel a balance of your emotional, social and spiritual health. This balance will give you a sense of accomplishment and will help you reach your full success potential as a life-coach and mentor for yourself and your family.

TEAMWORK AND YOUR FAMILY

Having your family work as a team does not mean becoming an exclusive unit, shutting out all others. Rather, it is vital for each family member to maintain her own individual character in order to be happy and successful. Think of your family as the hub of a wheel with each member as one of the spokes. The hub holds the wheel firmly together, but each spoke reaches out in a different direction.

Each person is the sum of her experiences, and the interests and knowledge she gains along the way make her who she is. A family unit that keeps too tight a reign on its members will only serve to stifle creativity and growth. You must remember that each person in your family has different ideas, interests and plans. Therefore, each person must be encouraged to develop and pursue her own interests, while maintaining a family teamwork goal. Each member will bring her own valuable skills to help fulfill the goals of the team. This can be a valuable tool for each individual in the family throughout her life, since most people have to work as part of a team, whether in school, in work or while participating in sports.

COACHING TIPS FOR INSTILLING TEAM SPIRIT IN YOUR FAMILY

The planning and execution of ideas brings people together to share thoughts and knowledge, and is of value to each individual. It is important to teach your children the value of being a team player. Demonstrate to your children that being part of a team can be fun. If children grow up as part of a family team, the transition to school or work team will be a natural one. They will be valued in various situations because of their ability to interact with others, while achieving both individual and group goals.

Below are some coaching tips that you and your children should discuss and incorporate within your lives. These are guidelines to achieve optimal success while working as a team in any environment. The tips are as follows:

1) Share.
2) Avoid blame.
3) Give and take.
4) Give wholeheartedly.

Tip 1: Share.

An important aspect of creating a spirit of teamwork is the essential social skill of sharing. It is vital to encourage your children to share both their possessions as well as their time. By doing this, you will create a climate of kindness, generosity and teamwork. **Sharing is the glue that holds a team together.**

Tip 2: Avoid blame.

Team members should not point a finger of blame; instead, they should share the responsibility equally, in both negative and positive instances. Team members share their victories, as well as their defeats. They share both the glory when things go right and the responsibility when things do not go as well as expected.

Tip 3: Give and take.

Your children must comprehend the fact that they are to "be there" for their teammates, instead of simply taking from others. When one team member is about to falter, the others need to help him by supporting him in any way possible. **There is no place on a team for superheroes with big egos;** instead, members should be valued for their own individual contributions, while working for the benefit of the team.

Tip 4: Give wholeheartedly.

Anyone who is part of a team must be willing to give 110% in order to achieve optimal success for the team. A team loses value if only some of its members participate, while others do nothing. Always do your best, not just for your own sake, but also for the sake of the team as a whole.

AN ASSESSMENT OF YOU AND YOUR FAMILY'S TEAMWORK SKILLS

As in all other phases of parenting and providing a life-coach model, you must prove yourself to be an effective team player. When you share responsibility for both the negative and the positive events that occur in your family, this behavior will be emulated by your children, both within the family and in life.

Before you and your children begin to plan your family function as a team, it is important for each family member to assess his own skills as a team player. The first assessment is to be completed by you, the parent. The assessment on the page after that is to be completed by your child.

These assessments will allow each person to take a look at the way he handles team situations. They will make him start to think about his strengths as a team player, as well as areas that can be improved upon. At the end of the assessments, you and your children can talk about their responses and share ideas on how teamwork can help your family. If you or your children respond with "No" to any of these statements, then that is something you may want to address as an individual goal.

An Assessment of Your Skills as a Team Player
(to be completed by the parent)

Please circle yes or no for the following statements.

1. I know how to be a great team player.

        Yes   No

2. I believe in working for the goals of the team, rather than exclusively on my own goals.

        Yes   No

3. I am very real and honest with others.

        Yes   No

4. I am a "people person."

        Yes   No

5. I respect the needs and desires of others.

        Yes   No

6. I contribute to the well being of my team.

        Yes   No

An Assessment of Your Skills as a Team Player

(to be completed by the child)

Please circle yes or no for the following statements.

1. I know how to be a great team player.

        Yes   No

2. I believe in working for the goals of the team, rather than exclusively on my own goals.

        Yes   No

3. I am very real and honest with others.

        Yes   No

4. I am a "people person."

        Yes   No

5. I respect the needs and desires of others.

        Yes   No

6. I contribute to the well being of my team.

        Yes   No

AN ACTIVITY TO IMPROVE YOUR FAMILY'S TEAMWORK

The best way to learn to work as a team is to actually do it. Now you're embarking on the most valuable part of hands-on teamwork training. In this section, you and your family will plan a group function. First, the entire family should spend time planning exactly what the activity is and what needs to be done. Choose a date for this activity, who will be involved (i.e., Are extended family members invited?), what type of activity it will be and other details.

Incorporate the input of everyone in the family team, ensuring that all members play an important role in completing this project. After all the basics have been decided upon, a list of responsibilities needs to be compiled, whereby each family member, according to age and ability, chooses a duty from an array of choices. In order to see what it is like to play a different role within your family, each person should have an opportunity to perform duties that another family member usually performs.

For example, imagine your family's activity is to plan an outdoor party. Decide on the details of this party, such as where this party will occur, who will be invited and what food or other items will be needed. Once you have the details all set, it's time to split up the list of responsibilities. Some of these responsibilities might include:

- Purchasing and sending invitations
- Purchasing and preparing food and drinks
- Decorating
- Planning party games
- Greeting guests

In the space on the following pages, write down the activity that you and your family decide upon. Include all of the details of the activity, such as who is doing what.

A few days after the party, follow up by having a family meeting to discuss how well it went, areas for improvement and what each family member thought of her new responsibilities. Be sure to congratulate family members for what they did well. Praise everyone's efforts, even if the results were not exactly as you had expected.

Our Family Activity

Planning

Activity:

Example: Planning an outdoor Hawaiian luau party

_____

_____

_____

Date and Time of Event:

Sunday, March 25 at 4:00 p.m.

_____

Duties to Fulfill:

Make and send invitations, decorate, greet guests

_____

_____

_____

Name:	**Responsibility:**
Jacky	*Greet guests*
Martha	*Help decorate*
_____	_____
_____	_____
_____	_____

_____   _____

_____   _____

_____   _____

_____   _____

How to Fulfill Duty:

Jacky   *Greet each guest with a lei*

Martha   *Decorate tables with coconuts*

_____   _____

_____   _____

_____   _____

_____   _____

_____   _____

_____   _____

_____   _____

Follow Up

Was the activity a success?

Yes, the party was a huge success. Everyone had a great time.

_____

_____

_____

How did each team member feel about the new duties and responsibilities?

Dad enjoyed cooking for a change. He feels empowered to do things he's never done before. Jacky loved greeting guests—she's not as shy as she thought.

_____

_____

_____

_____

_____

Can we do anything differently in the future?

Think about having someone come to give hula lessons. Add another dish to the party.

_____

_____

_____

_____

SUMMARY OF CHAPTER TWELVE

This chapter discussed teamwork and how it can help you and your family throughout your lifetime. You learned how you can incorporate teamwork into your life. I shared tips on how to instill team spirit into your family, and each member of your family assessed his own abilities as a team player. Your family planned a group function and assigned each family member specific duties for which he was responsible. In order to see what it is like to play a different role within your family, each person had the opportunity to perform duties that another family member usually does. After your activity, you followed up with your family to see how you can improve future events.

> ☆ Teach my children the importance of sharing and being part of a team.
>
> ☆ Praise my children for being team players, and encourage all family members to partake in activities.
>
> ☆ Take responsibility for my actions; avoid blaming others.

CONCLUSION

Throughout the course of reading this book, you have learned a great deal about yourself and about your children. You have become a better communicator, leader and problem-solver. You have learned the importance of empathy, motivation, teamwork, self-esteem and proper discipline. All of the tools you need to succeed are now in your hands. The skills you and your children have learned are a part of who you are.

Now that you have been educated, enlightened and empowered with the knowledge, I want you to run with it. Empower yourself to believe in your dreams and to reach for the stars. Always believe in yourself and the power within you to achieve your goals. This will enable you to impart the same message to your children, so that your whole family has the power to succeed in life.

Use this book as a reference guide that you can refer back to as needed, one chapter at a time, when you stray off course or simply want a reminder. Periodically come back to these pages and see how well you have been incorporating the strategies into your life.

It has been my pleasure joining you on your journey to happiness and success for you and your family. Good luck to you!

APPENDIX

INSPIRATIONS FOR YOU TO SHARE
WITH YOUR CHILD

I will teach you to believe in yourself.
I will teach you to trust your inner voice.
I will teach you to respect yourself and others.

We have shared dreams, yet separate goals and aspirations.
You will become everything you were ever meant to be and more...
Smart, strong and independent, with a kind, tender and passionate
heart.

I will do everything in my power to teach you how to fly.
As the years pass, I'll watch you spread your beautiful wings,
And I'll watch as you soar to new heights.

I believe in you, and in everything you are capable of achieving in
life.

ENDORSEMENTS FROM THE TOUGHEST CRITICS

Josh age 17

Ryan Age 11

Jono age 15

Scott age 14

Arielle Cohen (13)

Laura aged 8

RACHAEL Age 2

Michael aged 11

Matt Age 16

Claire age 15

Elyssa

Jason AGE 15

Daniel (12)

Jenny Age 7

FOR ADDITIONAL HELP

To find a psychologist in your area, call the American Psychological Association at 1-800-964-2000. If you live outside of the U.S. or Canada, contact a mental health facility or psychological association in your country. For immediate help, contact your local emergency services.

WALLET CARDS

Below are wallet cards you found at the end of each chapter. Cut out the cards and keep them with you to remind you of your goals.

Chapter One Wallet Card

☆ Focus on my assets.

☆ Offer only constructive criticism.

☆ Work on one change at a time.

☆ Repeat my positive affirmations daily.

☆ Emotional + Social + Spiritual Health = SUCCESS

Chapter Two Wallet Card

☆ Try a new activity.

☆ Decide on a life change I can make.

☆ Repeat my positive affirmations.

☆ Practice asserting myself.

☆ Embrace change.

Chapter Three Wallet Card

- ☆ Be knowledgeable, communicate my knowledge well and display confidence in my knowledge.
- ☆ Be loyal, be fair and be approachable.
- ☆ Remain calm, be organized and delegate responsibility.
- ☆ Be responsible by giving credit and taking blame.
- ☆ Be comfortable as a leader and laugh at myself.

Chapter Four Wallet Card

- ☆ Be a positive role model to my children.

- ☆ Be a manager in my home.

- ☆ Provide a warm environment for change in my family.

- ☆ Provide my children with unconditional love.

- ☆ Keep a positive attitude.

Chapter Five Wallet Card

☆ Each child is special; do not compare one child to another.

☆ Do not judge or criticize my children.

☆ Do not impose my own dreams on my children.

☆ Nobody is perfect.

Chapter Six Wallet Card

☆ Practice one attitude adjustment technique.

☆ Use motivation to help my children explore a new interest.

☆ Set realistic goals for my family and myself.

☆ Teach my children successful methods of goal-setting.

Chapter Seven Wallet Card

☆ Volunteer my time to those less fortunate.

☆ Plan a family volunteer day at a local charity.

☆ Listen to my children and realize that they each have special qualities.

☆ Show my children, by word and example, the importance of stepping into someone else's shoes.

Chapter Eight Wallet Card

☆ Watch my children carefully for signs of low self-esteem.

☆ Praise my children at least once each day.

☆ Find ways I can help my children improve their self-esteem.

☆ Plan a family meeting in which accomplishments can be praised.

Chapter Nine Wallet Card

☆ Think of five instances this week in which I could have communicated better.

☆ Be aware of my listening skills and work toward improvement.

☆ Have a conversation in I use good communication skills.

Chapter Ten Wallet Card

☆ Be a role model to my children when it comes to resolving conflicts.

☆ Effective conflict resolution can lead to success.

☆ Remember the Rule of the Five P's: Proper Preparation Prevents Poor Performance.

☆ Brainstorm with my family for new solutions to old problems.

Chapter Eleven Wallet Card

☆ Never punish in anger.

☆ Never embarrass my child in front of others.

☆ Try to analyze the underlying reasons behind my child's misbehavior before taking action.

☆ Keep in mind the temperament of my child when disciplining.

Chapter Twelve Wallet Card

☆ Teach my children the importance of sharing and being part of a team.

☆ Praise my children for being team players, and encourage all family members to partake in activities.

☆ Take responsibility for my actions; avoid blaming others.